The Torah REVOLUTION

The
Torah
REVOLUTION

Fourteen Truths That
Changed the World

Rabbi Reuven Hammer, PhD

For People of All Faiths, All Backgrounds

JEWISH LIGHTS Publishing

Woodstock, Vermont

The Torah Revolution:
Fourteen Truths That Changed the World

2011 Hardcover Edition, First Printing
© 2011 by Reuven Hammer

Library of Congress Cataloging-in-Publication Data
Hammer, Reuven.
The Torah revolution : fourteen truths that changed the world / Reuven Hammer. — 2011 hardcover ed.
p. cm.
Includes bibliographical references and index.
ISBN 978-1-58023-457-3 (hardcover)
  1. Bible. O.T. Pentateuch—Criticism, interpretation, etc. 2. God—Biblical teaching. 3. Equality—Biblical teaching. 4. Ethics in the Bible. 5. Jewish ethics. I. Title.
BS1225.52.H363 2011
222'.106—dc23
2011032680

10 9 8 7 6 5 4 3 2 1

Manufactured in the United States of America
❁ Printed on recycled paper.
Jacket design: Tim Holtz

Published by Jewish Lights Publishing
A Division of Longhill Partners, Inc.
Sunset Farm Offices, Route 4, P.O. Box 237
Woodstock, VT 05091
Tel: (802) 457-4000   Fax: (802) 457-4004
www.jewishlights.com

To our three great-grandchildren,
Eliya, Nadav, and Levi, and those who will come after—

You must be very strong and resolute to observe
faithfully all the Teaching that My servant Moses
enjoined upon you. Do not deviate from it to
the right or to the left, that you may be successful wherever you go.

Joshua 1:7

Contents

Preface

This book would not have been possible without the work of outstanding biblical scholars, whose insights into the background and basic meaning of the texts of the Torah have revealed much that was previously unknown and hidden. They are not responsible for what I have written, but without their work, I could never have conceived this book. The seminal work of Yehezkel Kaufmann, to which I was first introduced by Professor Shalom Speigel in my years at the Jewish Theological Seminary, forms the basis of my understanding of the early religion of Israel. It was also my privilege to study with Kaufmann at the Hebrew University. I must single out for special mention three of the greatest biblical scholars who unfortunately all passed away while I was working on this volume: Moshe Greenberg, Jacob Milgrom, and Yochanan Muffs. These extraordinary men were colleagues and friends from whose insightful works I have drawn liberally. The biblical commentaries and articles of the late Nahum Sarna and of Baruch Levine and Shalom Paul were also extremely helpful, as were the comments of Bezalel Porten. I owe special thanks to Jeffrey Tigay, not only for his work on Deuteronomy, but also for his generosity in commenting on my initial plans and providing me with helpful biographical material. Needless to say, these men are not responsible for my work and my conclusions, and all faults and errors are mine.

I have often consulted the 1985 Jewish Publication Society translation of the Bible for biblical quotations, but the translations also reflect my interpretations of the verses and vary accordingly. I have attempted to use gender-free language when referring to God and in other instances as well, although there are times when this has not been possible because of the awkwardness that resulted. Let it be clear, however, that gender is a realm that does not apply to God.

I must note that these fourteen truths are often closely related to one another. From time to time, this may result in the need to recapitulate material that has been mentioned before to clarify the specific matter under discussion. Nevertheless, I believe that each point is sufficiently important in itself to warrant an intensive discussion, and I ask the reader's indulgence.

I want to express my sincere thanks to my editor, Bryna Fischer, for her dedicated work and helpful suggestions in putting this manuscript into its final form. Lastly, my continual appreciation to my wife, Rahel, who has constantly but patiently encouraged me to turn my ideas into books.

Torat Moshe—
The Teaching of Moses

A previous book of mine, a commentary on each Torah portion, encompassed the entire Torah from *alef* to *tav*. Writing it was a unique experience. Usually Jews concentrate on one specific portion, or parashah, at a time. Even if we do that week by week in successive order, we still tend to see the trees and not the forest. Doing it this way—relating to the Torah as a whole, as a unity—I was able to discern what I see as the basic values and concepts underlying the entire Torah.

My intent, then, in writing this book was to discover and explore those core concepts on which the original religion of Israel was based, as expressed in the Torah. In doing this, I have concentrated on revealing what I believe to have been the ideas that were espoused when these documents were first conceived, as much as that is possible. Therefore, I have not dealt extensively with the later developments and changes that took place as the Torah was interpreted and reinterpreted time and again. To do so in depth would be beyond the scope of this volume. Not that I do not appreciate them and see their value. I do. As Solomon Schechter said, "A return to Mosaism would be illegal, pernicious and indeed impossible."[1] On the other hand, sometimes the plethora of interpretations and the layers of later meanings can make us forget or at least obscure the fundamental truths that started this revolution. Therefore, when I refer to postbiblical works, it is mainly to show how

1

they were influenced by these Torah truths and carried them forward. The entire Torah may not be the work of Moses in the most literal sense, but it certainly contains the concepts of Moses and his instructions to Israel as various schools of thought through the centuries that followed his existence interpreted them. As biblical scholar Jeffrey Tigay put it, "The great structure of Jewish law that eventuated from Moses's original teachings is ultimately his, even if he would not recognize the forms it would eventually take. In that sense the writers of Deuteronomy, too, have given us the Teaching of Moses, that is, a statement of his fundamental monotheistic teaching, designed to resist the assimilatory temptations of the writers' age and to preserve monotheism for the future."[2]

I am well aware that there are different strands within the Torah, that it reflects different groups, and that there are various emphases that each group brought. It is generally accepted in scholarly circles today that four main strands were blended into one: J, in which the four-letter name of God, YHVH, is used; E, which refers to God as *Elohim;* P, the Priestly code; and D, the Deuteronomic school. A Redactor, R—probably Ezra the scribe—likely oversaw the work of final redaction. See Nehemiah 9, where Ezra presents this document to the people as the constitution of the returned exilic community in 444 BCE. When all is said and done, the common ground among these groups far outweighs the differences, and the basic insights underlying them all create a whole that is greater than the sum of its parts.

The twentieth-century biblical scholar Jacob Milgrom once explained that he had no problem referring to the Torah as *Torat Moshe*—the Torah (Teaching) of Moses—even though all Milgrom's work was based on the assumption that the Torah we have was not brought into its final form until hundreds of years after Moses's death. Milgrom believed all of the documents of the various schools that were eventually put together to form our Torah were elaborations of Moses's basic teachings, which had been passed on from generation to generation. Unfortunately, we no longer have that urtext, that basic document, but it underlies the work we do have. Although each such group of teachers differed from the other in certain emphases and even in some basic theological conceptions, they were all influenced by what Moses had taught and built on his ideas. Indeed, I believe that certain basic concepts, which I have chosen to call "truths," informed all of these teachings. When I use the term "truths," I mean basic ideals presented in the Torah that rest on belief and not on scientific proof. Much as the American Declaration of Independence spoke about truths that were "self-evident," so too these truths contained in the Torah are self-evident.

If I am correct, Moses was a genius, a great original religious thinker, innovator, and revolutionary who transformed the important religious insights of the patriarchs, Abraham, Isaac, and Jacob, into a dynamic new religion. That religion of Israel, later known as Judaism, would go on to influence the world and yield a new way of understanding God and the meaning of human life.

Behind the teachings of the Torah stands the extraordinary personality of this man Moses—Moshe. We can never know more of him than the Torah itself tells us. All the rest is speculation. Although everything in the Torah is ascribed to divine revelation, so that all the laws and concepts are deemed to be the authorship of God and not of Moses, who is only the conduit, nevertheless this conduit was not an empty vessel. Whatever our conception of divine revelation, the intellect and the moral and ethical sensitivity of Moses deserve appreciation. We tend to look in admiration at his courage and his leadership in undertaking, however reluctantly, the liberation of a powerless slave nation from the greatest power on earth. We forget that he also had to deal with the ideals and institutions that would be needed to make that group first into a people and eventually into a nation. It is not my contention that all of the laws as we have them in the Torah were the fruit of Moses's mind. Undoubtedly, many of these formulations were the product of individuals and groups that followed him, but the fundamental concepts on which they were based can, I believe, be ascribed to him.

Moses was a great religious innovator with a broad view of humanity and the world who had a vision, perhaps too utopian, of what a godly society should be. It is that vision I have attempted to explore in revealing the basic truths on which the Teaching of Moses, the Torah, is based.

The Torah based on Moses's insights is a radical book, a revolutionary book. We tend to think of documents such as the English Magna

Carta, the French Declaration of the Rights of Man, and the American Declaration of Independence as radical and revolutionary in the good sense of those terms. But the Torah was and is no less radical. It was a revolution in its day, and the amazing thing is that now—some three thousand years later—it has not lost its radical flavor.

When dealing with the story of creation I wrote:

> Like a bolt of lightning, Genesis shattered ancient myths and replaced the chaos of paganism with the light of the belief in one power—one God—whose will is supreme.[3]

That sentence very much captures my feeling about the entire Torah—it shattered ancient beliefs and replaced them with profound new insights and beliefs. They are givens that serve as the basis of the Torah's faith, even though they were not always lived up to in actual life or even in all of the Torah's laws and texts. The implications of these new concepts are not always carried to the furthest point of implementation. Sometimes that took generations, and sometimes there were retreats from the purity of these ideas. Some have yet to be fully realized. I am reminded of the fact that America was founded on the statement that "all men are created equal," yet it took one hundred years before blacks were freed from slavery and ostensibly made legally equal. It took longer than that before women were permitted to vote. A similar thing has happened with the Israeli Declaration of Independence, which is far from having been realized. The implications of basic ideas and the implementation of these ideas are often not simultaneous with their first utterance. The text of the Torah represents the time in which it was given and the then current conditions of life and often does not reach the ultimate goal inherent in the truths contained therein.

I have identified fourteen revolutionary, radical ideas in the Torah. Some are more important, some less so; and they are often interrelated. Understanding these concepts helps us understand the narratives and the laws in the Torah. They did not emerge in a vacuum. The following is a brief description of each truth. The chapters of the book will explain them in depth.

1. The first of these revolutions, as indicated, lies in the very concept of God. All the elements of myth are absent. God is not in nature but above nature. God is in essence unknowable—but not unknown. Such a concept is liberating, freeing not only our understanding of a God of limitations and a bondage to fate, but also freeing the human being to create an image of God that is constantly changing and expanding to meet the challenges such new knowledge brings.

2. There is no supernatural evil force in the world—only the inclination of humans toward evil. Other religions posited many gods or sometimes only two—good and evil, light and darkness. The Torah rejects the idea that there is any such evil force in the world.

3. Morality is God's supreme demand on all human beings, as witnessed by the stories of the flood and of Sodom and Gomorrah. The prophets emphasize this time and time again, but the origins are in the Torah itself.

4. The purpose of worship changes from providing the gods that which they need and conducting rituals that have an effect on them into an act for the benefit of the human being. This allowed for the development of verbal worship—prayer—divorced from sacrifice, which in turn led to an institution—the synagogue—a place of worship without sacrifice that revolutionized human worship.

5. The fifth revolutionary concept is the value of human beings. Humans are differentiated from all others in that they are created in the image of God. Therefore, human life is sacred; it is an absolute value.

6. Next is the equality of all human beings. There is only one common ancestor for us all, regardless of race or religion. The Torah and the rest of the Hebrew Bible never make Jews—Israelites—superior to other human beings. This also leads to the idea that each individual is important and is unique.

7. The seventh is the equality of men and women. Unfortunately, this equality was not carried out to its ultimate end in legislation

where, especially with respect to marriage, men are given greater rights.

8. Human beings are granted free will and are not in the hands of fate; the concept of choice is the very opposite. No one is doomed in advance. All of human responsibility comes from this idea. The High Holy Days as they exist today are predicated on the idea of choice.

9. The sovereign—if there is to be one—has limitations and is subject to the rules of the Torah because God is the only absolute Sovereign. Even if there were to be a human sovereign, he would not be a supreme leader, and certainly not a god.

10. The priesthood is given an entirely new meaning, totally divorced from magic, healing, or rites that bring about any divine action. Priests have no special powers. They can pronounce God's blessing but cannot themselves cause either blessing or curse. They can teach the people Torah but possess no secret knowledge that is kept from the public.

11. The Torah contains several laws governing economics. They include the equitable distribution of land, including the return of the land and the forgiveness of debts in the Jubilee year. This economic plan may be totally unrealistic, but it sets an impressive and challenging standard.

12. Another given is the virtual abolition of Israelite slavery. The experience of Egypt caused us to be sensitive to the plight of the slave and to mitigate all slavery.

13. The impoverished, the needy, and the stranger must be treated properly. This, too, is based on the experience of Israel in Egypt. We were strangers and know what that means.

14. The institution of a day of rest for all—servants and animals included—is a radical social concept. Everyone is entitled to that most elementary thing—time off.

Taken together, these fourteen truths paint a picture of the world, of human beings, of society, of religion, and of morality that is surprisingly modern and relevant. They are not provable in any scientific way, nor can they be disproved. They are givens based on prophetic insight or, if you will, on divine revelation. They teach that humanity is one, as God is one. That magic and superstition are falsehoods. That humans are responsible for their actions and have the choice to do good or evil. That poverty and deprivation, slavery and hatred are evils that must be eradicated. That the earth is not ours to destroy. That love of others is a divine command. A society based on these principles would revolutionize the world.

Part I
DIVINITY

1

God Is Unique

Revolutionary Truth #1: There exists one sole God, eternal and without physical needs, above nature and above fate, not controllable by magical rites, just and merciful.

> YHVH alone is God; there is none beside Him.
> *Deuteronomy 4:35*

> For YHVH your God is God supreme and Lord supreme, the great, the mighty, and the awesome God, who shows no favor and takes no bribe.
> *Deuteronomy 10:17*

> Who is like YHVH our God, who, enthroned on high, sees what is below, in heaven and on earth?
> *Psalm 113:5*

The quiet, seemingly innocuous way in which God is introduced in the first verse of the Torah is indicative of the revolutionary concept of the Divine that permeates the entire Torah: "In the beginning, God created the heavens and the earth" (Gen. 1:1).[1]

It is as if the main character in a play were to appear with no explanation and no background information. We know nothing about God. When was God born? What is God like? Where does God live? God is presented to us in this first verse as a given.[2] What is not said is as significant as what is said. God has no history. God lives, but mythology is dead.[3]

That is not the case with the stories told of the gods of other nations at the time these books originated. Neither Abraham (ca. 1800 BCE), the first Hebrew, nor Moses (ca. 1200 BCE), to whom the Torah is ascribed and whose ideology is its driving force, was the product of a civilization that would have portrayed a god in that way. The gods of Mesopotamia and the gods of Egypt, the two great civilizations of the ancient Near East, may have been different, but they all shared certain commonalities: they were not supreme and self-sufficient, and they had a history. They were born, they had a home, they had families. You knew all about them. You could make images of them; you could tell stories about their lives.[4] Not so the God of Israel. The God of Israel simply is. As a matter of fact, the very name YHVH, by which this God is known to Moses, is derived from the Hebrew root meaning "to be, to exist."

When God first appears to Moses at the burning bush, Moses wants to know God's name (Exod. 3:13). In pagan mythology, this was a crucial question, for the name of the god was needed to be able to invoke and control that god through magical incantations. God replies, "*Eheyeh asher Eheyeh*"—"I am that I am" or "I am what I am" (Exod. 3:14)[5]—a phrase based on the Hebrew verb "to be" or "to exist," as if to say, "I have no 'name.' I cannot be controlled by any magic." Although this phrase was later reworked into a name, the four letters *yod hey vav hey*—YHVH, a third-person form of the verb "to be" usually translated as "Lord"—it is not so much a name as a description. It indicates that God is the One who is, the One who causes all else to be—existence itself!

The very name and its explanation indicate a God whose essence is unknowable. As the biblical scholar Moshe Greenberg puts it so well, "My presence will be something undefined, something which, as my nature is more and more unfolded in history and the teachings of the prophets, will prove to be more than any formula can express."[6]

The philosopher Martin Buber preferred to translate *Eheyeh asher Eheyeh* as "I am and remain present." In that case, YHVH means "The One who is here" or "The One who will be present."[7] The God of the Torah is not some primordial force who created the universe but has no further connection to it, but a God who is present and active at all times, concerned with human life and involved with historical events.

Abraham was a child of Mesopotamia. He was born in Ur, a great metropolis that was the center of the worship of the moon goddess, Sin. The religion on which he was nurtured was based on the epic poem known as *Enuma elis*—"When on high"—which tells the story of creation and was reenacted publicly at each new year's celebration. There are seven tablets on which the epic is related, and unlike the Torah, the first three of them are devoted to the story of the birth of the gods, who themselves emerged from other beings that already existed, Apsu and Tiamat. Marduk emerges as the most powerful god. He battles against the primordial monster Tiamat, slays her, splits her body in two, and creates the heavens from the top half and the earth from the bottom.[8]

Abraham rejected these beliefs. In the words of biblical scholar Yochanan Muffs, "Abraham got up and left, and the echoes of this revolutionary exodus are still reverberating in the world today."[9] He rejected all the heavenly science, all the marvelous literature, and all the esoteric theosophy of the Babylonians. The Torah reflected this rejection. In one bold stroke, Genesis completely eliminated those first three tablets and thus gave us a new understanding of God—a God who creates but was not created, a God with no ancestors and no descendants, a God who reigns alone and who brings the world into being with a word and not with a sword.[10]

Because there was a multiplicity of gods in the Mesopotamian pantheon, all decisions had to be made in the assembly of the gods, where unanimity and harmony were seldom achieved.[11] There was no one supreme god who ruled the world alone, no single being on whom worshippers could depend. Noted assyriologist and biblical scholar E. A. Speiser has posited that this was the basic weakness of Mesopotamian religion, which came to rely more and more on cumbersome rituals and less on spiritual truths. Monotheism would be the solution to this crisis, but to conceive of such an idea, initially, without any known precedent in the experience of mankind, called for greater resources than those of logic alone. It required a resolute rejection of common and long-cherished beliefs, a determined challenge to the powers believed to dominate every aspect of nature, and the substitution of a single supreme being for that hostile coalition. The new belief, in short, would call for unparalleled inspiration and conviction, a true revolution. Without that kind of call, notes Speiser, Abraham could not have become the father of the biblical process.[12] The Torah, in its very first words, represents exactly that unparalleled revolution and continues it in all its teachings about God. This teaching could be summarized in the phrase "ethical monotheism."

This new concept of one God lays the foundation for a new understanding of the world in which we live. It is one world, a place not of chaos and struggle but of harmony. Humankind is also one in origin and in purpose, even if diverse in its manifestations. All humans answer to one God. There are no competing divinities and no power of evil to challenge the one God, as will be explained in chapter 2.

The Nature of God

Oneness alone, however, is not the essence of Israelite monotheism. It is important to emphasize that Israelite monotheism is not simply a reduction of the number of gods to one. It is a complete change in understanding of the nature of the Divine. The God of Israel described by the Torah is not subject to fate. God is not a part of nature but the creator of nature, not subject to physical needs, and not to be influenced or changed by magical manipulation. That is very much implied in the phrase "I am that I am." To quote Buber again:

> "I do not need to be conjured for I am always with you … but it is impossible to conjure me." It is necessary to remember Egypt as background of such a revelation: Egypt where the magician went so far as to threaten the gods that if they would not do his will he would not merely betray their names to the demons, but would also tear the hair from their heads…. In the revelation at the burning bush religion is demagicized.[13]

In that sense, Israelite religion was the first monotheistic religion. The brief period in Egypt of the worship of the sun god Aton as the only god is often cited as a predecessor of Israelite monotheism, but it is not, because the worship of the sun was no different from the worship of any other natural phenomenon in essence.[14] When the Egyptian Pharaoh Akhenaton reformed religion by decreeing the sole worship of Aton, he created a kind of monism that was no less pagan than the religion that had preceded it. True monotheism requires the belief in a God "who is above nature, whose will is supreme, who is not subject to compulsion and fate, who is free of the bonds of myth and magic."[15]

The important thing is not whether there was one god or many, but the nature of these deities. Pagan deities were physical in nature, depending on other forces for their existence. They needed food and drink. They could be manipulated by magic. They were born and often died. In other words, they were little different from human beings in essence, albeit human beings writ large. Often they were also personifications of natural phenomena.[16] Not so the God of Israel, and that was the great revolution created by the religion of Israel:

One God unbounded and unfettered by physical needs

One God who neither was born nor died and whose will was supreme

One God who could not be identified with nature or with any object in nature such as the sun or the moon

One God who could not be manipulated by magic[17]

One God who was righteous, just, merciful, and loving

One of the wonderful things about this radical and revolutionary idea is its reluctance to dwell on the exact nature of God and God's being. Just as the strict monotheism of Israelite religion makes God one, unique and alone, so it voided any possibility of speaking about the "life of God." God has no interaction with others of a godly nature, other than some use of super–human beings known as angels or messengers for specific purposes.[18] Therefore, there is no story to tell of the gods. The action, then, moves to another dimension, the history of God's interaction with human beings.[19]

Even though at the early stages of Israelite religion physical manifestations of God were believed to exist, the Torah strictly forbids the making and worshipping of images of God. Images may have been forbidden so that people would not believe there was any divine power in the images themselves. Furthermore, whatever form God may have taken, the true God—YHVH—could not be captured in a humanly constructed image. Imagery would only confine and diminish our understanding of God. The book of Deuteronomy is especially insistent on this, reminding the people that at Sinai they saw no image. They only heard a voice.[20]

Even if the Torah envisioned God as corporeal, it never ascribed physical needs,[21] sexual characteristics, birth, or death to God. In the most essential ways, the God of Israel was always considered "Other," not a part of nature and not in any sense a human being. The magnificent description of God's appearance to Isaiah (chapter 6), with its proclamation of "Holy, holy, holy" (v. 3) as the only adequate reaction to God's presence, and the unequalled chapters of Job describing a God beyond human comprehension (38–41) would never have been possible without the Torah's concept of an imageless God. In a sense, the words of Job are the only possible response to such a concept: "Indeed, I spoke without understanding of things beyond me, which I did not know" (Job 42:3).

This worship of a God who was not usually seen and who could not be confined to any statue eventually led to the further freeing of the concept of God when Maimonides made it a principle of Jewish faith that God has no physical being, no body.[22] Although there were those who insisted that Maimonides was wrong and that Judaism was consistent with the notion of a physical God, his concept was overwhelmingly accepted as part and parcel of Jewish belief, so that all physical references to God's body are today taken as metaphorical, no matter what they might once have meant.

Being incorporeal, however, does not mean being totally abstract with no consciousness, a mere force rather than a being. The Torah ascribes feelings and emotions to God. God is concerned, God loves, God sorrows and rejoices.[23] Although it is difficult for us to fathom, it is obvious the Torah assumes a God who is capable of feelings that somehow parallel human emotions yet exceed them. Perhaps the best way to understand that is to say it presents a God who is more than an abstract force and more than a first cause. God is greater than, not lesser than, human beings. God's consciousness is more than human consciousness and ultimately unfathomable to our minds.

The Torah's message concerning God is given succinctly in the verse proclaimed by Moses to Israel as they stood on the other side of the Jordan ready to enter the land: "Hear, O Israel: YHVH is our God. YHVH is one" (Deut. 6:4). Known as the *Shema*, this extremely brief and simple verse has become the Jewish creed. In it, Moses inculcates the very essence of the new concept of God: first, that Israel's God is the Divinity known as YHVH—the essence of all being, the Creator of all that exists; and, second, that this God YHVH is the only one and is unique, different than anything else that exists in the world.

It is true that the Hebrew verse can be translated in various ways. The new Jewish Publication Society version has "The LORD is our God, the LORD alone." The commentator on Deuteronomy, Jeffrey Tigay, prefers this translation and suggests that the major import of this verse is not so much monotheism but a demand for Israel to give total allegiance to YHVH. Israel must worship only YHVH. That there are no other gods has already been stated in Deuteronomy 4:39, "Know therefore and keep in mind that YHVH alone is God in heaven above and on earth below; there is no other."[24]

The Torah's concept of God, so different from all concepts that had come before, has great advantages in freeing our understanding of God of all subservience to other forces and to magic, thus transforming ritual from matters that meet God's need or force God's actions to matters that benefit human beings. God and nature are also separated. The forces of nature are God's creation, but they are not divine. The world becomes a place of order, not chaos.

The Origin of Monotheism

Did monotheism originate with Abraham or with Moses? Both of these men grew up in societies where polytheism and idol worship, replete with its mythological gods, were in full flourish. Obviously, both of them also broke with this; in the case of Abraham, however, exactly in what way and to what extent remain unclear. He never voices any struggle against idolatry, as does Moses, although Abraham remains totally committed to the one God whom he worships exclusively. It is impossible to know to what extent Abraham understood the ramifications of his new belief, but in the teachings ascribed to Moses, it is fully realized and becomes the basis for Israelite religion.

There is a hint that it remained for Moses to completely realize the meaning of the worship of this one God, YHVH, when God says to him, "I appeared to Abraham, Isaac, and Jacob as El Shaddai, but I did not make Myself known to them by My name YHVH" (Exod. 6:3). It is not that they did not know the name, but that its full implications were not yet understood. To quote Moshe Greenberg, "However the passage is interpreted ... it must mean that with the advent of Moses a new and fuller perception of God was achieved."[25] Moses inherits the God of the fathers, the God of Abraham, Isaac, and Jacob, and carries the understanding of that God to a higher level than ever before, making clear the concepts that were inherent in the teachings of the fathers.

The idea that one God and only one God exists naturally resulted in the belief that all nations should acknowledge that God.[26] This is expressed openly in many of the psalms that call on all peoples to praise YHVH, for example: "Ascribe to YHVH, O families of the peoples, ascribe to the Lord glory and strength" (Ps. 96:7) and "Praise YHVH, all you nations" (Ps. 117:1). The prophets taught that the day would come when YHVH would be truly one in that all nations would acknowledge YHVH as the only God. As Zechariah says, "YHVH will be king over all the earth; on that day YHVH shall be one and His name one" (14:9).

This leaves us with the expectation that the day will come when all will worship the only God who exists, although it is not always clear exactly how this will occur or if this will mean that the religion of Israel will become the religion of all. It is more likely that each nation will worship God in its own way.

Monotheism remained confined to Israel alone for well over a thousand years. Although there were individuals from other peoples who joined Israel and worshipped Israel's God—Ruth is an obvious example—monotheism was not adopted by non-Jews in any significant number until some time in the late Second Temple period, when it began to spread throughout the Roman Empire. Unfortunately, the political and military defeat of the Jews in 70 CE put an end to that. It was not until Christianity and later Islam blossomed that monotheism truly conquered the Western and Middle Eastern worlds.

Different Approaches to Belief in God

Within Judaism, there were many different approaches to the monotheism taught by the Torah, from mystical concepts found in Kabbalah to Maimonidean thought in which God had not only no body but also no emotions, since to Maimonides any change even in feelings meant imperfection. Thus, anything written of that sort in the Bible had to be understood as simply "the language of human beings." As noted earlier, as important as what the Torah says God is, is what it says God is not. Maimonides said we could only speak of God in negatives. Heavily influenced by Greek philosophy, Maimonides posited a God very different from the God that mystical thought in Judaism—Kabbalah—described. Kabbalah developed an entire complicated system of spheres and manifestations of God that seem perilously close to polytheism. Yet, both based themselves on the God of the Torah. In a sense, both approaches had to move beyond the simple meaning of the text without betraying it.

The Torah posits the existence of God; it does not attempt to prove it. As we have seen, it begins with the assertion "In the beginning God created" (Gen. 1:1). At that time, the existence of gods was taken for granted. The Torah is concerned with the exclusivity of the one God and with combatting the beliefs that existed then regarding the existence of many gods, all of whom were of a very different nature than the God Moses worshipped. The way in which God was understood and negated all previous beliefs was—and is—revolutionary. It enables our understanding of God to grow, change, and be refined to fit the knowledge we have today that was not known earlier. Just as Maimonides was able to refine his understanding of the Torah and his concept of God in light of the best scientific and philosophical knowledge of his day, so too have we been able to do so today.

In modern times, theologians such as Mordecai Kaplan have posited a nonsupernatural idea of God,[27] while others, among them

Abraham Joshua Heschel, stressed a very personal God. For Heschel, the wonder of the world, the astonishment of being alive, was sufficient proof of the existence of what he termed "the Ineffable."[28]

Modernism and rationalism have tended to play down the descriptions of God in the Torah so as not to seem too simplistic and to avoid teaching the "old man in the sky with a beard" version of God. In so doing they have often shied away from the depiction of a God who is concerned and who is moved, a God who can love but can also be angry and disappointed. Yochanan Muffs terms this idea "the Personhood of God" and states that in portraying God in this way the Torah presented a God who "could be worshipped by man since He was so much like him" and "provided the models that man so needed to survive and flourish."[29]

If the problem that the Torah dealt with was pagan polytheism, the problem of our age is atheism or agnosticism. This is the result of many things. Science has taught us that much that we took for granted is not so, making it difficult, if not impossible, for us to believe literally in many of the stories of the Torah or that every event of nature is the result of the immediate will of God. Miracles—defined as supernatural events that contradict the laws of nature—have been brought into question. For others, the presence of evil in the world makes belief in God—at least in a good God—questionable. When the former chief justice of Israel Aharon Barak was asked in an interview if he believed in God, he remarked, "I do not believe that God exists. In my view the Holocaust is irreconcilable with the existence of God." I am sure Barak is not the only one with this viewpoint. These problems indeed raise questions that must be dealt with, and they may even cause us to refine our concept of God, but they do not disprove God's existence.[30]

The mistake atheists make is that they assume belief in God must be equated with ancient ideas of God they cannot accept, rather than admitting we can build on past traditions and create concepts of God that are more acceptable to the modern mind. The theologian Rabbi Milton Steinberg, for example, points out that the universe is dynamic, creative, rational, and purposive and contains consciousness. In his view, the entire universe is the outward manifestation of Mind-Energy, of Spirit, or, to use the older and better word, of God.[31] It may be possible to dispute Steinberg's claim, but it certainly seems plausible. When we consider the wonder of the universe in which we live, a wonder that becomes greater and greater as we explore the extent of the universe, and when we consider the wonders of the human mind and human creativity, the idea that there is no intelligence in the world other than our own seems implausible. In other words, although there is reason to believe, we believe not because of reason but rather because of our feelings and experiences.

In view of all we know today about the world and all the scientific knowledge that we have, what we need is a concept of God that is great enough to encompass the magnificence of the universe in which we live. In place of a God who acts on the world in "supernatural" ways, we may conceive of a God manifested in the evolution of the universe and of humanity, a God working through the forces of history and human nature in a much more complex way than we might have previously thought. Impulses, possibilities, and capabilities come from God. Application comes from human beings. Like a power line, the world surges with divine forces we must learn to harness. We are God's partners in the work of creation. God does not change, but our understanding of God changes with the growth of knowledge. An understanding that does not grow can lead to misunderstanding and to rejection of the idea of the existence of God. To quote Steinberg again:

> If the believer has his troubles with evil, the atheist has more and graver difficulties to contend with. Reality stumps him altogether, leaving him baffled not by one consideration, but by many.... This then is the intellectual reason for believing in God: that though this belief is not free from difficulties, it stands out, head and shoulders, as the best answer to the riddle of the universe.[32]

Given the choice between accepting the existence of God even though much cannot be explained or understood and rejecting it—thus leaving the complexity of the universe and the existence of life and consciousness unexplained—I believe that the former is the more acceptable.

Neither science nor logic can offer proof. They cannot disprove the existence of God, but neither can they prove it. In the end, it always comes down to a matter of belief—to our reaction to the wonders of the universe and of life itself—that is not contrary to reason but rises above it. The revolutionary concept of God that the Torah teaches is as relevant today as ever and provides the needed theological basis for an understanding of God acceptable to moderns.

2

No Divine Power of Evil Exists

Revolutionary Truth #2: There is no supernatural evil force in the world. Other religions posited many gods or perhaps only two—good and evil, light and darkness. The Torah rejects that and denies the existence of a superhuman force of evil. The only divine force is God, and God is good.

> And God saw all that He had made, and found it very good.
>
> *Genesis 1:31*

> I am YHVH and there is none else; beside Me there is no god....
> I am YHVH and there is none else,
> I form light and create darkness,
> I make weal and create woe–
> I YHVH do all these things.
>
> *Isaiah 45:5–7*

The Torah's monotheistic concept, the idea that there is only one God in the world, a God who is the embodiment of all good and is bound by no other power, represented a total rejection of the generally accepted idea that evil has a divine or supernatural source. Paganism in its various forms deals with the problem of evil—woe—in the world by simply positing the existence of evil forces as well as good ones. The Torah has no such option. Any acknowledgment of a demonic force would impinge on the exclusive divinity of the one God who created the world without struggle simply by uttering words. This concept of a world in which evil has no ultimate cosmic power was revolutionary for its time. In a sense, the idea changed the rules concerning how human beings related to the natural world and to their own nature as well.

Yehezkel Kaufmann, a pioneer in the study of biblical religion, characterizes the pagan religions that existed prior to the religion of Israel as ones in which there existed

> many independent power-entities, all on a par with one another, and all rooted in the primordial realm. This radical variety finds particular expression in the dichotomies of good and evil gods, equal in their divine rank and power, because both derive independently from the primordial realm. The battle between good and evil, between holy and impure is conceived of as an everlasting struggle between hostile divine twins.[1]

In paganism, the realm of evil is autonomous and just as powerful as the realm of the good. There is an eternal struggle between these two realms, the pure and the impure.

Nothing of the sort is found in the Torah, where the realm of the unclean is simply that which the one and only God has decreed to be unclean. That realm has no intrinsic impurity in it, nor does it belong to any independent realm of evil or impurity. There is no connection between the unclean and some primordial evil. Israel is commanded to make a distinction between clean and unclean beasts because they are creatures "that I have set apart for you to treat as unclean" (Lev. 20:25) or because "they are unclean for you" (Deut. 14:7–8). In one version of the flood story, Noah is commanded specifically to take one pair of unclean animals into the ark as well as seven pairs of those that are clean (Gen. 7:2). The unclean are also the creations of God and are to continue to exist in the new world about to be born. There is no explanation of their status and no hint that they in any way represent a demonic force in the world. They are simply animals that God has set apart and will later forbid Israel to eat or to sacrifice.

The clearest, most radical formulation of the concept of evil as an independent force is found in the Persian religion Zoroastrianism, which is based on the continual struggle between two equal divinities: Ormazd, the realm of light and goodness, and Ahriman, representing darkness and evil.[2] Many interpreters, going back to Jewish philosopher Saadia Gaon, have seen in the verse from Isaiah quoted above—"I form light and create darkness, I make weal and create woe" (45:7), in which the word translated as "woe," *ra*, also means "evil"—a specific reference to and refutation of the belief in two gods. Even those who do not think that the prophet was specifically referring to Zoroastrianism see this verse as an assertion that only one divinity exists in the world and that YHVH is the source of everything—the creator not only of light, as in Genesis 1:3, but of the darkness that preceded it as well. Nor are catastrophes, woe, created by other divine forces. None exist.[3]

Nowhere in the Torah—nor in the entire Hebrew Bible, for that matter—is there a struggle between God and forces of evil. The only evil that God confronts is that committed by human beings. The struggle has moved from the mythical realm of the gods to the interaction of God and human beings. God does not have to struggle against forces of nature to control them, nor does God ever engage in battle with demons or evil gods—or even with good ones, for that matter. The contest conducted by Elijah with the priests of Baal (1 Kings 18:20–40) is no contest. It is merely an opportunity for Elijah to demonstrate that no god exists except YHVH. So too are the plagues in Egypt, which "mete out punishments to the gods of Egypt" (Exod. 12:12) only in the sense of demonstrating that those so-called gods have no power. They are, in the phrase of Deuteronomy 32:17, "no gods."

Angelic Creatures

It is true that the Torah does conceive of "heavenly creatures" aside from God, but they are not divinities with independent power. Angels appear often in the stories of the patriarchs. The first appearance of an angel is to Hagar, when she runs away from Sarah (Gen. 16:7). Three angels appear to Abraham at Mamre, although the text at first calls them men (Gen. 18:2) and only later names them angels (Gen. 19:1). Jacob sees creatures identified as "angels of God" (Gen. 28:12). Jacob also struggles with a man (Gen. 32:25) but is later said to have wrestled with "a divine being" (Gen. 32:31). An angel of YHVH appears to Moses in the flames of the burning bush (Exod. 3:2), but it is YHVH who then calls and speaks to him (Exod. 3:4). In the Torah, angels have no individuality or personality. They serve as messengers of God and sometimes disappear as God takes their place. It is only during later, postexilic times that angels with specific names or functions appear in Hebrew texts. The Hebrew word for "angel" also means "messenger," and that seems to be their function. In the description in Psalm 78:49 of punishments that God inflicted on the Egyptians, the expression "angels [messengers] of woe [evil]" is used. There are no "evil angels" as opposed to "good angels," only angels who are sent to afflict those God wishes to punish. As Yehezkel Kaufmann points out, destructive agents "do not constitute a domain opposing YHVH; like the rest of the angels, they are his messengers only."[4]

Early Folklore

Evil divine forces simply do not exist in the Torah or the rest of the Bible. They begin to appear as "harmful creatures" in Babylonian Jewish folklore and play a part along with many other superstitious practices in Talmudic lore. The people in the wilderness may have believed in demons and even sacrificed to them (Lev. 17:7), as did Israel once settled in its own land (Deut. 32:17), but the Torah does not ascribe reality or power to them and commands Israel not to worship them.

Satan

The figure of Satan as a truly evil force, a rival of God attempting to seduce human beings into acts of evil, does not appear in biblical literature. Satan as described by Milton in *Paradise Lost*, for example, is a far cry from anything that appears in the Torah or even in later biblical books:

> *To do ought good never will be our task,*
> *But ever to do ill our sole delight,*
> *As being the contrary to his high will*
> *Whom we resist. If then his Providence*
> *Out of our evil seek to bring forth good,*
> *Our labour must be to pervert that end,*
> *And out of good still to find means of evil.*[5]

The serpent in the garden—identified by Milton and Christianity in general as Satan—in the Torah is simply "the shrewdest of all the wild beasts that YHVH God had made" (Gen. 3:1) and, as punishment for its sin, is demoted and made to crawl in the dust (Gen. 3:14). By specifying that the serpent, too, is a creation of YHVH, the verse denies the existence of an independent power of wickedness.

The word "satan" appears first as *ha-satan*—the Adversary—in Job 1:6, where it is not a proper name but a descriptive title. The tale of Job pictures God as presiding over a heavenly court, a description that occurs in the psalms as well. In Psalm 82:1, for example, we read that "God arises in the divine assembly." The Adversary is a kind of prosecuting attorney who attempts to put to trial those whom he suspects are not as pious as they appear. When questioning Job's piety, God allows the Adversary to put Job to the test with certain limitations. The Adversary never appears to Job or tries to tempt him. Rather, the Adversary makes Job suffer in a way that could cause him to give up his loyalty to God. This figure—the Adversary—appears only one other time in the Bible, in the book of postexilic prophet Zechariah (3:1). It is clear that from this conception, a figure of evil could develop. The closest the Bible comes is one reference in the late postexilic book 1 Chronicles: "Satan arose against Israel and incited David to number Israel" (21:1). It is indeed possible, as the biblical scholar Robert Gordis contends, that the development of such a figure, even in the way he appears in Job, is due to the influence of Persian thought, in which there is a cosmic battle between good and evil. Nevertheless, as Gordis writes, "For the ancient Hebrews, who could not conceive of God's existence apart from His governing the world, to attribute evil to any other power beyond His sway would be tantamount to a denial of God."[6]

God and the Problem of Evil

In his modern verse drama updating the Job story, *J.B.*, the poet Archibald MacLeish puts the problem succinctly:

> *If God is God He is not good*
> *If God is good He is not God.*[7]

If God is all-powerful, He must be the source of any evil that exists. If not, if God is only good, then He is not all-powerful.

Of course, the prophet's assertion in Isaiah 45:7 that God is the source of both "weal and woe" can be problematic as well, especially given that, as pointed out above, the Hebrew word for "woe," *ra*, can also be understood as "evil." This may be the reason that when the verse was later incorporated into the morning prayer service, blessing God for creating the world that has both light and darkness, the word *ra* was changed to *ha-kol*, "everything": "forming light and creating darkness, making weal and creating everything." Unfortunately, the theological problem of the existence of evil in the world created by a good God cannot be solved that easily.

How do we define "evil"? The Hebrew *ra*, as we have already seen, can mean simply anything that causes suffering, with no pejorative implication. In the Torah, suffering is sometimes seen as punishment for evil conduct. Was the suffering caused by the biblical flood or by the destruction of the evil cities of Sodom and Gomorrah itself evil? No, not if it was deserved punishment brought by a just God. Nor can the woe caused by the Ten Plagues in Egypt be called evil, although the Hebrew term *ra*, or "woe," would be appropriate. What, then, is God's relationship to the suffering that occurs due to natural disasters—volcanic eruptions, earthquakes, tsunamis, floods? Unless we presume that God has deliberately brought these to punish us—a presumption that is very hard to believe—then these are "evils" in the sense of sufferings that have no explanation. The Torah mentions famines without indicating that they were brought specifically by God (Gen. 12:10, 26:1). Other books of the Bible speak of earthquakes or famines without describing them as heavenly punishments (Amos 1:2, Zech. 14:5, Ruth 1:1). Although

God punishes Miriam with a kind of leprosy (Num. 12:10), there is absolutely no indication that all those afflicted with skin diseases are sinners (Lev. 13:2). Unless the Torah has specifically stated that an event was a punishment, there is no warrant for seeing it as such.

Another kind of *ra* is that which human beings cause to others. Cain kills Abel, defying God's word. Abel is innocent, not a sinner; he does not deserve to die. Humans murder or rape innocent victims. People are killed in automobile crashes or airplane disasters; they drown on the *Titanic*. In a good world, should that happen?

Human evil is easier to deal with. As we will see in chapter 8, given the Torah's belief in human free will, humans have the ability to do evil, and God does not stop these individual acts. What causes human beings to do such things? The Torah's explanation is that humans have an inclination toward evil—the *yetzer ha-ra*—that they can resist but often do not. As God said to Cain, "Its urge is toward you, yet you can rule over it" (Gen. 4:6–7). This is the cause of much of the evil, the suffering and woe, in the world.[8] Wars and even the Shoah are the result of human actions. God is not the cause, yet we may question why God permits such things to happen or why humans were created with this evil impulse. The answer is that without God's granting freedom of action to all, which of necessity includes the possibility of doing evil, humans would be no different from animals or robots. Indeed, we cannot conceive of human life without the freedom to choose and even to disobey. That may not be a satisfactory answer, since we could hope that somehow a divine force would stop such massive catastrophes before they happen.

This questioning of God is voiced by the second-century *Tanna* Rabbi Shimon bar Yochai in one of the most daring midrashim. Commenting on the phrase "to Me" in the verse, "Hark! Your brother's blood cries out to Me from the ground!" (Gen. 4:10), he says:

> This matter is difficult to say and impossible for the mouth to explain—it may be likened to two athletes who were wrestling before the king. Had the king so wished, he could have separated them. One overpowered the other and was killing him—and he shouted, 'Who will bring my cause before the king!'[9]

He cries out to the king—as did Abel's blood—because the king is responsible, since he could have separated them and instead permitted the fight to continue so that one killed the other. Rabbi Shimon has no answer to the question he hardly dared utter.

The Rabbis, borrowing biblical terminology, coined the idea of God's "hidden face" (*hester panim*) for such times. This idea at least has the virtue of saying that God did not actively permit these things; they do not represent God's will. As Abraham Heschel once remarked, "History is the realm in which the will of God is defied."

Paganism has no problem with evil perpetrated by human beings, as it has no problem with evil in general. Since evil is inherent in the very makeup of the world, where forces of good and evil exist and are in constant conflict, human evil is a natural part of that struggle. Although Christianity, following Judaism, does not ascribe evil to God, it has elevated the role of Satan to that of a supernatural power of evil and has also created the doctrine that human beings are born inherently sinful. Because of original sin, humans are incapable of freeing themselves from this by their own power.[10]

Judaism's view of human beings is less pessimistic. Nevertheless, the power and force of human evil, the strength of the *yetzer ha-ra*, is never underestimated, and we ignore it at our peril. The Torah is quite explicit on this point, and later, Rabbinic Judaism emphasized it as well. "The evil inclination is so described because it entangles human beings as if among thorns," they taught.[11] If ever there were proof of the human capacity for evil, it is the events of the twentieth century, an age of enlightenment and human progress, when human beings perpetrated on one another evil undreamed of before.

Although there are numerous psalms that question why God permits suffering or does not answer the call of the righteous—see, for example, Psalms 13, 22, 38, 70, 71, and 88—the only book of the Bible to really attempt to deal with the problem that the Rabbis called "the suffering of the righteous" (*tzadik v'ra lo*) is Job. The poetic sections of the book, as opposed to the earlier prose framework, gave the poet the opportunity to explore the question of human suffering and to reject the easy answers, such as "You sinned and therefore you are being punished," the implication of which is that anyone who suffers must deserve that suffering.

What answers, if any, does the author of Job give to this question, aside from rejecting the traditional connection between suffering and sin? One answer is simply to concede that abuses are found in the world but that it is impossible even for God to deal with them all. This is the implication of the way in which God, in effect, challenges Job to take the position of ruler of the world and do better!

> *And as you see each proud sinner—abase him!*
> *As you look on each arrogant one—bring him low,*
> *And tread down the wicked in their place.*
> *Bury them all in the dust,*
> *Press their faces into the grave.*
>
> (*Job 40:11–13*)[12]

In the magnificent concluding speeches of God, describing the great universe that God has created and that is beyond human comprehension, the message according to Robert Gordis is that "just as there is order and harmony in the natural world, though imperfectly grasped by man, so there is order and meaning in the moral sphere, though often incomprehensible to man."[13] Moshe Greenberg put it somewhat differently:

> Man's capacity to respond with amazement to God's mysterious creativity, and to admire even those manifestations of it that are of no use or benefit to him, enables him to affirm God's work despite its deficiencies in the moral realm. Such deficiencies, like so much else in the amazing cosmos, stand outside human judgment … for mankind wisdom consists of fearing God and shunning evil; more than that he cannot know.[14]

The answers the author of Job does not give are that God is unjust or that there is another power—an evil one—that causes suffering.

Although traditional Jewish philosophical thought accepts no limitation on the power of God, Rabbinic Judaism recognized there is such a thing as "the world works in its own way" (*olam k'minhago noheg*), which would be the equivalent of natural law. Even God does not supersede that. Thus, the Rabbis taught that "if a man stole wheat and sowed it in the ground, by rights it should not grow, but the world works in its own way.... Similarly, a man has intercourse with his neighbor's wife, by rights she should not conceive, but the world works in its own way" (Talmud, *Avodah Zarah* 54b). The Mishnah (*Berachot* 9:3) teaches that when a woman is pregnant, one is not allowed to pray that the child be a boy or a girl; the sex is already determined. But could not God—the All-Powerful—change that? There are rules of nature that remain inviolable.

On the other hand, the theologian Milton Steinberg writes about the role of chance:

> I am inclined ... to accept the limitation on God's power which is implied in the concept of the surd and of chance. God is indubitably the power of rationality, of design, of order, of meaningfulness, yet ... the concept of surds, of the irrational, of the fortuitous, of the chance events that crop out of the normal stream of life, seems true to reality.... The concept of irrational evil prevents us from ascribing to God that which probably should not be ascribed to Him. God is exempted, not from the struggle, but from the responsibility for the elements of chance within His universe. Both He and His creation are then faced with a common task and a common battle.[15]

Einstein may have been convinced that "God does not play dice with the universe." Yet, science seems to say that there is a great element of chance in the natural world. As Kohelet put it long ago, "Not to the swift in the race and not to the mighty the battle ... for time and mishap will befall them all" (Eccles. 9:11).

The problem of evil remains unsolvable, but the problem of the existence of the universe is equally unsolvable if we say that because of evil, we cannot believe there is a God, a power beyond ourselves. It is tempting to posit dualism, granting divinity to evil just as we acknowledge the Divinity of the Good, but we are then left with a world that is not a harmony but a chaos, a constant battleground between competing forces. In short, it returns us to the chaos of paganism. Better a world that is not totally explainable but is the work of a benevolent Creator than one that is hostile to human beings.

While retaining the belief in one God and only one God, Moses and those who later interpreted his teachings could have posited some evil force less than God but greater than human beings. They did not do so, not willing to compromise the supremacy of YHVH in any way, nor could they ascribe evil to God. This revolutionary idea left us with unsolved and perhaps unsolvable problems of understanding, but it also bequeathed us the blessing of the view of a world that is not the battleground of conflicting forces and in which evil could wreck havoc and even prevail.

3

Morality Is God's Supreme Demand

Revolutionary Truth #3: Morality is God's supreme demand of all human beings. Ritual is secondary to right conduct.

> I am El Shaddai. Walk in My ways and be blameless.
> *Genesis 17:1*

> For I have singled him out, that he may instruct his children and his posterity to keep the way of YHVH by doing what is just and right.
> *Genesis 18:19*

> *Who may ascend the mountain of YHVH?*
> *Who may stand in His holy place?—*
> *One who has clean hands and a pure heart.*
> *Psalm 24:3–4*

Abraham and the God of Justice

According to the Torah's tradition, as far back as Abraham, the very first Hebrew, it was a given that God was a God of justice. Although Abraham's exact concept of the nature of that God is not spelled out, the Torah makes clear that he knew that his God was a righteous God who placed supreme value on justice and righteousness in human conduct above any considerations of ritual or correct worship. This can be seen from the story of the cities of Sodom and Gomorrah. Although Abraham believed that his God was a God of justice, it was not justice in the sense of harshness, but justice combined with mercy. Therefore, Abraham could reason with God and say, "Shall not the judge of all the earth deal justly?" (Gen. 18:25), utilizing a play on words, because both "judge" and "justly," *shofet* and *mishpat*, come from the same Hebrew root. After all, what Abraham asks of God is not simply to save the righteous in the city, which would be strict justice, but to save an overwhelming number of sinners if there were even ten righteous people. The Sages understood this when they ingeniously turned that question into a statement, so that according to them, Abraham said to God:

> The judge of all the earth *shall not* do justice. If You want the world to exist, there cannot be strict justice. If You want strict justice, the world cannot exist. You are trying to hold the rope by both ends. You want both the world and strict justice. If You do not let strict justice go, there will be no world.[1]

Therefore, there must be justice tempered with mercy. A God who is the embodiment of such justice also requires it of human beings above all else. God's decision to destroy these cities is not based on their idolatry, but on one consideration alone: immoral conduct, as exemplified by the cruel treatment of the angels, whom the inhabitants thought were simply strangers (Gen. 19:4–11). Instructive, too, is the fact that God informs Abraham of what is to happen so that he will teach his progeny to do "that which is right and just" (Gen. 18:19). Ethical monotheism in the Torah and the later teachings of the prophets of Israel were based on the belief that justice and righteousness were the very foundations of religion.

The God of Mercy

Moses also learns and imparts to Israel the ethical and merciful nature of God. In the story of the Golden Calf, Moses asks to see God's "Presence" (Exod.

33:18), meaning to understand God's nature.[2] Although the answer—"You will see My back; but My face must not be seen" (Exod. 33:23)—means that no one can fully understand the Divine, God does reveal to Moses what has come to be known as the Thirteen Attributes of God:

> YHVH! YHVH! a God compassionate and gracious, slow to anger, abounding in kindness and faithfulness, extending kindness to the thousandth generation, forgiving iniquity, transgression, and sin; yet He does not remit all punishment, but visits the iniquity of parents upon children and children's children, upon the third and fourth generations.
>
> (Exod. 34:6–7)

These words themselves are an enlargement of the expression of God's qualities—particularly that of mercy—in the Ten Commandments, where God is described as "visiting the guilt of the parents upon the children, upon the third and upon the fourth generations of those who reject Me, but showing kindness to the thousandth generation of those who love Me" (Exod. 20:5–6).

In an act of exegetical daring that is typical of the development of later Rabbinic Judaism, when editing the verses in Exodus 34 for use in Jewish prayer—where they appear as a plea for God to act mercifully and forgiving—the Sages broke off the Hebrew of the second verse in a way contrary to its meaning, so it would read not "yet He does not remit all punishment" (v. 7) but rather "and remitting all punishment." Thus, the Rabbinic Sages went a step further in their desire to emphasize the merciful nature of God and minimize God's punishment.

In one of his last orations to the Israelites, Moses gives his understanding of the nature of God, a three-part summation of all he has attempted to teach them in their forty-year journey:

> For YHVH your God is God supreme and Lord supreme, the great, the mighty, and the awesome God, who shows no favor and takes no bribe, but upholds the cause of the fatherless and the widow, and befriends the stranger, providing him with food

and clothing. You too must befriend the stranger, for you were strangers in the land of Egypt.

(*Deut. 10:17–19*)

In the first section, Moses asserts the supremacy of God and God's greatness and power, painting an awesome portrait of an unimaginable Divine Power. In the second part, he depicts a God who is the very essence of morality and who cares for the indigent and the needy, even providing them with the basic necessities of life. Finally, in the third section he comes to the important point: each of you—the Israelites—must imitate God's qualities of honesty, morality, and care. This teaching informs all of the Torah and influenced the teachings of the prophets and of later Judaism as well. Its meaning is clear: morality—ethical living, acting justly and mercifully—is the absolute demand of God. Rituals, as important as they may be, are secondary. As scholar of Jewish thought Louis Finkelstein writes, "The dominant principle of the Torah, whether love for man or obedience to God, obviously expresses itself in every commandment—ritual, moral, or legal. But perhaps we may take it that from the viewpoint of the School of Hillel, the legal and moral law reflects the ideas of Torah directly and the ritual system only indirectly."[3] This radical and revolutionary idea dominates the stories and the legislation of the Torah and is at the very heart of the ancient religion of Israel.

The religion of Israel teaches that all of the laws of the Torah stem directly from God. Moses is not the originator of these statutes; rather, the Torah depicts him as the prophet who conveys God's will to the people, the mouth of God. In this way, the legislation of the Torah is differentiated from that of other ancient Near East civilizations where the king—Hammurabi being the best-known example—was always the lawgiver. The laws and their enforcement were his domain. "I established law and justice in the language of the land, thereby promoting the welfare of the people. At that time (I decreed)," reads the prologue to the Code of Hammurabi.[4] Not so in Israel, where instead the laws are preceded by "YHVH spoke to Moses, saying: Speak to the Israelite people thus," or similar words. Because of this, all laws—or, as they came to be known, *mitzvot*, "commandments"—whether concerning civil matters or ritual ones, attained the status of God's will. This in itself was revolutionary because it elevated rules of ethical conduct from being merely laws of the welfare of the community to being statutes directly stemming from the divine will. At the same time, these demands of ethical living became the *supreme* demands, expressing the very essence of God's being and desires for human beings, and carrying with them a religious purpose, the achievement of sanctity—"You shall be holy" (Lev. 19:2)—a holiness predicated on ethical living. Not to act justly is not merely a violation of a social norm or a crime against the state; it is a sin against God.[5]

Penalties Lenient and Strict

Many of the civil statutes are similar to laws found in other ancient codes, but frequently they differ in the nature of penalties for their violation. Some of these differences are because of a tendency toward greater leniency and mercy. Some can be attributed to basic concepts of Israelite religion that differed from those of other religions of the time. Moshe Greenberg has pointed out that the Torah's view of both the sanctity of human life and the absolute nature of God-given rules account for many of these differences. For example, a woman's adultery in the Torah is not solely an offense against the husband but an offense against God as well. Therefore, whereas in Mesopotamian law the husband could decide not to punish the wife,[6] in the Torah he has no say in the matter (Lev. 20:10; Deut. 22:22). Mesopotamian law allowed the king to pardon capital offenses and permitted ransom for murder.[7] A life could be compensated for monetarily or by another life. That is impossible in the Torah because human life is sacred (Exod. 21:12–17; Gen. 9:5–6).[8] Later on, this same concept led the Rabbis to enact rules of evidence so strict that capital punishment was virtually impossible.[9] In a discussion that was purely theoretical because the right of the Sanhedrin to execute anyone had ceased decades before, a court that executed a person once in seven years was called "murderous." Rabbi Elazar ben Azariah said that this was so even if it was only once in seventy years, and both Rabbi Tarphon and Rabbi Akiba declared that "had we been members of the Sanhedrin, no one would ever have been executed." Only Rabban Shimon ben

Gamliel protested, saying that if so, they would have multiplied murderers in Israel (Talmud, *Makkot* 1:11).

The Role of Rite

Religion by definition has always included rituals in which the worshipper serves the realm of the Divine. In this, Israelite religion was no different. The rituals that were held in the Temple were called "the service" (*avodah*), and in later Judaism, prayer was termed "the service of the heart" (*avodah she-balev*). The difference lay in the meaning, emphasis, and content of such worship, and the fact that morality was no less a part of obedience to God than ritual, but rather the opposite: morality was the very essence of obedience to God. This difference was made possible by the new understanding of the nature of God that we discussed in chapter 1.

To briefly recapitulate: Near Eastern religions, whether those of Abraham's Mesopotamia or Moses's Egypt, all worshipped gods who were dependent on their followers to supply their needs, both physical and metaphysical. Since the gods themselves were subject to external forces, had physical needs for food and drink, and could be dominated by magic and incantation, even needing these to sustain their power, these deities were truly in need of human beings. The elaborate rites celebrated in the gods' magnificent temples provided those needs, including food and shelter. The God of Israel was above all of that. YHVH could dispense with sacrifices and could even raze the Temple—YHVH's "dwelling"—because God was not in need of any physical dwelling. Solomon's statement at the dedication of the First Temple that "even the heavens to their uttermost reaches cannot contain You" (1 Kings 8:27) is an expression of that conviction. All worship, therefore, was simply for the benefit of Israel, to bring the worshipper closer to God. What need, then, does this God have for human beings?

God Needs Human Beings

In his inspirational book *God in Search of Man*, Abraham Joshua Heschel notes that "Where are you?" is God's first question to Adam (Gen. 3:9). It is the basic question asked of every human being. God searches for and needs to find human beings, not for the purpose of serving God's personal needs but to create the human society that God wishes to see on earth. "All of human history as described in the Bible may be summarized in one phrase: *God in search of man.*"[10]

The new understanding of God as presented in the Torah thus changes the very nature of our relationship to God and redefines the purpose and importance of ritual. In its place comes the imperative to imitate God, a God whose very essence is morality. "You shall be holy, for I, YHVH your God, am holy" (Lev. 19:2). The Holiness Code, as this section has come to be known, includes ritual laws because these are needed to connect humans with the presence of the Divine, but the vast majority of the laws there are moral imperatives: leave gleanings for the poor and the stranger, practice honesty and truthfulness, treat workers properly, love your fellow and the stranger, care for the aged. This idea is repeated in Deuteronomy 10:17–19, quoted above. Exodus teaches that God is not only just but also merciful and compassionate (Exod. 34:6). As Rabbinic Judaism later taught, "Walk in the ways of YHVH. As God clothes the naked so should you clothe the naked, as God visited the sick, so should you visit the sick, as God comforted mourners, so should you comfort mourners" (Talmud, *Sotah* 14a). The God of the Torah is a just and merciful God who commands those following God to be just and merciful as well. In the words of Heschel:

> The moral imperative was not disclosed for the first time through Abraham or Sinai. The criminality of murder was known to men before.... What was new was the idea that justice is an obligation to God, *His way* not only His demand; that injustice is not something God scorns when done by others but that which is the very opposite of God; that the rights of humans are not legally protected interests of society but the sacred interests of God. God is not only the guardian of moral order, "the Judge of all the earth," but One who cannot act unjustly (Gen. 18:25).[11]

There is no capriciousness in God's handling of human beings as recounted in the Torah. Unlike the tales told in Mesopotamian and Babylonian texts, the Torah's stories of the flood are explicit in stating that the sin of that generation was a moral one. "YHVH saw how great was man's wickedness on earth, and how every plan devised by his mind was nothing but evil all the time" (Gen. 6:5). "The earth became corrupt before God; the earth was filled with lawlessness" (Gen. 6:11). In the Mesopotamian epic, on the other hand, the flood occurs because the god Enlil was disturbed by the noise made by human beings: "Oppressive has become the clamor of mankind, by their uproar they prevent sleep."[12] The hero in the Mesopotamian story is saved only because he is the favorite of one god.[13] There is no mention of his character. Noah, however, is saved because "Noah was a righteous man; he was blameless in his age" (Gen. 6:9). The generation of the Tower of Babel, however, was punished not for immorality but for hubris, a kind of rebellion against God, and they are not destroyed, only scattered. Such hubris is a lesser offense to God than lawlessness and violence. As we have seen, the cities of the plain are morally corrupt, as the story of the way they treat the strangers illustrates; indeed, "their sin is very grave" (Gen. 18:20). Even the sins of the Canaanites that will cause the land to spew them out (Lev. 18:25) are not ritual sins, but sins of sexual immorality (Lev. 18:1–24). It is not idolatry that causes them to be cast out but wickedness.

The Teachings of the Prophets

The primacy of morality and ethics was emphasized by the prophets and became their central message, but they did not invent it. They simply built on the concept that was inherent in the Torah's ideology, namely, that "God's covenant had a moral-legal, rather than a cultic purpose."[14] The prophets make it very clear that God rejects cultic sites when people violate the laws of justice and love.[15] Such an idea was unknown to pagan religions. Jeremiah's polemic, uttered at the Temple site itself, illustrates this boldly. It is an illusion, he tells the people at the gate of the Temple, to think that the presence of the Temple will save them from destruction. Rather, they must change their ways. They will be saved, he says, "if you execute justice between one man and another; if you do not oppress the stranger, the orphan, and the widow; if you do not shed the blood of the innocent in this place; if you do not follow other gods" (Jer. 7:5–6). They have made it a "den of thieves"; therefore, just as God destroyed the shrine at Shilo "because of the wickedness of My people Israel," so God will destroy the Temple in Jerusalem and send the Israelites into exile if they do not change (Jer. 7:11–15).

Jeremiah's cry for just living and his scorn for worship unaccompanied by morality were preceded by the words of Amos (eighth century BCE). Amos speaks of the sins of Israel that will not be forgiven and begins with: "Because they have sold for silver those whose cause was just, and the needy for a pair of sandals. Ah! You, who trample the heads of the poor into the dust of the ground, and make the humble walk a twisted course" (Amos 2:6–7). He castigates them for turning "justice into wormwood" (Amos 5:7) and urges them to "seek good and not evil.... Hate evil and love good, and establish justice in the gate" (Amos 5:14–15). Amos goes to the extreme, saying, in the name of God, "I spurn your festivals, I am not appeased by your solemn assemblies. If you offer Me burnt offerings—or your meal offerings—I will not accept them.... But let justice well up like water, righteousness like an unfailing stream" (Amos 5:21–24). He goes so far as to question the very institution of sacrifices: "Did you offer sacrifice and oblation to Me those forty years in the wilderness, O House of Israel?" (Amos 5:25). Small wonder that Amaziah the priest wanted King Jeroboam to exile the prophet as a danger to the kingdom (Amos 7:10–13).

In the end, Amos's interpretation of God's concerns and not Amaziah's prevailed. As Jewish scholar Shalom Speigel pointed out in his brilliant speech (given at the Jewish Theological Seminary in the presence of then U.S. Supreme Court Chief Justice Earl Warren):

> Amos vs. Amaziah makes justice the supreme command, overriding every other consideration or obligation.... Justice becomes the categorical imperative, transcending all the other requirements of the law.... Worship in biblical religion could never be an end in itself, for God is not in need of ritual, as in magic religions of antiquity.... In Israel, worship is God's favor to man.... Worship

is meant to inspirit man with passion for justice, to purify and prepare him for the encounter with God.... Worship and ritual are means, while justice and righteousness are ends.[16]

No less indicative of the relative importance of morality as opposed to ritual is the prophecy in Isaiah 58, in which the prophet speaks to the people who have called a fast to overcome some calamity. Their fast, he proclaims, is of no value "because on your fast day you see to your business and oppress all your laborers" (v. 3). Fasting and putting on sackcloth and ashes are not a true fast (v. 5); rather, Isaiah states, "This is the fast I desire: to unlock fetters of wickedness, and untie the cords of the yoke, to let the oppressed go free; to break off every yoke. It is to share your bread with the hungry, and to take the wretched poor into your home; when you see the naked, to clothe him, and not to ignore your own kin" (vv. 6–7). How appropriate that these words were chosen by the Rabbis to be recited specifically on the most sacred fast day of the year, Yom Kippur.

These prophets of Israel make explicit what was already implicit in the teachings of the Torah. Lest there be any misunderstanding, they pointed out specifically that just behavior is God's true desire, not sacrifices or libations. "With what shall I approach YHVH, do homage to God on high? Shall I approach Him with burnt offerings, with calves a year old? Would the Lord be pleased with thousands of rams, with myriads of streams of oil? ... What does YHVH require of you? Only to do justice, to love mercy, and to walk humbly with your God," proclaims Micah (6:6–8). What courage it took on the part of Micah and other prophets to utter such words, yet all they were doing was expressing what the Torah taught and taking it to its ultimate, extreme meaning. "The prophet's word is a scream in the night," writes Heschel. "While the world is at ease and asleep, the prophet feels the blast from heaven."[17]

Moral Emphasis in the Psalms

The pervasiveness of this outlook in Israel is seen by the fact that the book of Psalms, so closely connected to the Temple and its rites, contains calls for morality in terms that are no less fervent than those of the prophets, if less provocative in never explicitly questioning the value of ritual. A prime example is Psalm 24, in which those who want to enter the Temple are told that only those who have "clean hands and a pure heart" and have not "sworn deceitfully" are worthy to ascend the mountain of YHVH (Ps. 24:4). Similarly, Psalm 15:2–3 describes those worthy of dwelling on God's holy mountain: "He who lives without blame and does what is right and in his heart acknowledges the truth; whose tongue is not given to evil; who has never done harm to his fellow." Ritual commands are not even mentioned. "Shun evil and do good," cries the psalmist (Ps. 37:27)— words that could have been uttered by any prophet. "Judge the wretched and the orphan, vindicate the lowly and the poor, rescue the wretched and the needy; save them from the hand of the wicked," says God to the divine beings in Psalm 82:3.

The morality of the Torah is unique and, indeed, revolutionary in grounding itself, as Kaufmann writes, "in the absolute command of God, revealed and imposed on mankind by him.... Morality is not a private matter.... Society as a whole is under a covenant obligation to eradicate evil from its midst and cause justice to prevail."[18]

As for the Torah's laws of ethical living, they are exhortative in nature and not merely a dry legal compilation. "Do what is right and good in the sight of YHVH" (Deut. 6:18), exhorts Moses in a saying that was traditionally understood to mean that strict observance of the laws was insufficient. Rather, all actions should be judged on the basis of being right and good, not merely legal. "Love your fellow man" (Lev. 19:18) and "Love [the stranger] as yourself" (Lev. 19:34) in the Holiness Code hardly qualify as legally enforceable rules. The same may be said about Moses's call, "Justice, justice shall you pursue" (Deut. 16:20).

Ethical Emphasis in Later Judaism

In the Rabbinic period, the Sages of Israel agree that the very basis of all of the Torah is ethical behavior. The earliest to voice this clearly is Hillel, in his famous reply to the request that he teach a non-Jew the entire Torah while standing on one foot. Paraphrasing and interpreting Leviticus 19:18, "Love your fellow as yourself," in Aramaic, Hillel replies, "That which is hateful to yourself do not do to your fellow. All the rest is commentary. Now go and learn" (Talmud, *Shabbat* 31b). Some two hundred years later, Rabbi Akiba is asked to say which verse in the Torah is the one on which all else is based, the general rule of all of Judaism. His answer is that same verse, "Love your fellow as yourself."[19]

In one of the most famous passages of Rabbinic literature, Rabbi Simlai tries to show that the *mitzvot* are not mere legal formulas or unrelated fragments, but rather are all part of a unified scheme: "Six hundred and thirteen *mitzvot* were given to Moses, 365 negative, equaling the days of the year, and 248 positive, corresponding to the parts of the human body." The midrash continues, showing how in each generation these were reduced to smaller numbers of basic principles:

> Micah came and comprised them in three: It has been told you, O man, what is good and what does YHVH require of you—only to do justice, love mercy, and walk humbly with your God (6:8).
>
> Isaiah came and comprised them in two: Keep justice and do righteousness (56:1).
>
> Amos came and comprised them in one: Seek Me and live! (5:4).
>
> (*Talmud*, Makkot 24a)

According to Rabbi Simlai, then, the system of *mitzvot* has as its goal creating a person who will constantly seek to live according to godly ways and to be always in God's presence.

Thus the infinite value of ethical living runs directly from Abraham to Moses and the commandments of the Torah, and thence to the psalms and to Amos and the other prophets. It is a central truth that has had an enormous impact on Judaism and has set a standard of moral living for all humanity. Once this was established, ritual was forever relegated to second place in the order of God's priorities, so that the essence of religion became not rite but right.

4

Worship Is for the Benefit of Humans

Revolutionary Truth #4: God neither needs nor requires sacrifice. Worship is for the benefit of humanity, not of God.

> And let them make Me a sanctuary that I may dwell among them.
>
> *Exodus 25:8*

> But will God really dwell on earth? Even the heavens to their uttermost reaches cannot contain You, how much less this House that I have built!
>
> *1 Kings 8:27*

> These are the set times of YHVH, the sacred occasions, which you shall celebrate each at its appointed time.
>
> *Leviticus 23:4*

> You shall rejoice in your festival, with your son and your daughter, your male and female slave, the Levite, the stranger, the fatherless, and the widow in your communities.
>
> *Deuteronomy 16:14*

The Torah's new and revolutionary concept of God, discussed in detail in chapter 1, demands a new and no less revolutionary way of worshipping God. The first two commandments of the Decalogue address this problem and begin by giving us two prohibitions that were unknown in the ancient world. The first is the demand that Israel worship only YHVH: "You shall have no other gods besides Me" (Exod. 20:3; Deut. 5:7). The second commandment prohibits the making and worship of images, not only of other gods, but even of YHVH: "You shall not make for yourself an idol of the visage of anything that is in the heavens above,[1] or on the earth below, or in the waters below the earth" (Exod. 20:4; Deut. 5:8). It then details the kinds of worship that are prohibited: "You shall not bow down to them or serve them" (Exod. 20:5; Deut. 5:9).

The Prohibition of Images

The prohibition of images was expanded in Deuteronomy when, before recapitulating the words of the Decalogue, Moses warns the people that because they saw no shape when God spoke to them at Horeb, they are not to "make for yourselves an idol or the visage of anything, a statue which is the likeness of a man or a woman, the form of any beast on earth, the form of any winged bird that flies in the sky, the form of anything that creeps on the ground, the form of any fish that is in the waters below the earth" (Deut. 4:16–18). Moses then adds that it is prohibited to bow down to the sun, the moon, and the stars themselves (Deut. 4:19). Jeffrey Tigay explains the connection between not making idols and the fact that the Israelites saw no shape when God spoke to them: "Idolaters used idols to bring deities near and thereby secure their blessings or receive communications from them, but ... since God spoke to Israel directly from heaven, without the mediation of idols, it sees that idols are not necessary for these purposes."[2] Not only are idols not needed, but they also detract from the worship of the one true God by seducing the worshipper into believing that the idols themselves have a measure of divinity.

Idols are prohibited, even those that would represent the true God, not because God has no image—the Torah does not actually state that, and it was not until the Middle Ages that Maimonides established it as a basic belief of Judaism—but because no idol, no image, is God or contains God. To worship an idol of any sort, then, is to worship something other than YHVH, and that is forbidden.

Israelite worship was radically different from anything that existed at that time in being imageless. It required its adherents to worship a God they could not see and of which they had no visual representation. All the more important, then, that there be some tangible symbol of the presence of God. That symbol was the Ark of the Covenant, described in detail in Exodus 37:1–9. The Ark was placed in the holiest part of the sanctuary. Made of wood overlaid with gold inside and out, the Ark had a cover of pure gold, on either side of which were figures of cherubim with outstretched wings. These were not considered a violation of the prohibition against images. The cherubim seem to represent the pedestal on which the invisible presence of God would rest, or the guardians of the contents of the Ark. Inside were the tablets on which were inscribed the Ten Commandments as well as scrolls containing other commands of God. God spoke to Moses from the Ark. During the period of the Tabernacle and the First Temple, the Ark was the closest thing to a tangible representation of God's presence that Israel had. When it disappeared at the time of the destruction in 586 BCE, it was never replaced. The Second Temple had a Holy of Holies, but it was an empty room.

The incident of the Golden Calf emphasizes the danger of idols. The people grow fearful when Moses remains atop Mount Sinai and does not return to them. Believing themselves leaderless, they approach Aaron: "Come, make us a god who shall go before us, for that man Moses, who brought us from the land of Egypt—we do not know what has happened to him" (Exod. 32:1). We might think that because it was "that man Moses" who was missing, the Israelites would ask for another man to lead them. Instead, they ask for a god. Moses was charismatic enough that they could manage without a visible god. Without him, they need a more concrete god to lead them. Aaron makes a calf, but whether he intends it to be a representation of a god is unclear. Like the calf that was made centuries later in the temple of the northern kingdom (1 Kings 12:28),[3] it may have been a pedestal for God's presence, just as the cherubim were.

But for the people, it is a god, and they begin to worship it, exclaiming, "This is your god, O Israel, who brought you out of the land of Egypt!" (Exod. 32:4). The idol becomes more than a representation of a god; it *is* the god. The result of this terrible breach of the commandments against idol worship is that God threatens to destroy the Israelites. Only Moses, who himself breaks the tablets of the covenant, symbolic of the broken relationship with God, prevents this and, after destroying the rebels, brings about a reconciliation (Exod. 32:9–34:28).

The Tent of Meeting

A major component of worship is the place where it occurs. The Israelites had just emerged from spending hundreds of years in Egypt. No place in the ancient world rivaled Egypt for the magnificence of its temples of the gods. The mysterious rituals of the Egyptian religion were performed in buildings and courtyards the size and grandeur of which knew no rivals. Even today, to walk through the ruins of those structures is to experience the feeling of awe that they were intended to inspire. These temples were, of course, replete with idols and pictures of the gods and of the mythical events of their existence. That pictorial aspect was totally negated in Israel by the prohibition against idols and images.

To duplicate the grandeur of the Egyptian temples would have been impossible for this group of former slaves. Even had they not had to wander for forty years, they would still be traveling and not settled down; therefore, they need something portable. When they set out, their journey was to have been quite short, but even so they required a place of worship they could transport with them. Their experience of God at Sinai had to be kept alive in their daily lives, and this could be done best by a tentlike structure in which God could continue to be present as at Sinai. What is striking, however, is that the Torah makes no mention of and no provision for the erection of any permanent structure once the Israelites arrive at their new homeland. The portable structure, then, was not solely a concession to the conditions of wilderness life. It was a deliberate rejection by the Israelites of the grandeur of Egypt in favor of a much more humble and modest structure to serve as the house of the God of Israel.

That structure, described in detail in Exodus 35–38, has many purposes. It was termed "a Tent of Meeting" because it was a place in which God would meet with Moses, just as God had met with him on Mount Sinai. "There I will meet with you, and I will impart to you—from above the cover, from between the two cherubim that are on top of the Ark of the Covenant—all that I will command you concerning the Israelite people" (Exod. 25:22).[4] This prophetic function of the Tent of Meeting basically vanished when Israel entered the land of Canaan.[5] In addition, there was another type of meeting: "And there I will meet with the Israelites, and it shall be sanctified by My Presence" (Exod. 29:43). This meeting between the God of Israel and the people of Israel remained the purpose of the temporary sanctuary and of the permanent building that eventually was built, as it is written, "Three times a year all your males shall appear before the Sovereign, YHVH" (Exod. 23:17).

Although it may be true that the Tent of Meeting as described in Exodus contains "generous legendary embellishments,"[6] there seems little reason to question that a tentlike structure did exist in which the Ark was housed and where sacrifices took place. Furthermore, although nothing is known about what happened to it after the people entered Canaan, we do know that the Ark continued to be housed in similar temporary structures until the time of Solomon.

The fact that the Torah does not command the building of a permanent Temple is unusual because it easily could have done so. Even Deuteronomy, which reached its final form after the Temple had been built, does not acknowledge that fact. Deuteronomy limits worship to one sanctuary alone, in the place that God "will choose to establish His name" (Deut. 26:2), but makes no attempt to describe the structure in which this will take place. The only structure so described in the Torah is the portable sanctuary, which seems to indicate the original plan was for Israel's place of worship to be a modest temporary structure, one that would contrast with the elaborate temples of Egypt rather than compete with them. The God of Israel neither needed nor desired a magnificent palace for a dwelling.

When David brings the Ark to his city, he houses it in a tent (2 Sam. 6:17). Later, when he thinks it proper to build a house for God (2 Sam. 7:2), the prophet Nathan tells David that God does not want that:

"From the day that I brought the people of Israel out of Egypt
to this day I have not dwelt in a house, but have moved about
in Tent and Tabernacle. As I moved about wherever the
Israelites went, did I ever reproach any of the tribal leaders
whom I appointed to care for My people Israel: Why have you
not built Me a house of cedar?"

(2 Sam. 7:6–7)

Although Nathan continues by stating that God will permit David's son
and heir to build such a house, the prophecy sounds more like a concession to a new reality than a reflection of God's true desire. It bears a
resemblance to the way in which, immediately after the giving of the Ten
Commandments, God tells Moses that the Israelites are not to make any
images. Rather, God says, "Make for Me an altar of earth and sacrifice on
it your burnt offerings and your sacrifices of well-being, your sheep and
your oxen; in every place where I cause My name to be mentioned I will
come to you and bless you" (Exod. 20:21). This is followed by "And if
you make for Me an altar of stones, do not build it of hewn stones; for by
wielding your tool upon them you have profaned them" (Exod. 20:22).
Why is an altar of stone even mentioned as a possibility if God commands the creation of a simple altar of earth? It is a concession to a popular desire to build something more permanent and more beautiful. If
the Israelites insist on doing that, then at least let them refrain from
using metal instruments. Here, too, God is content with a Tabernacle,
but if the people must have a palatial structure, then let it be built by
Solomon after David's death. All of this reflects the reality of a new society, based on urban living and intent on proving itself no less sophisticated than the other kingdoms nearby.

The Purpose of Sacrifices

If Israelite worship constituted a deliberate rejection of Egyptian worship,
it is nevertheless true that many of the specific forms of worship described
in the Torah bear an uncanny surface resemblance to well-known pagan
rites. This is particularly true of sacrifice. A careful examination, however,

shows that there is always a difference.[7] There is a hint of this in the way the Torah recasts a detail in the Mesopotamian story of the flood. When the flood is over, the Torah recounts that Noah builds an altar and offers sacrifices, after which "YHVH smelled the pleasing odor" (Gen. 8:21). This disturbing anthropomorphism seems strange and unnecessary until we read the way the story is told in the ancient Mesopotamian version. There, after days without food—because during the flood no sacrifices were offered—when the hero brings a sacrifice, "the gods smelled the savor, the gods smelled the sweet savor, the gods crowded like flies about the sacrificer."[8] They come eagerly to devour the offerings because they were literally starving. The God of Israel does not starve and does not eat, so the most the Torah will allow itself is the phrase "YHVH smelled the pleasing odor."

This is emblematic of the entire approach to sacrifices, which were the main form of worship in pagan religions and play such a central role in the Torah as well. In pagan worship, the sacrifices were for the benefit of the gods who needed them, either for sustenance or, in some cases, as part of rituals that magically restored the life and potency of the divinities. Not a trace of that remains in the Torah, and it is for that reason that the Torah and the later prophets could imagine God destroying the sanctuary and doing without sacrifices.

Everything about the sacrifices seems to point to preparation for a meal, but there is no mention of the meal being consumed by God. For example, shewbread, or "display-bread," consists of twelve loaves that the priest would arrange "before YHVH regularly every Sabbath day" (Lev. 24:8). God does not consume them in any way, unless seeing them is considered consuming. Rather, "they shall belong to Aaron and his sons, who shall eat them in the sacred precinct" (Lev. 24:9). In other words, they are only set out before YHVH, and they remain on the table for a week before being eaten by the priests. Ancient forms of sacrifice, found in the religions of Mesopotamia and Egypt, were retained, but they were emptied of their original pagan content and given new meaning in keeping with the Torah's concept of God. As Yehezkel Kaufmann writes, "Religion customarily conserves forms that have become emptied of meaning. Such terms and rites mean only that at one time sacrifice was considered food for the god. For biblical religion, however, it is decisive that the mythological setting of this conception is entirely wanting."[9]

Since sacrifices were not essential to God, the only purpose they served was to benefit human beings. There is no need to go into all the complex forms of sacrifices outlined in the Torah, but the common purpose of them all is clear. They allow people to express their thankfulness and gratitude and provide a means of showing regret for misdeeds and of attaining atonement for sin. Through the bringing of offerings, people feel a closeness to God. By participating in worship, they establish their relationship to the Deity. Leviticus 17:3–7 also indicates that one of the reasons for sacrifices and for limiting them to the Tent of Meeting was to prevent people from sacrificing to satyrs, "that they may offer their sacrifices no more to the goat-demons after whom they stray." Thus, all slaughter had to be done in a sanctuary and performed by a priest (Leviticus 17). Deuteronomy, written at a time when there were many small places of worship as well as larger ones in Jerusalem and Bethel, goes further and permits only one sanctuary, as a further guard against idolatry and polytheism (Deut. 12:4–7): "Look only to the site that the Lord your God will choose amidst all your tribes as His habitation" (v. 5). There was always a danger that people might retreat from the Torah's strict new monotheism and adopt superstitious or pagan practices.

Why use these forms at all when their core meaning has vanished? Maimonides understood the psychology behind it very well:

> It is impossible to go suddenly from one extreme to the other; it is therefore according to the nature of man impossible for him to discontinue everything to which he has been accustomed…. The custom which was in those days general among all men, and the general mode of worship in which the Israelites were brought up, consisted of sacrificing animals in those temples that contained certain images, to bow down to those images, and to burn incense before them…. He did not command us to give up and to discontinue all those manners of service; for to obey such a command would have been contrary to the nature of man, who generally cleaves to that to

which he is used.... For that reason God allowed these kinds of service to continue; He transferred to His service that which formerly served as a worship of created beings.[10]

The Temple of Silence

The sacrifices were brought in silence. This is in total contrast to pagan rituals, which constantly combine sacrifice, ritual actions, and specific incantations.

"In Egypt, Babylonia, and in the pagan world in general word and incantation were integral parts of the cult; act was accompanied by speech. The spell expressed the magical essence of cultic activity," notes Kaufmann.[11] The daily ritual in the temple of Amon-Re at Karnak has been preserved and tells exactly what was done to awaken the god. It is headed, "The beginning of the utterances of the sacred rites which are carried out for the House of Amon-Re, King of the gods, in the course of every day by the major priest."[12] As the rite progresses, it lists the utterance for each action that the priest performs. We can search the Torah in vain for any references to such utterances that are to be recited as part of the Temple sacrificial rituals.

The Torah records one act of speech that is to take place in the sanctuary, the declaration made when bringing the first fruits, and it is recited not by the priest but by the farmer who brings them. He "shall go to the priest in charge at that time and say to him, 'I acknowledge this day before YHVH your God that I have entered the land that YHVH swore to our fathers to assign us'" (Deut. 26:3), after which the priest takes the basket and sets it down in front of the altar. The farmer then recites verses that give a brief historical summary of the way in which God brought Israel into the land of Canaan, and concludes, "Wherefore I now bring the fruits of the soil which You, O YHVH, have given me" (Deut. 26:10). It is very clear that this is a declaration for commoners to recite. The priest says nothing when he receives the first fruits. His only task is to place it in front of the altar.

Similarly, in the rite of expiation that is performed on the Day of Atonement, the high priest brings several bulls as offerings of expiation for himself, for his household, and for the whole congregation of Israel. In each case, he slaughters the animal and sprinkles its blood. This effects a purging of the shrine from its ritual impurities. Nothing is said. The only time he speaks, according to the Torah, is when he makes a confession of sins on the head of the goat that is sent off live into the wilderness, carrying on it "all their iniquities to an inaccessible region" (Lev. 16:22). Thus, he never speaks when slaughtering an animal, only when sending it off alive. Even then, what he says is not a blessing, a spell, or anything else that might be thought to have special potency, only a confession of sin.

In the time of the Second Temple, things were very different. According to the Mishnah, the high priest then spoke each time he offered an animal and when sprinkling the blood. He made a verbal confession in which he also uttered the exact name of God. When those in attendance heard God's name pronounced, they prostrated themselves and responded, "Blessed is the name of His glorious Majesty forever and ever" (*Mishnah Kippurim* 3:8). By that time, the religion of Israel was well established, and the fear that the use of speech in rituals would lead to pagan ways no longer existed.

By creating a dichotomy between sacrifices and offerings in the Temple and verbal utterances, the Torah opened the way for the eventual development of formal verbal worship without sacrifice. Just as sacrifices required no verbal prayers or blessings, so verbal prayers could be uttered in the absence of sacrifices. Prayer, both individual and collective, is often recorded in the Torah with no mention of sacrifice or other rituals being performed. Exodus 15, the Song at the Sea, is a prime example. We might expect that in gratitude to YHVH for their salvation, the Israelites would have offered a sacrifice, as Noah did after the flood, but none is mentioned, only the singing of this glorious ode. Abraham builds altars to God and "proclaims the name of YHVH" (Gen. 12:8), but there is no mention of a sacrifice. Jacob also prays and gives thanks without offering a sacrifice (Gen. 32:25–33). When the Temple was built, psalms were written and recited there, but not as a part of the sacrificial service. All of this eventually led to the creation of places of worship where there was only verbal prayer and no sacrifice. In that sense, the

Torah's lack of any insistence on incantations or indeed any verbal usage when offering sacrifices also gave an impetus to a later revolution in human worship: synagogues, places for prayer in which no sacrifices were or could be offered.

New Meanings for the Festivals

Just as there is no hint of sacrifices being needed by God, so the main occasions for worship, which were celebrated by the bringing of sacrifices and other rituals, have no connection to any events in the life of God. Pagan holidays celebrated and reenacted stories in the mythology of the lives of the gods. The closest we come is celebrating the Sabbath because God "rested on the seventh day" (Exod. 20:11). The purpose of the major festivals described in the Torah is not to help God, but to allow all the people to rejoice and to have "nothing but joy" (Deut. 16:15).

The two main holidays in the Torah are the spring and the autumn festivals, both of which have obvious origins in nature, celebrating the harvests and the birth of spring lambs. In paganism, nature festivals were connected to the gods. As Yehezkel Kaufmann explains:

> The most solemn [pagan festivals] celebrate occasions in their lives. The festival is rooted in divine events reflected in nature or in the life of the tribe and recurring in the fixed cycle. All forms of paganism know the cultic drama, in which the gods are both actors and acted upon. The human celebrant participates in the divine mysteries, suffers with the gods, mourns their death, triumphs in their resurrection. His rites crucially affect the destiny and vitality of the gods.[13]

In the Torah, these nature holidays are given parallel historical meaning. They celebrate events in the history of the Israelite people and their relationship to God. The spring festival, an amalgam of the farmer's wheat festival and the shepherd's lamb-birthing festival, becomes the celebration of the Exodus from Egypt, the redemption of Israel from bondage. The wheat becomes the bread of affliction; the lamb becomes the paschal offering, reminding the Israelites of the lamb whose blood was used as a protective sign on their homes (Exodus 12–13). It is not myth in the sense of the story of the lives of the gods, but rather the tale of God's actions in Israel's history.[14]

The autumn harvest holiday, while largely retaining its connection to nature, is also given a historical significance. It is interpreted as the remembrance of dwelling in *sukkot* in the days of their wandering in the wilderness. You are to observe it "in order that future generations may know that I made the Israelite people live in booths when I brought them out of the land of Egypt" (Lev. 23:43). Again, there is no reference to mythology; the focus is on God's interaction with the people Israel.

Worship in early Israel was divested of all pagan elements, even while it retained some similar outward forms. The focus turned from what the worshipper could do for the gods to what worshipping the one God could contribute to the life and happiness of the worshipper. Instead of concentrating on the life of the gods, it concentrated on the history of the people Israel and God's assistance to them. The history of Israel, rather than the history of God, was the focus. All elements of magic and incantation were removed, and the place of sacrifice was so changed that eventually official public worship totally devoid of sacrifice could occur. This led to the development of the synagogue and, later, the church and the mosque. The grandeur and the mystery of Egyptian religion gave way to the simpler, more modest worship of God in a temporary dwelling, a meeting place for God and humans.

Part II
HUMANITY

5

Human Life
Is Sacred

Revolutionary Truth #5: Humans are differentiated from all others in that they are created in the image of God. Therefore, human life is sacred; it is an absolute value.

> And God said, "Let us make the human being in our image, after our likeness. They shall rule the fish of the sea, the birds of the sky, the cattle, the whole earth, and all the creeping things that creep on earth. And God created the human being in His image, in the image of God He created him, male and female He created them.
>
> *Genesis 1:26–27*

> *What is man that You have been mindful of him,*
> *mortal man that You have taken note of him;*
> *yet You have made him little less than divine,*
> *and adorned him with glory and majesty.*
>
> *Psalm 8:5–6*

With these words, the psalmist has captured the revolutionary assertion of Moses's teaching, proclaiming the value of human beings and their inestimable worth. Because Judaism also teaches that compared to the expanse of the heavens and the eternity of the universe, the human being is "like a breath; his days are like a passing shadow" (Ps. 144:4), we might think that humans are hardly worth God's consideration or care. Not so. Humans are but "little less than divine" and are adorned "with glory and majesty."

This belief in the ultimate worth of human life is based on the depiction of their creation in the opening chapters of the book of Genesis. The Torah's concept of the place of human beings in the scheme of creation is stated there quite clearly. Human beings are the pinnacle of creation, differentiated from all else that exists. They and they alone are created in the image of God.

Such a concept is not to be taken for granted, neither in modern times, when the value of human life has been denigrated by one vicious regime after another, nor in ancient days, when the religious texts accepted by the greatest civilizations painted quite a different picture of the value and purpose of human life.

Consider, for example, the description of the creation of man in the ancient Akkadian creation epic. The god Marduk says:

> *Behold I will establish a savage, "man" shall be his name.*
> *Verily, savage-man I will create.*
> *He shall be charged with the service of the gods*
> *That they might be at ease.*

In the same text, the creation of a human being is accomplished through the slaying of the monster Tiamat.

> *Out of his blood they fashioned mankind ...*
> *And "imposed upon it the service of the gods."*[1]

Similarly, an old Babylonian text reads:

> *Thou art the mother-womb,*
> *The one who creates mankind.*
> *Create, then, Lullu [the savage] and let him bear the yoke!*

The yoke he shall bear ...
The burden of creation man shall bear!

Of Lullu it is then written:

He who shall serve all the gods,
Let him be formed out of clay, be animated with blood![2]

Three times the purpose of the creation of humans is stated: to serve the gods. Since the ancestors of those who created the Torah were natives of Mesopotamia, the center of these ancient civilizations, it stands to reason that the early Hebrews were familiar with these texts or similar ones, at least orally. They would have heard them recited at ritual occasions. Yet although there are echoes of these texts in the Torah, on this subject the Torah deliberately departed from them in radical ways. Not only is the method by which humans were created different, but also the very purpose of their creation and their nature. There is no hint in the Torah that God created Adam and Eve so that they might be God's slaves or servants. Rather, the task they are given is to rule the world (Gen. 1:28).

On the contrary, the Torah considers human beings to be God's supreme creation, formed in "the image of God" (Gen. 1:27) and therefore distinguished from all other forms of life. This is a value judgment, a self-evident truth, not to be confused with scientific fact. Science may indeed be able to prove that humans are related to certain species of mammals, yet because the Torah is not a scientific work but a religious tract, teaching values rather than scientific facts, this in no way negates the importance of the Torah's teaching.

The Creation of Human Beings

To return to Genesis, modern biblical studies posit that in many instances the Torah contains more than one version of the same story. That is the case of the tale of the creation of humans. There are two different versions stemming from two different ancient schools of religious thought within the religion of Israel. They can be differentiated in many ways, as noted earlier, including the fact that the first uses only the word *Elohim* to refer to God, while the second adds the name *YHVH*, commonly translated as "Lord." Yet the positive attitude toward human beings is expressed in both of these myths of creation, albeit in different ways. The basic value concept underlying them both remains the same: humans are the crown of God's creation of living creatures, endowed with immeasurable worth. They alone are worthy of and capable of interaction with the Divine.

Let us examine these two accounts. Genesis 1–2:3, stemming from the source known in scholarly circles as P, the Priestly school,[3] is spare in detail, austere in vocabulary, yet filled with grandeur in the scope of its canvas. It describes creation in terms of divine fiat. The creation takes place in six stages, each of which is termed a "day." The process moves from the inanimate to the animate, with the last step being the creation of human beings. Everything leads up to this moment. The human is thus the very peak of creation, the one who is given the task of ruling over and caring for everything that has been created on earth (Gen. 1:26, 1:29–30).

Exactly how humans were actually created is never described in source P. Instead, we are simply told that after deciding to create humans, God did so (Gen. 1:27). The uniqueness of that creation is indicated with great subtlety in that only in the case of creating humans is the formula "And God said" missing. Rather, the creation is described thus:

> And God created the human being [*ha-adam*] in His image, in the
> image of God created He him; male and female He created them.
> (Gen. 1:27)

This phrase, "the image of God," was mentioned in the previous verse (1:26) as well. God says, "Let us make a human [*adam*] in our image, after our likeness," using the plural "us," either—as Rabbinic interpretation had it—speaking to the angels or as the plural of majesty.[4]

Indeed, whenever the creation of human beings is mentioned, P makes certain to remind us that they were made in the image or the likeness of God! A similar phrase, "the likeness of God," is used again in Genesis 5:1, "When God created Adam, He made him in the likeness of God." The phrase "the image of God" is also found in Genesis 9:6 in God's poetic charge to Noah and his family forbidding murder:

> *"Whoever sheds the blood of the human being [ha-adam],*
> *by the human being shall his blood be shed,*
> *for in His image did God make the human being."*

As the outstanding biblical scholar Moshe Greenberg demonstrates, whatever the specific meaning of "the image of God" may be, it had consequences in the laws of the Torah.[5] The most important of these has to do with murder. Paradoxically, because humans are made in God's image, there is no way in which human life can be compensated for through money or any other means.

> Compensation of any kind is ruled out. The guilt of the murderer is infinite because the murdered life is invaluable; the kin of the slain person are not competent to say when that person has been paid for. An absolute wrong has been committed, a sin against God that is not subject to human discussion. The effect of this view is, to be sure, paradoxical: because human life is invaluable, to take it entails the death penalty. Yet the paradox must not blind us to the judgment of value that the law sought to embody.[6]

This is exactly the opposite of the laws in other ancient literature, where monetary compensation for human life was the norm.[7]

As the Rabbis later explain, the shedding of human blood or the taking of human life is equivalent to reducing the image of God in the world. They give this parable:

> A king of flesh and blood entered a city and people erected icons and images of him and struck coins [in his image]. Later they upset his icons, broke his images and defaced his coins, thus reducing the images of the king.[8]

The meaning of the phrase "the image of God" has been the subject of much interpretation over the centuries. It is difficult to know exactly how literal the Sages were in their understanding of that phrase. Hillel the Elder seems to have taken it to mean that the human body is actually the physical image of God's being. Thus, he once said that when going to wash himself he was actually performing a commandment, just as an idol worshipper would if he were going to clean the statue of a god he worshipped![9]

At the opposite end would be the teachings of the medieval philosopher Maimonides that God has no physical form, the third of his thirteen principles of faith.[10]

As the biblical scholar Umberto Cassuto remarks, when we use this phrase today, speaking of humans being created in God's image, we do not have a physical likeness in mind. Rather, we think that although humans are similar to animals in having a physical being, we are closer to the Divine in our thinking and in our moral consciousness. Thus, although in ancient times the phrase may have originated as likening humans physically to the gods, the only question is: when did its meaning change—before or after it was used in the biblical text? On the basis of the abstract usage of language in Genesis 1 in all its descriptions of God and of the creation, Cassuto believes that the change came earlier.[11]

A more recent scholar, Nahum Sarna, points out that the phrase "the image of God" is immediately followed by the command to rule over the rest of creation (Gen. 1:28). Therefore, being in the image must include "all those faculties and gifts of character that distinguish man from the beast and that are needed for the fulfillment of his task on earth, namely intellect, free will, self-awareness, consciousness of the existence of others, conscience, responsibility and self-control."[12]

The Torah itself is silent on the exact meaning of the phrase.[13] Nevertheless, it seems clear that its importance lies in its indication that the human being—and only the human being—shares a likeness with the Divine. This could be physical, moral, or intellectual. The practical consequence, as we have seen, is that human life is of inestimable value. It cannot be measured in any way. P, the first biblical account, then, gives no details of the creation of humans but indicates the supreme value of human life by making humans the last of the creation. Their position at the end of the progression indicates their special status in being created in God's image and gives them the authority to rule over the world and all the creatures in it. That is the purpose and the meaning of human's creation.

The story told in Genesis 2:4–4:26 is quite different, although the importance and value of human life is no less. This section is ascribed by biblical scholars to a source known as J because throughout it uses the personal name of God—YHVH, J standing for the letter *yod* (Y).[14] Unlike P in Genesis 1, J gives no account of the creation of the universe, but concentrates rather on the earth itself, ignoring the heavens. Whereas Genesis 1 begins with "When God began to create heaven and earth" (1:1) and repeats that order at the conclusion—"The heaven and the earth were finished" (2:1)—J's account begins with "When YHVH God made earth and heaven" (2:4), placing earth before heaven. Its main concern is the story of humankind, their creation, their nature, and their fate.[15] Incidentally, this allowed the redactor of the Torah to place the two accounts together easily, as if the first one were a general description of the creation of the entire universe, while the second goes back and gives the details of the creation and history of humanity.

J emphasizes that *adam*—the human being—was the most important creation of God. At the beginning there was "no shrub of the field" and no "grasses of the field" for two reasons. First, God had not yet sent any rain; second, "there was no human to till the soil" (Gen. 2:5). Therefore, God "formed the human from the dust of the earth" (2:7).[16] The earth could not be sustained; nothing on it could grow without *adam*. Thus it is that immediately after creating the human, God plants "a garden in Eden, in the east, and placed there the human He had formed" (2:8), causing all the trees to grow there (2:9). The human is put in the garden "to till it and tend it" (2:15); just as in P's telling, humans were given the role of ruling over the earth "and mastering it" (1:28). In neither case are humans created to care for and help the gods or to be their slaves.

Although this version of creation does not mention the concept of "the image of God," J does add that God "blew into his nostrils the breath of life, and man became a living being" (2:7), something that is not stated when the animals are created. This breath, coming from God, is a reflection of the Divine. Many centuries later, the teacher known as Kohelet refers to this when, describing death, he writes, "And the dust returns to the ground as it was, and the life breath returns to God who gave it" (Eccles. 12:7).

All of this emphasizes the uniqueness of the human being in the eyes of the Torah. According to J, the human is the very purpose of creation, created before any other living creature. Without the human, there would be no vegetation on earth. Without the human, there would be no other animate life.

These teachings—perhaps even more than those of Genesis 1— stand in stark contrast to everything that science teaches us about the origins of life and of the universe and to the depiction of humans in the religious literature of the ancient Near East. They are an expression of the Torah's deeply held view of the sacredness and the value of human beings and human life and led to an idea of the value of human life without which civilization as we know it would be impossible. As such, it is a religious credo, a sacred value that stands alone, dependent on belief and not on scientific validity.

Human Imperfection

J's account, however, is also concerned with the nature of human beings. Humans may be unique and even "little less than divine," but they also are imperfect and inclined to transgress. The story of Adam and Eve in the Garden of Eden reflects that truth as well. It is intended to teach that humans are subject to urges and desires that lead them to disobedience. However, this urge, which the Sages later termed "the evil inclination" (yetzer ha-ra), could be overcome by free will.

In J's account, the first human is commanded not to eat of the tree of knowledge of good and evil, "for as soon as you eat of it, you shall be doomed to die" (Gen. 2:17). The symbolism is clear. Adam and Eve represent the childhood of humankind, the time when, lacking knowledge and experience, we are unaware of all the possibilities of good and evil in the world. Once we attain that knowledge, we are also mortal. Adam and Eve are responsible for their actions even before attaining that knowledge, and therefore they are punished. The story thus accounts for the presence of suffering and evil in the world by placing it on the head of human beings and the fact that they have free will.

In Akkadian accounts of the attainment of knowledge, the man, Enkidu, gains it through sexual adventures, after which he is told, "You are wise Enkidu, you are like a god."[17] Although many have interpreted Genesis as connecting sex with Adam and Eve's disobedience, the text conspicuously does not state that. At the very moment of Eve's creation, sexual activity is alluded to in a positive way: "Hence a man leaves his father and mother and clings to his wife, so that they become one flesh" (Gen. 2:24). The specific mention of sexual activity, however, is found only in Genesis 4:1, after Adam and Eve have been banished from the garden.

All human beings share imperfection. God voices disappointment in the human race in two of the saddest verses of the Torah: "And YHVH saw how great was the wickedness of the human being on the earth, and that the inclination of all the thoughts of his heart was nothing but evil all the time. And YHVH regretted that He had made the human being on the earth, and His heart was saddened" (Gen. 6:5–6). After the flood, that verse is echoed, but with a difference: "Never again will I doom the earth because of the human being, since the inclination of the heart of the human being is evil from his youth; nor will I ever again destroy all living beings as I have done" (Gen. 8:21). The Torah, speaking of God in anthropomorphic terms, expresses a change of heart, the realization that the power of the inclination of evil within human beings led to the flood and destruction. Now that same realization leads to a pledge never to destroy the world again! Noah was saved not because of any fundamental difference between him and others but because of his righteous conduct. The lesson God learns, as it were, is not to expect perfection from human beings. They will err; they will do wrong. They need rules and regulation, discipline, to overcome the same fundamental flaw in all of them.[18]

Human beings, unique and created in the image of God, are not divine and are not perfect. The urge—the inclination that is part of our makeup—can lead us astray if we let it. Yet we have the power to overcome it. Are humans innately sinful? No, but they are capable of sin. Are they doomed to sin? No. They have the freedom of will to conquer that inclination so that their full godlike potential may be realized.

In this matter Judaism's daughter religion, Christianity, differed, developing a doctrine of original sin in which the sin of Adam and Eve, known as the Fall, was passed on to all human beings through all generations. Human sinfulness has nothing to do with the actions of individuals and requires "salvation" that can only be attained through the sacraments of Christianity.[19] Although there may have been some teachings in late classical Judaism that emphasized Adam and Eve's sin, nothing further developed in that direction, and it certainly never became a dogma of Judaism. The biblical story that was the basis for the Christian doctrine was interpreted very differently by Rabbinic Judaism.[20] Rabbi Leo Baeck, leader of German Jewry at the time of the Shoah, writes that the idea of original sin originated not in Judaism at all, but in the Orphic mysteries and that "Paul found a place for it in the biblical narrative and clothed it in biblical language."[21] It is hardly accidental that one of the few mentions of Adam and Eve in Jewish liturgy, for example, is in the blessing recited at weddings, which does not concern sin at all but rejoices at marriage. It asks God to "grant perfect joy to these loving companions, as You did for the first man and woman in the Garden of Eden." Perhaps this was Judaism's way of asserting that sexual relations had no connection to sin and reminding everyone that the command to "be fruitful and multiply" was God's blessing to human beings (Gen. 1:28); becoming one flesh was the purpose of the creation of man and woman (Gen. 2:24).

Returning to the Torah and Moses's doctrine of the value of human beings, recall that the story of Adam and Eve's disobedience is not mentioned or referred to again in the Torah. The creation of human beings is mentioned only positively, as a reminder that humans were created in the image of God and that therefore human life is sacred and human blood must not be shed (Gen. 9:6). "But for your own life-blood I will require a reckoning: I will require it of every beast; of the human being, too, will I require a reckoning for human life, of every human being for that of his fellow human being" (Gen. 9:5).

This extraordinary concept has not yet been incorporated into the conscience of the world. The twentieth century, which was to be the century of progress and technologically saw more advances than all the previous centuries combined, was also the bloodiest century of all time. The value of human life reached its nadir when millions died at the whim of Stalin, a Soviet tyrant, and Germany, aided and abetted by people from many other nations, treated human beings as if they were vermin, using technology to exterminate millions. Twenty-first-century terrorism has not shown an improvement in the regard for human life. The Torah's teaching was never better expressed than in the Mishnah's elaboration on the fact that in Genesis 2:7 only one human being was created: "Whoever destroys one human life is considered to have destroyed the entire world, and one who saves one human life is considered to have saved the entire world" (*Mishnah Sanhedrin* 4:5).

6

All Human Beings Are Equal

Revolutionary Truth #6: All human beings have the same common ancestors; they are descendants of one human father and mother. Therefore, all are equal. No race or nation is superior to any other.

> YHVH God formed the human being from the dust of the earth. He blew into his nostrils the breath of life, and the human being became a living being.
>
> *Genesis 2:7*

> This is the record of the begettings of humankind [Adam]. At the time of God's creating humankind, in the likeness of God did He make it, male and female He created them and gave blessing to them and called their name: Humankind! on the day of their being created.
>
> *Genesis 5:1–2[1]*

The Unity of Humanity

Only one human being was created in the world … in order to create harmony among humans so that one cannot say to

another, "My father is greater than your father," ... and to proclaim the greatness of the Holy One who created each person
in the image of the first human and yet no one is exactly like
another. Therefore each person can say, "For my sake was the
world created."

(Mishnah Sanhedrin 4:4)

In this Rabbinic teaching, found in the Mishnah (ca. 200 CE) and based
on the Torah's account of the creation of *ha-adam*, the human being,[2] the
Sages clearly articulate the revolutionary truth that all humans are
descendants of the same common ancestor and are therefore equal. With
this bold statement, they give the lie to all concepts of superior and inferior races, the doctrine that has led to so much hatred and enmity and
that created the basis for the Holocaust and other instances of human
barbarity toward so-called inferior creatures.[3] The Sages correctly understood that the Torah clearly posits that all of us are "the children of
adam," one human being who fathered one human family. As the
psalmist writes, "The heavens belong to YHVH, but the earth He gave to
the children of *adam*" (Ps. 115:16). This is articulated by the renowned
biblical scholar Moshe Greenberg, who coined the phrase "Adamites" to
refer to human beings, called in Hebrew *B'nei Adam*. "Hebrew history,"
he writes, "begins not with the patriarch Abraham, but with the father of
the human race, Adam. Its proper subject is man as the self-conscious
creature and subject of God: Israel arrives on the scene late, after several
fruitless experiments with previous generations of man."[4]

We have already seen in the previous chapter how the Torah
expresses God's concern for all human beings. Before the creation of the
people of Israel, the concern for all of humankind is expressed in the
command to Noah and his sons that "whoever sheds the blood of a
human being, by a human being shall his blood be shed; for in His
image did God make the human being" (Gen. 9:6). All of humanity is
included in this command. The emergence of Abraham and his progeny
did not change the Torah's conception of humanity as one family. Israel
may have eventually come into being and become God's own people,
God's "firstborn son" (Exod. 4:22), but this in no way contradicts or

eliminates the idea that all humans are equal and of concern to their Creator. On the contrary, the concept of the firstborn son implies that all of the others are also sons of God. As Rabbinics scholar Jacob Z. Lauterbach put it, the responsibility of the elder brother is to be an example and a helper for the younger brothers. Thus, even the idea of chosenness implies the relationship of a teacher to a pupil, rather than a belief in inherent superiority.[5]

Of course, the equality of all human beings is not a "truth" in any scientific sense. According to evolution, the origin of human beings is much more complicated than that. Although evolution posits not only that all humans are related but also that we are related to all living creatures, no one knows exactly how many "fathers" we may have had and how we came to be the creatures that we are. However, as I have remarked before, the Torah is a book not of science but of moral truth. The unity and equality of all human beings is based not on science but on an ethical insight that may be seen as divine revelation. It is a fundamental belief, a basic concept, not a scientific fact. It is a belief that was instinctively understood by the founding fathers of America, who began the Declaration of Independence with the words: "We hold these truths to be self-evident, that all men are created equal." These words were considered so important that they were incorporated into the constitutions of many of the individual states as well. They express the basic belief of the founding fathers, who thus declared war against the prevailing belief in England and the Old World that society was divided into classes, some of which were more equal than others. Almost a hundred years after the Declaration of Independence, Abraham Lincoln famously quoted this phrase in his Gettysburg Address: "Fourscore and seven years ago our fathers brought forth on this continent a new nation, conceived in liberty and dedicated to the proposition that all men are created equal." Yet the founding fathers did not follow this truth to its logical conclusion. They never recognized that women had equal rights or that nonwhites were equal and therefore must not be enslaved, even though these concepts were implicit in that statement.

There is something absurd about saying that "all men are created equal" when it is blatantly false. As the midrash quoted above (*Mishnah*

Sanhedrin 4:4) so accurately puts it, "no one is exactly like another." We do not look exactly like one another, each person has a unique set of fingerprints, and we are not equal in our abilities. Some are strong, some weak, some brilliant, others less so, some talented in one thing, some in another. Yet there is a profound truth in saying that we are all created equal if we understand the statement as the midrash understood the Torah—that even though we are not exactly alike, each of us is created in the image of the first human, who was in turn created in the image of God, and therefore we are all siblings and cannot say, "My father is greater than your father." Similarly, Rabbi Meir teaches that the first human being was created from dust "gathered from all parts of the earth" (Talmud, *Sanhedrin* 38a), another way of saying that all human beings are equal and that no group from any part of the earth can claim superiority to any other group.[6] This leads inevitably to the conclusion that all humans have equal rights to such things as life, liberty, and the pursuit of happiness, equal rights to justice and freedom. If the law codes, whether Jewish, American, or other, do not achieve this, then they are still imperfect and need to be improved.

Righteous Gentiles in the Book of Jonah

The Torah's teaching of the equality of human beings comes to full expression in the book of Jonah. In this magnificent text, God sends the Hebrew prophet on the task of warning the people of Nineveh—if anything, enemies of the Israelites—that they are to be judged by God, "for their wickedness has come before Me" (Jonah 1:2). The purpose of this mission is not merely to inform them of approaching doom, but to give them an opportunity to avoid destruction by changing their ways. Jonah understands that all too well and therefore attempts to avoid this task. As he says after the Ninevites have indeed repented and been spared, "That is why I fled beforehand to Tarshish. For I know that You are a compassionate and gracious God, slow to anger, abounding in kindness, renouncing punishment" (4:2). How does Jonah know that about God? Because that is exactly how God is revealed and described to Moses in Exodus 34:6–7. Although there the context is God's quality of mercy and forgiveness as applied to Israel, it is clear to Jonah that God's mercy extends to all God's creatures, even the people of Nineveh. As YHVH says to Jonah in the final speech of the book, "Should I not care about Nineveh, that great city, in which there are more than a hundred and twenty thousand persons who do not yet know their right hand from their left, and many beasts as well?" (Jonah 4:11).

This message of human equality is all-pervasive in the book of Jonah. The king of Nineveh, a pagan, proclaims a fast and calls on the people to abandon their evil ways (3:8). The non-Hebrew sailors are depicted as extremely concerned not to injure Jonah and are termed "God-fearing" (1:16), the same expression used to describe the righteous midwives who saved the Hebrew infants in Egypt (Exod. 1:21).[7]

Although the book of Jonah goes much further in making this point clear and in positing repentance as a possibility, the same idea of the equality of all humans in the sight of God is also found in the much earlier story of Sodom and Gomorrah. Even though Abraham has family there, when he pleads with God to save the cities if there are a sufficient number of righteous people therein, he does not ask for his kin alone to be delivered but for all to be saved from destruction—the blameless and the guilty alike. The righteous that he speaks of are not his family, but any human beings in the city who are innocent (Gen. 18:23–32).

There are times when the Torah singles out a group as being unworthy or even cursed. It is never because of an inherent flaw making them inferior, but because of bad conduct. Following the flood, for example, Noah curses Canaan, the son of Ham, because "Ham, the father of Canaan, saw his father's nakedness and told his two brothers outside" (Gen. 9:22). Therefore he says, "Cursed be Canaan: the lowest of slaves shall he be to his brothers" (Gen. 9:25) and twice he says, "Let Canaan be a slave to them" (Gen. 9:26–27). This strange curse of the son when the father committed the offense has been explained either as an ellipsis—that is, the phrase "cursed be Canaan" really indicates "cursed be Ham, the father of Canaan"—or that it is assumed that Canaan took part in the disgraceful act even though he is not mentioned.[8] Note that it is not God who curses Canaan and makes the Canaanites slaves, but Noah. From a historical point of view, the text may also be justifying the generally negative attitude of the Torah toward the Canaanites, who are accused of immoral conduct, defending the loss of their land by pointing to the immoral conduct of their ancestor (Deut. 12:29–31). Just as in the Torah the conduct of the progenitor of a tribe of Israel is taken as representing the future history of the tribe, so too the conduct of an ancestor is symbolic of their future way of acting. Nevertheless, even here, it is their immoral conduct that earns them punishment and not any inferiority within them.

Similarly, when Deuteronomy will not permit Moabites or Ammonites to "be admitted into the congregation of YHVH," it is not because of their race but because of their conduct toward Israel (Deut. 23:4–7). Perhaps the story of Ruth, who was from Moab, was a quiet protest against that view. Even the Amalekites, against whom Moses proclaimed, "YHVH will be at war with Amalek throughout the ages!" (Exod. 17:16), are blamed in this way because of their actions, not because of any inner flaw making them less than human. The demonization of human beings goes against the grain of the ideals of the Torah.

The concept of the equality of all human beings is embedded in all parts of the Hebrew Bible. In the section known as Writings, the repository of wisdom literature, for example, we find Job, who is not a Hebrew, depicted as a man "blameless and upright; he feared God and shunned evil" (Job 1:1)—the finest descriptions of a truly righteous and religious man. This is similar to the Torah's description of another non-Hebrew, Noah, "a righteous man, blameless in his age" (Gen. 6:9). When Job protests his innocence and his goodness, he states that he treats his male and female slaves in such a way that they never have a complaint against him. "Did not He who made me in my mother's belly make him? Did not One form us both in the womb?" (Job 31:15). There is no better expression of our common humanity than that.

The Torah's concern with humanity as a whole is also frequently echoed in the book of Psalms. As cited above in chapter 5, Psalm 8, basing itself on Genesis's account of creation (Gen. 1:26–30), speaks of all humanity as God's creation and concern: "What is man that You have been mindful of him, mortal man that You have taken note of him, that You have made him little less than divine, and adorned him with glory and majesty; You have made him master over Your handiwork, laying the world at his feet" (vv. 5–7). Psalm 104 similarly speaks of God's graciousness to all humans: "You make the grass grow for the cattle, and herbage for the labor of a human being that he may get bread out of the earth, wine that cheers human hearts, oil that makes the face shine, and bread that sustains the life of human beings" (vv. 14–15).

The book of Psalms is also filled with references to all of the nations who are depicted as worshippers of the true God. "From east to west the name of YHVH is praised" (Ps. 113:3), a strange assertion considering the fact that all of the nations were considered to be worshippers of mere fetishes! "Their idols are silver and gold, the work of men's hands" (Ps. 115:4). Yet they are called on to praise God: "Praise YHVH all you nations, extol Him, all you peoples" (Ps. 117:1). "Let all the ends of the earth pay heed and turn to YHVH, and the peoples of all nations prostrate themselves before You, for sovereignty is YHVH's and He rules the nations" (Ps. 22:28–29). The postexilic prophet Malachi goes so far as to say that YHVH is worshipped throughout the world—this at a time when the only monotheistic religion in existence was that of Israel. "From where the sun rises to where it sets, My name is honored among the nations, and everywhere incense and pure oblation are offered to My name; for My name is honored among the nations—said YHVH of Hosts" (Mal. 1:11). The potential for realizing the truth concerning God may be found among all nations because all are equally God's children and God's creation.

The prophet Amos is clear about this idea when he teaches, "To Me, O Israelites, you are just like the Ethiopians—declares YHVH. True, I brought Israel up from the land of Egypt, but also the Philistines from Caphtor and the Arameans from Kir" (Amos 9:7). Not only is God the universal God—given that Judaism posits there is only one God, it can hardly be any other way—but even if God has a special covenantal relationship with Israel, all human beings are objects of God's concern and are not set apart as if they were different in substance and essence from the people Israel. Even when that same prophet refers to the covenantal relationship—"Concerning the whole family that I brought up from the land of Egypt: You alone have I singled out of all the families of the earth—that is why I will call you to account for all your iniquities" (Amos 3:1–2)—he speaks of Israel as a part of one humanity, "the families of the earth."

In the same vein as Amos speaks of the past, Isaiah prophesies about the future: "In that day, Israel shall be a third partner with Egypt and Assyria as a blessing on earth; for YHVH of Hosts will bless them, saying, 'Blessed be My people Egypt, My handiwork Assyria and My very own Israel'" (Isa. 19:24–25). The prophets envision the day when all will worship YHVH: "To Me every knee shall bow, every tongue swear allegiance" (Isa. 45:23). The Torah begins with the creation of the one human being from whom all humanity springs. The prophets conclude with a messianic vision in which all humanity is united in the worship of the one Creator.[9]

This concept is articulated in the ancient *Aleinu* prayer that concludes every Jewish worship service. Written in the Hellenistic period before monotheism had spread outside of Judaism, *Aleinu* begins by asserting that Israel is differentiated from all the nations in one way only— that Israel recognizes and worships the true God, while the others worship "nothingness and vanity." It concludes with the hope that this differentiation will disappear because all nations will abandon false worship and "all mortals will call upon Your name." Then YHVH will truly be one.

The Rights of "Strangers"

The influence of the ideal of the equality of all humans can be felt in the laws of the Torah found in the last four books, Exodus through Deuteronomy, even though the laws therein are intended for the people of Israel alone. They envision Israel living in its own land—the Land of Israel, formerly Canaan, that had been promised to Abraham, Isaac, and Jacob—and form the constitution of the new state of the Israelites. Nevertheless, the Torah makes provision for non-Israelites who will be dwelling there, grants them many rights, and cautions the Israelites concerning their treatment. These people are known as *gerim*, "strangers," or literally "dwellers." It is a term that Abraham had used to describe himself in relation to those who lived in the land to which he had come. "I am a *ger* and a resident among you," he said and then asked for permission to buy land (Gen. 23:4). Although there is no explicit ruling in the Torah prohibiting the resident stranger from owning land, most scholars assume that this was the case. The exilic prophet Ezekiel states that when the people of Israel return to the land and divide it among the tribes, "You shall allot it as a heritage for yourselves and for the strangers who reside among you, who have begotten children among you. You shall treat them as Israelite citizens; they shall receive allotments along with you among the tribes of Israel" (Ezek. 47:22). Certainly, this was an innovation; in the original division of the land among the tribes, there is no such provision for a "stranger," but this innovation is very much in the spirit of the Torah's revolutionary concept of human equality.[10]

Similarly, there is no specific prohibition in the Torah against selling land to a non-Israelite; such prohibitions were enacted in Jewish law against idolaters at a later period, when Jewish independence was no more and Jews did not control the land. Within Jewish law, there were different opinions as to who was prohibited from owning land and, in general, who was referred to whenever the laws spoke of "idolaters." Although some sages took it as referring to all non-Jews, others restricted it literally to those who worshipped idols. The most liberal position on this question was taken by a thirteenth-century rabbi from Provence, Menachem Hameiri, who held that any such prohibitions applied only to the seven Canaanite nations who no longer existed and certainly not to people who were "guided by religious norms," which included both Christians and Muslims.[11] Although there may be harsh statements against non-Jews found in the vast works of Jewish tradition, these reflect the agony and suffering of Jews under their oppressors at various times in Jewish history and as such are understandable. Such harsh words, however, "did not thereby become Jewish religious teachings and are not to be considered as an authoritative statement of Judaism."[12]

Rabbi Haim Hirschensohn, an early twentieth-century Orthodox Zionist thinker, taught that the Torah is democratic in viewing all citizens as equal before the law, including the Jew and the stranger—the non-Jew—in their midst. As paraphrased by the philosopher Eliezer Shweid, "In principle, Hirschensohn insists, the Torah advocates complete social, political and moral equality between Jews and Gentiles, in the sense that any demand based on human morality applies equally to all…. The differences in religious and ritual considerations do not in the slightest impinge on the full equality between Jew and Gentile in the eyes of the Torah."[13]

As Lauterbach puts it, "For we are mindful of the fundamental principles of our religion, that we all have one Father in heaven and that every human being is made in the image of the Father and that we sin against God if we harm any man."[14]

Common Ancestry in Rabbinic Judaism and Beyond

Rabbinic Judaism went far in developing and emphasizing this concept. A late midrash expresses the idea that all are equal in the sight of God: "I call heaven and earth to witness, that whether one be Gentile or Jew, man or woman, slave or handmaid, the Holy Spirit will rest upon them according to their deeds!"[15] As we have already pointed out, the Sages used the Torah's creation story to indicate that we all have one common ancestry. The early sage Hillel taught that we should be like Aaron, "loving all those created [by God] and bringing them closer to the Torah" (*Pirkei Avot* 1:12). Hillel does not say "loving Israelites" but "loving all those created," which specifically includes non-Jews. Rabbi Akiba well understood the meaning of this and taught, "Beloved is the human being, for he was created in the image of God. The human being is exceedingly beloved in that it was made known to him that he was created in the image of God" (*Pirkei Avot* 3:18). Hillel's contemporary, Shammai, taught that one was to greet "every human being with a cheerful face" (*Pirkei Avot* 1:15).

In an interesting discussion between Akiba and Ben Azzai on the question of which verse of the Torah is the basic verse on which everything else depends, Akiba suggests, "Love your neighbor as yourself" (Lev. 19:18). Ben Azzai objects, contending that "this is the record of the begettings of humankind. At the time of God's creating humankind, in the likeness of God did He make it" (Gen. 5:1) was an even greater verse.[16] Although Ben Azzai does not explain himself, we may assume that he felt that "your neighbor" could be understood to mean your fellow Israelite alone, whereas Genesis 5:1 speaks of all humanity as being in God's likeness and would therefore apply the Torah's ethical principles and concern to them all. The eighteenth-century mystic Pinhas Eliah Hurwitz reinterprets the verse from Leviticus that Akiba chose to apply to all human beings:

> The essence of neighborly love consists in loving all mankind, all who walk on two legs, of whatever people and whatever tongue, by virtue of their identical humanity.... The meaning of the verse "You shall love your neighbor as yourself" is not confined to Jews only, but the sense is "your neighbor who is a human being as yourself"—people of all nations are included, any fellow humans.[17]

Perhaps that was the way that Akiba had understood it. Walt Whitman, the nineteenth-century poet of America and American ideals, expresses much the same idea in the opening verses of his *Leaves of Grass*:

> *I celebrate myself,*
> *And what I assume you shall assume;*
> *For every atom belonging to me, as good belongs to*
> *   you....*
> *In all people I see myself—none more, and not one a*
> *   barleycorn less,*
> *And the good or bad I say of myself, I say of them.*

At the conclusion of the Second World War, Henry Alonzo Myers of Cornell University wrote a book titled *Are Men Equal?* He viewed that war as the ultimate struggle between Jefferson's ideal of the equality of men and Hitler's ideal of the inequality of men. Myers acknowledges that this doctrine was much older than Jefferson, having been stated in the Torah thousands of years earlier: "From beginning to end the Bible teaches the fatherhood of God and the brotherhood of man. The story of the creation of Adam and Eve, the parents of all men, is the first lesson."[18] Because of the importance of that struggle, Myers attempts to strengthen the grounds for the belief in human equality:

The lessons of history are clear enough. The doctrine of superiority has always been, even in its noblest forms, a means of dividing men, of setting one class or one people over others and against others. The proposition of equality, on the other hand, by its very nature implies the unity of men. Already a giant force in world politics, it will in time prevail over armed force—if men believe it to be true.[19]

It is ironic that the Torah's concept of human equality was so well expressed in German in the words of Friedrich von Schiller, which were later immortalized and sung so gloriously in the finale of Beethoven's Ninth Symphony: *"Alle menchen weirden bruder"*—"All humans shall be brothers." Had these words been taken to heart in twentieth-century Germany, the great tragedy of that time would have been averted.

7

Men and Women
Are Equal

Revolutionary Truth #7: Women are not inferior; rather, men and women are created equal.

> And God created humankind in His image, in the image of God did He create it; male and female did He create them.
>
> *Genesis 1:27*

> At the time of God's creating humankind, in the likeness of God did He then make it, male and female He created them and gave blessing to them and called their name: Humankind! on the day of their being created.
>
> *Genesis 5:1–2[1]*

The verses above from Genesis are remarkable in the absolute way they proclaim the equality of male and female, created in the image of God, with no distinction between them. The strange shift between the singular "it" (which could also be translated as "him") to the plural "them" is the basis of the interesting Rabbinic midrash that the human being was created two-sided, one male and one female, and then later divided into two separate beings, a man and a woman.[2] As biblical scholar Nahum

Sarna remarks, "Both sexes are created on the sixth day by the hand of the one God; both are made 'in His image' on a level of absolute equality before Him."[3] The verses had no need to spell out "male and female." By doing so they emphasize the equality of the sexes. These two verses, then, articulate an article of belief, a received truth: the equality of male and female.

As noted earlier, the second creation story in Genesis 2:4–24 is from a different source.[4] It describes the creation of Adam and Eve and seems somewhat less absolute regarding gender equality; it clearly posits that the male was created first and only later the female in answer to Adam's need for an appropriate companion. Nevertheless, it does state that the woman was created from the man and is therefore a part of him. "This last one is bone of my bones and flesh of my flesh. This one shall be called woman, for she was taken from man" (Gen. 2:23). The story of the creation of man—*adam*—from clay is similar to the story of the creation of the first human in the old Babylonian myth—"Let him be formed out of clay, be animated with blood"—but there is no parallel story in the latter to the creation of woman, nothing that indicates the close bond between male and female.[5] The Torah then goes on to explain the basis for marriage: "Hence a man leaves his father and mother and clings to his wife, so that they become one flesh" (Gen. 2:24). In a sense, we have come full circle to the original human of Genesis 1, who, at least according to the midrash, was indeed one flesh, male and female. Becoming one flesh is a clear indication of equality. It is interesting to note that after eating the forbidden fruit, Adam and Eve work together as partners and "sewed together fig leaves and made themselves loincloths" (Gen. 3:7).

The Portrayal of Women in Narrative Texts

Before discussing women's legal status, let us consider the image of women in some of the stories of the Torah, where they play a crucial role, as well as in later biblical writings.

The first story in which a female is depicted is that of Adam and Eve in the Garden of Eden (Genesis 3). It has been commonly assumed in European writings that Eve was a temptress and the source of human misery.

She is depicted thus in classical art and literature. For example, "God created Adam master and lord of living creatures, but Eve spoilt it all."[6] But that is not what the text of the Torah actually says. The serpent did not tell her to disobey God but gave her a different version of God's command to Adam—a command she had never heard directly from God—and she believed it. Eve may have been naïve to accept the serpent's word, but she did so because it seemed good to her, desirable and useful for imparting wisdom (Gen. 3:6). She handed some of the fruit to Adam, and without a word of protest, he—who *had* heard God's command—ate it. If anyone truly disobeyed God it was Adam, and God's words to him emphasize that: "Because you did as your wife said and ate of the tree *about which I commanded you, 'You shall not eat of it'*" (Gen. 3:17).[7] Adam attempted to put all the blame on Eve, but God would not have it. Therefore, Adam's punishment is at least as severe as Eve's. The first woman, the mother of us all, may have been gullible, but she was not evil. She and Adam were equal in their creation and equal in their guilt. Nevertheless, this story also indicates that women will be governed by their husbands (Gen. 3:16), which is indeed a reflection of the status of women in biblical times.

In the stories of the founding families of Israel, although it is clear that a patriarchal society is being described in which men are dominant, the role of the matriarchs is not inconsequential. These matriarchs are clearly subordinate to their husbands, but they are by no means mere chattel lacking independence and initiative.

Sarah, Rebekah, and Rachel are all described as being beautiful (Gen. 12:11, 12:14, 24:16, 29:17). They are also intelligent, independent, and active in determining the fate of the nation. When Abraham wants Sarah to do something for him, he does not command her but asks for her help: "Please say that you are my sister" (Gen. 12:13). When Sarah tells Abraham to take some action, God says to him, "Whatever Sarah tells you, do as she says" (Gen. 21:12). The extraordinary care Abraham takes in finding an appropriate burial place for Sarah says something about her worth and the relationship between them (Genesis 23). No wonder a prophet saw fit to mention her specifically together with Abraham: "Look back to Abraham your father and to Sarah who brought you forth" (Isa. 51:2).

Rebekah is depicted as being extraordinarily kind and generous (Gen. 24:19–20). She is consulted concerning her marriage and has to give her consent (Gen. 24:57–58). She resembles Abraham and Sarah in being willing to leave her family and journey to far-off Canaan, an indication of her independence. Although the marriage was an arranged one, we are informed that "Isaac loved her" (Gen. 24:67). The same is said of Jacob and Rachel, a true love story if ever there was one (Gen. 29:18). Rebekah's initiative is also seen in her role in obtaining the blessing of the firstborn for Jacob (Genesis 27). Although we may question the propriety of such a deception, she obviously is acting out of a sense of what is necessary for the future of the family and is attempting to fulfill the prophecy she heard when she was pregnant (Gen. 25:23). Rebekah is anything but a passive figure.

The stories connected with the birth of Moses continue the tradition of the matriarchs in showing women as positive factors in determining the future of Israel. Shiphrah and Puah, the Hebrew midwives who resist Pharaoh's command to kill male babies, are the very symbol of righteous conduct (Exod. 1:17). They are given the highest compliment when the Torah says that "they revered God." Joheved, Moses's mother, is equally brave in defying Pharaoh and saving her son (Exod. 2:2–4). The same could be said of Pharaoh's daughter, who pities the child and saves him, knowing full well that he is one of the Hebrew babes whom her father has condemned to be killed (Exod. 2:6). Moses owes his life to these four women, and also to his sister, Miriam, who watched to see what would become of him. Miriam herself is termed a prophetess, one of the troika that led the people, and she is also a religious leader who led the women in joyful and thankful song and dance (Exod. 15:20). It cannot be accidental that five women—and only women, no men—are deemed responsible for the life of Moses, without whom Israel would never have attained freedom from Egyptian bondage. Nor should we ignore Moses's wife, Zipporah, who takes drastic and courageous action to save the life of Moses when they are on the way back to Egypt (Exod. 4:24–26).

In addition to Miriam, we know of another prophetess, Huldah, who lived at the time of Jeremiah and was so prominent that when a scroll was found in the Temple, it was she to whom King Josiah's men turned to verify its authenticity and sacredness (2 Kings 22:14). Perhaps there were other women prophets who were simply not mentioned in the chronicles of the time.

Another woman, whom we usually refer to as a judge, is also deemed to have been a prophetess: "Deborah, the wife of Lappidoth,[8] was a prophetess; she led Israel at that time … and the Israelites would come to her for decisions" (Judg. 4:4–5). As a judge, she leads the nation, the equivalent of a president or prime minister today. Deborah even participates personally in the battle against Sisera, the Canaanite general, and defeats him (Judg. 4:9–16). Sisera himself is slain by Jael, another courageous woman (Judg. 4:17–21), who takes on herself a task usually assigned to men, thus breaking the stereotype of the proper roles of men and women.

The story of Dinah, Jacob's only daughter, is instructive in showing how women were expected to conduct themselves and how they were regarded in patriarchal societies. "Dinah … went out to visit the daughters of the land. Shechem son of Hamor the Hivite, chief of the country, saw her, and lay with her and mistreated her" (Gen. 34:1–2). The word translated here as "mistreated" is sometimes translated as "forced." Its usual meaning, however, is to cause affliction or harm. Although the story is often taken to mean that Shechem raped her, biblical scholar Tikva Frymer-Kensky convincingly demonstrates that is not necessarily the case.[9] Dinah may have consented; her "going out" was already an indication of her not acting in an appropriate fashion, as would become a proper virginal daughter. Shechem's mistreatment or humiliation of her comes from his having intercourse with her before marriage. It does not sound as if Shechem was a brutal rapist. On the contrary: "Being strongly drawn to Dinah … and in love with the maiden, he spoke to the maiden tenderly" (Gen. 34:3). In stark contrast with the story of Amnon and Tamar (2 Sam. 13:14), where Amnon brutally rapes Tamar and then discards her callously, Shechem wants to marry Dinah. Whether she consented or not is of little importance here;[10] in either case, the family's honor has been maligned. As Simeon and Levi say to their father after they have avenged this dishonor in a dishonorable way, "Should our sister be treated like a whore?" (Gen. 34:31). A whore is not raped. To have a sister with whom other men feel free to lay as they would with a whore is a disgrace to the family, to the father and brothers who could not keep that from happening.

Two biblical books are called by the names of women who are the heroines of their stories, Ruth and Esther. Some have even speculated that they may have been written by women.[11] Ruth, a novella set in the period of the Judges, depicts the travails of women who have no men to provide for them. The solution to the problem is to find a relative who will take on himself the task of redeeming Ruth, the widow of his kin. Ruth, a Moabite woman who decides to accompany her Israelite mother-in-law Naomi and assumes the nationality and religion of Naomi, is the very embodiment of loyalty and loving-kindness (Ruth 2:11–12, 4:15). The irony of this story is that it has as its heroine a woman who comes from a people who were considered the enemies of Israel. Moabite women caused the disaster of the plague at Baal-peor (Num. 25:1–9), and now a Moabite woman is the ancestress of David, the king of Israel and progenitor of the Messiah. The message is that Moabite women are not to be scorned. They, too, can be accepted into Israel and can be bearers of future leaders. The book of Ruth may also be understood as protesting Ezra's actions at the return from Babylon in demanding that foreign wives be renounced (Ezra 10).

Esther risks her life to save the Jewish people in exile when they are threatened with extermination by the evil Haman (Esther 4:16). Although Mordecai might be seen as the true hero of the story because it is he who convinces Esther of what she has to do and eventually becomes second only to King Ahasuerus (Esther 10:3), it is Esther who continually intercedes with the king and to whom he gives authority. The book is not called Mordecai but Esther, attesting to her power and the esteem in which she is held.

Song of Songs, often thought of as a problematic book because of its frank and erotic depictions of male and female sexuality, is unique in allowing a woman full freedom and complete equality with a man in all things. She is no more or less a sex object than is her male beloved. When she says, "I am my lover's and my lover is mine" (Song 6:3), she expresses beautifully the mutuality of their love. Benjamin Segal, in his commentary to Song of Songs, writes, "The Song departs from the Bible's androcentric view of love relationships … and the Song is certainly revolutionary in that regard. However, there may be biblical parallels to this approach. Some feel that the Song's egalitarianism reflects the original harmony of another story—the Garden of Eden."[12]

For the only truly misogynist picture of women in the Bible, one must turn to the book of Ecclesiastes, in which the anonymous wisdom teacher called Kohelet, who masquerades as King Solomon, has little good to say about them: "Now I find woman more bitter than death; she is all traps, her hands are fetters and her heart is snares" (Eccles. 7:26). He does manage, however, to recommend enjoying happiness "with a woman you love all the fleeting days of life that have been granted you" (Eccles. 9:9). The writer of that book has many ideas that are strange to the rest of the Bible and may have been influenced by the denigration of women that is found in classical Greek thought.[13]

Fortunately, this attitude finds few echoes in other parts of the Hebrew Bible, although in another wisdom book, Proverbs, there are warnings to youth about designing women who entrap them with sexual wiles (Prov. 5:1–19, 7:1–27). More typical would be the chapter at the conclusion of Proverbs:

> O to find a capable wife!
> Her worth is far beyond rubies.
> Her husband puts his confidence in her
> And lacks no good thing.
> She is good to him, never bad,
> All the days of her life.
>
> (Prov. 31:10–11)

This woman, sometimes described as "a woman of valor," takes total control of her household, conducts a business, treats the poor charitably, and makes and sells cloth. "Her mouth is full of wisdom, her tongue with kindly teaching" (Prov. 31:26). "Her husband praises her" (v. 28).

It should be pointed out, on the other hand, that we are never told the names of the wives of either Cain or Noah or the daughters of Lot. When the names of all who lived are given in 1 Chronicles 1, women are largely omitted, including the matriarchs.

Women and Worship

Miriam's leading the women in song to praise God after the salvation of Israel at the Red Sea (Exod. 15:20–21) indicates that women were expected to participate in the worship of God. Deuteronomy often goes out of its way to specifically mention women, wives, or households to include women in participation in cultic rites and worship. Thus, they are included in rejoicing in Jerusalem (Deut. 12:12, 14:26, 15:20, 26:11) and in resting on the Sabbath (5:14). Although the laws are written as if addressed specifically to men, they include women as participants in the major rituals of Israelite worship. In Deuteronomy 31:10–12, Moses tells the people specifically that every seventh year at Sukkot, all Israel, "men, women, little children," are to gather to listen to the Teaching being read aloud. Exodus 38:8 also mentions "women who performed tasks at the entrance of the Tent of Meeting," although exactly what they did remains unknown.[14] In two places in Leviticus, 12:6 and 15:29, women are specifically required to bring sacrificial offerings to the sanctuary to achieve ritual purification. Biblical scholar Meyer Gruber points out that in the Priestly legislation in the Torah, "neutral, nonsexist expressions *nefesh* and *adam*, both meaning 'person,'" are used referring to cultic acts that can be performed by either men or women.[15] Women as well as men played in the orchestra in the Temple in David's time (1 Chron. 25:5–6) and sang in the choir during the postexilic period (Ezra 2:65 and Neh. 7:67).[16]

That women did participate in worship is seen in the anecdotal stories of Hannah, who "went up to the House of the Lord year after year" to worship (1 Sam. 1:7) and of the Shunamite woman whose husband questions why she is going to see Elisha the prophet when "it is neither the new moon nor Sabbath" (2 Kings 4:23).[17] Within the family, although it was undoubtedly patriarchal, the mother was not ignored.

The Legal Rights of Women

On the basis of Genesis's expression of equality, we could expect that despite minor exceptions of matters concerned directly with women's sexuality and role in procreation, there would be no distinction between men and women in their rights and their treatment under the law. Of course, that is not the case. Things are not that simple. The Torah, after all, is not a utopian book but a product of its times, and ancient societies were patriarchal, often much more so than in Israel. Men controlled women and their lives and were dominant in all matters. The Torah accepts that world-view and does not truly reform it, although in some ways the Torah modifies what was happening elsewhere. What is crucial is that the Torah acknowledges that, as the Genesis story teaches, both men and women are human and are equal. As Tikva Frymer-Kensky writes, "The role of women is clearly subordinate, but the Hebrew Bible does not 'explain' or justify this subordination by portraying women as different or inferior. The stories do not reflect any differences in goals and desires between men and women."[18] The initial insight is of great importance and influence, but it was not carried to its ultimate implications in the Torah any more than it was in Western societies. After all, a constitutional amendment proclaiming the equality of men and women has yet to be approved in the United States.

When we consider the laws pertaining to women in the Torah, we find specific laws in which women are treated differently than men and have fewer rights. Nevertheless, we can also detect the effect of the idea of equality in provisions intended to give women certain rights and protection. This becomes clear when we compare the Torah's legislation to that of other Near Eastern societies. It must be stated, however, that we never can be certain if the laws of the Torah were ever really enforced, or if some of them were theoretical or polemical. This is particularly true when we see that the laws in one corpus do not always agree with those in other sections. Deuteronomy, for example, is generally considered a later book than the others, and many scholars feel that its laws had no juridical application but were more homiletical in nature.[19]

One major area of legislation is in the area of sexual relations, in which the woman's virginity is paramount. In many ancient societies, and Israel was certainly one of them, a woman's virginity was highly prized.[20] An unmarried woman who lost her virginity voluntarily dishonored her family by demonstrating that her father had no control over her. "Real men have the strength and cunning to protect and control their women."[21] The case of Dinah, discussed above, is an example of that. Lack of virginity threatens not only social status, but also economic viability of the family.[22]

Deuteronomy 22:13–21 discusses the case of a bride whose husband accuses her of not being a virgin. If the charge is proved correct, the woman faces the death penalty. If the charge is proved false, the husband is flogged and fined, and he can never divorce her. Although the woman's feelings are not taken into account, the law benefits her because the deliberate harshness of the penalty in either case may serve to discourage the accusations from ever being made public.[23]

Strangely enough, the evidence—the sheet with blood on it— remains in the hands of the bride's parents, whereas in other cultures it belongs to the groom.[24] Her parents could, should they so desire, manufacture false evidence. Thus, her fate is in their hands. Indeed, parents controlled not only daughters but also sons, as the law of the rebellious son demonstrates (Deut. 21:18–21). All of this indicates that the purpose of this law was not so much to punish the bride as it was to protect the woman, given that under Mesopotamian law a man could simply divorce his wife by claiming lack of virginity without her having any opportunity to defend herself.[25]

This concern for the woman and her rights is also shown in Deuteronomy 22:28–29, where a man who has raped an unmarried woman must not only pay a fine, but must also marry her and may never divorce her. On the other hand, in Exodus 22:15–16, when a man seduces a woman, her father has the right to refuse the marriage and just take the money.[26]

Even a law that today seems to degrade women may originally have been intended to protect them. In Deuteronomy 25:5–10, a childless woman whose husband has died is expected to marry her husband's brother. If the brother refuses to marry her, he must undergo a ceremony in which he is shamed and even spit on. To us, insisting that a woman marry someone she may not want to marry may seem a way of degrading the woman, but in biblical society, in which an independent woman had no protection, it guaranteed her future livelihood and sustenance. Giving her the rights to call on the brother to do so and to publicly shame him if he did not was a recognition of her independent status and her right to protect her own needs.[27]

Similarly, the law of the captive foreign woman—in which the man who wishes to cohabit with her must give her time to lament her parents before making her a wife, with all the privileges thereof, and may not sell her if he tires of her but must emancipate her (Deut. 21:10–14)—is a far cry from the usual practice in ancient warfare, and some modern as well, of taking women at will.

Exodus 21:2, speaking of the limitation of six years of service for a person who sold himself into indentured servitude, uses the expression "a Hebrew slave"—in the masculine form. In contrast, Deuteronomy 15:12 states that "a fellow Hebrew, man or woman" goes free after six years. Exodus 21:7 also speaks of a man who sells his daughter and says specifically that "she shall not be freed as male slaves are." It seems likely that Deuteronomy is amending the slavery laws of Exodus to prevent a woman from being sold into perpetual concubinage-slavery by her father.[28] In Exodus 21:8–11, the law provides a certain measure of protection for girls sold that way by insisting that her master cannot sell her to others nor withhold any rights from her if he marries someone else. In those cases, she simply goes free. Nor is a man permitted to sell his wife into slavery while remaining free himself, as other societies allowed.[29]

The Decalogue, in Exodus 20:12 and again in Deuteronomy 5:16, states that mothers are to be honored along with fathers, while Leviticus 19:3 even places the mother first in the command "You shall each revere his mother and his father."

The *Sotah* Law

Perhaps the most controversial law concerning women is that of the *sotah*, the woman suspected of adultery when there are no witnesses to the act and no proof (Num. 5:11–31). If the woman does not confess to it but protests her innocence, she is made to undergo an ordeal, the only such instance in the Torah. She drinks "bitter waters" in which the ink from the writing of a curse has been placed together with earth from the floor of the sanctuary. If her belly distends and her thigh sags, she is considered guilty; the consequence is that she becomes unable to bear children. If innocent, nothing happens to her and she becomes fertile. This ordeal has its parallels in the Code of Hammurabi, although there are significant differences, the main one being that in the latter, if proved guilty she is put to death.[30] Torah law was very strict in permitting the death penalty only where there are two witnesses to the crime (Deut. 19:15). The *sotah* ceremony certainly shames the woman, but it also has the effect of clearing her where there is doubt, thus permitting the marital relationship to be restored. It also saves her from the possibility of being wrongly divorced or even physically abused. It most certainly takes the matter out of the hands of her husband and places it under the judgment of God.[31]

According to the Rabbinic law code, the Mishnah, this law was made inoperative by Rabban Yochanan ben Zakkai during the first century CE, "when the number of adulterers grew large" (*Mishnah Sotah* 9:9). Nevertheless, the Mishnah devotes an entire section to it, as does the Talmud. The thrust of the Rabbinic reinterpretation of the law is to make it more difficult to bring a woman to this ordeal. For example, the husband must have warned her in the presence of two witnesses against speaking with a certain man, after which she secluded herself with that man (*Mishnah Sotah* 1:1–2). The Rabbis also require the paramour to be there at the ordeal and state that it would test him as well (*Mishnah Sotah* 5:1), thus addressing the inequality in the Torah's description, which totally ignores the man involved and tests only the woman. In the words of Talmudic scholar Judith Hauptman, "The rabbis sharply reduced the number of instances in which a man could subject his wife to the ordeal of the bitter waters because they recognized that, by their standards, this section of the Torah treats women unfairly."[32]

Marriage and Divorce

Perhaps the most problematic laws concern marriage and divorce. The man acquires the woman as his wife; therefore, it is he who can dismiss her. She has no such rights. Rabbinic Judaism sought to remedy this situation at least in part by the institution of the *ketubah*, the marriage document in which the woman is given financial protection in case of divorce. Whereas under Roman law a divorced woman received only the dowry she brought to the marriage, the *ketubah* specified an additional sum that the husband would have to give her (*Mishnah Ketubot* 1:2). In addition, the Mishnah spells out other ways in which a wife is protected, such as receiving medical care and being supported from his estate should her husband predecease her (*Mishnah Ketubot* 4:8–9). In Hauptman's words, "In a sense this is a complete insurance policy."[33]

Divorce is even more problematic than marriage. According to the Torah, if a wife fails to please her husband in that "he finds in her something obnoxious," he simply "writes her a bill of divorcement, hands it to her, and sends her away from his house" (Deut. 24:1). The term "obnoxious" is not defined, and commentators ancient and modern are divided as to its meaning. The school of Shammai confined it to sexual matters (*Mishnah Gittin* 9:10), but in general, it has been given the much broader interpretation of "any conduct the husband finds intolerable."[34] Thus, the right of divorce is totally in his hands. We have already seen that the Rabbis protected her financially through the *ketubah*'s regulations, but that does not solve the basic problem: that divorce is totally the man's prerogative. Of course, in that society, it would be unlikely that a woman would want a divorce, because it left her basically destitute and unprotected.

In several places, the Mishnah inaugurates the idea of a forced divorce in which the Rabbinic court has the right to require the man to grant a divorce, even against his will (*Mishnah Ketubot* 7:9–10; *Mishnah Gittin* 9:8). In *Arakhin* 5:6, the Mishnah states, "We force him until he says, 'I am willing!'"[35] In pre-Emancipation Jewish society, prior to the French Revolution, the problem posed by the Torah's divorce laws was generally solved by community pressure on the husband to grant a divorce if the wife desired one. In modern-day Jewish life, enforcing this has become much more difficult. Many rabbinical groups have therefore adopted changes in the *ketubah* or prenuptial agreements stipulating that the bride and groom grant the rabbinical court the right to decide if a divorce must be granted. Nevertheless, the problem of the *agunah*, the woman who cannot remarry because the husband will not grant a divorce, remains a vexing one in Jewish life.

The Rabbis certainly did not eradicate the patriarchal basis of Jewish law and grant women full equality, but they were aware of the problem and attempted to at least alleviate it. To quote Hauptman again, "They began to introduce numerous, significant, and occasionally bold corrective measures to ameliorate the lot of women.... They broke new ground, granting women benefits that they never had before, even at men's expense."[36]

Inheritance

The laws of inheritance seem to be an exception to the Torah's more lenient approach to women; ancient Sumerian law, for example, granted daughters equal inheritance rights, while the Torah grants them only to sons. The famous case of the daughters of Zelophehad, who had no sons (Num. 27:1–11), is the exception. The daughters come to Moses protesting that when the land of Canaan is divided among all the tribes, their father will have no portion. God informs Moses that their plea is just, and the law is formulated so that if there is no son, the daughters will inherit the property. However, it is later stipulated that they must marry within the ancestral clan (Num. 36:5–12). Why the Torah was so far behind the laws of other groups in this matter is puzzling. A plausible explanation has been offered by Jacob Milgrom. He states that the reason is to be found in the different structures of these societies. Mesopotamian societies were centralized, urban societies, while the Torah, "in its earliest stages, presumes a tightly knit clan structure; the foremost goal of its legal system was the preservation of the clan."[37] Allowing daughters who may be married to men from a different clan to inherit would destroy that structure.

We see, therefore, that although Genesis 1 clearly assumes the equality of women, this ideal was not reflected in all parts of the Bible. The reality was that there existed a patriarchal society in which women were controlled and protected by father and husband, but they could also serve as true partners in love and as religious and political leaders. Women could be busy not only with the house but also in business and commerce and could be thought of as a source of wisdom. Although some laws of the Torah regarding women may be unacceptable today, in their time they generally served to protect women in a society that was far different from that which is currently acceptable. Biblical scholar Eckart Otto goes so far as to claim:

> The family laws in the book of Deuteronomy had a progressive and protective attitude toward the legal status of women. They were deeply concerned with the restriction of male predominance … in modern eyes this may be too little and by no means enough—but in antiquity and for women living at that time it meant very much … [and] paved the way for the modern emancipation of women.[38]

8

Human Beings
Have Free Will

Revolutionary Truth #8: Human beings are endowed with free will and can choose their actions.

> Life and death have I have set before you, bless-
> ing and curse—choose life so that you and your
> offspring would live.
>
> *Deuteronomy 30:19*

> God made man unrestrained and free, acting
> voluntarily and of his own choice, to the end
> that, being acquainted with bad things as well as
> good, and acquiring conceptions of honorable
> and shameful conduct, and thinking clearly
> about right and wrong and all that has to do
> with virtue and vice, he may habitually choose
> the better and avoid the contrary.
>
> *Philo[1]*

What role does fate play in our lives? How free are we to make choices, even choices that will harm us? Verdi wrote an opera titled *The Force of Destiny* (*La forza del destino*) dedicated to the concept that destiny dic-
tates our lives, while another of his operas, *Rigoletto*, concludes with the

despairing jester crying out against the curse that brought about the tragedy the protagonist laments, the death of his daughter.

Shakespeare, too, often invokes the concept of fate dictating the lives of his characters. Could Macbeth have done other than live out the events that the witches predicted? Even Hamlet despairs, "There's a divinity that shapes our ends, rough-hew them how we may" (Act 5, Scene 2).[2] Long before Shakespeare, it was taken for granted in ancient Greece that a person had no way to escape his destiny. In *Oedipus*, Sophocles's play built on the legend of the doomed king, Oedipus's wife-mother Jocasta recounts, "It was told him [Laius] that it was fate that he should die a victim at the hands of his own son, a son to be born of Laius and me."[3] Oedipus himself relates how he was told by a seer that "I was fated to lie with my mother ... and I was doomed to be a murderer of the father that begot me."[4] Fleeing to avoid this, he nevertheless fulfills the prophecy. "Would not one rightly judge and say that on me these things were sent by some malignant God?"[5] he asks. Oedipus is doomed from birth to kill his father and marry his mother; he has no way of escaping this terrible fate.

The idea of fate, known to the Greeks as *moira* and to the Romans later as *fatum*, is integral to ancient pagan religions. Even the gods have no control over it. Time after time in Greek legends, notes biblical scholar Yehezkel Kaufmann, heroes such as Achilles and even the gods themselves are told of what fate has in store for them and have absolutely no way of avoiding it.[6]

This idea of freedom of will also seems to fly in the face of much that modern science teaches us. As we learn about the influence of hormones on our actions, as we see how drugs and pharmaceuticals can shape our behavior, it often seems that there remains little room for choice. If rats and other animals can be trained to Pavlovian responses, are not humans susceptible to similar programming? Physical and psychological forces beyond our control shape our actions and therefore our destinies. What, then, remains of our free will, our ability to make decisions free of coercion? As theologian Abraham Joshua Heschel puts it, "What makes a human being human is not just mechanical, biological, and psychological functioning, but the ability to make decisions constantly."[7]

One of the world's most famous scientists, Albert Einstein, said, "I am a determinist. I do not believe in free will. Jews believe in free will. They believe that man shapes his own life. I reject that doctrine. In that respect I am not a Jew."[8] In his famous credo *What I Believe*, written in 1930, he states clearly:

> I do not at all believe in free will in the philosophical sense. Everybody acts not only under external compulsion but also in accordance with inner necessity. Schopenhauer's saying, "A man can do as he wills, but not will as he wills," has been a real inspiration to me since my youth: it has been a continual consolation in the face of life's hardships, my own and others', and an unfailing wellspring of tolerance.[9]

It may be a source of consolation to think that if we made wrong choices, it was not our fault because everyone acts under compulsion, but does it not also relieve us of responsibility for our actions? Would this not mean the end of all ethics? To his credit, Einstein conceded that "I am compelled to act as if free will existed, because if I wish to live in a civilized society I must act responsibly."[10]

Unlike Einstein, and unlike many ancient and modern religions, including various interpretations of Christianity and Islam that are predicated on the idea that the actions and fate of humans are predestined,[11] the Torah insists that human beings do indeed have free will. We can choose blessing or curse, life or death, good or evil. The Torah may tell us how we should decide—"choose life" (Deut. 30:19)—but it cannot force us to do so. Our choices have consequences—consequences that are often spelled out in advance—but the choice remains ours.

Certainly there are tremendous limitations on human freedom of action. We are limited by the physical and mental abilities with which we are born, although we seldom if ever reach their maximum capacities. We are limited by the place in which we live and the time into which we are born. Obviously, there are forces—nature and nurture—that shape our lives; the debate continues as to which is more influential and how much each determines our actions. Yet, even given all of those limitations, the Torah asserts as an unprovable but basic religious truth that we have freedom of will, freedom of choice. As Viktor Frankl puts it, "Man's freedom is no freedom from conditions but rather freedom to take a stand on whatever conditions might confront him."[12]

The Choice Between Good and Evil

All of the early stories of Genesis, which are clearly intended to explain the nature of human beings and of human life, emphasize choice and free will. Even the first tale, that of Adam and Eve in the Garden of Eden, presents these two naïve creatures, who have no life experience and no history of the past to guide them, as free agents. Before the creation of Eve, Adam is given one commandment: not to eat of the tree of knowledge of good and evil, "for as soon as you eat of it you shall die" (Gen. 2:17). Commentators, ancient and modern, have spilt a great deal of ink over the meaning of that verse. What exactly is "knowledge of good and evil"? Yehezkel Kaufmann's interpretation, that it means "the knowledge of, and desire for, evil, without which man's comprehension is incomplete," is compelling.[13] Whatever the meaning, one thing is clear: Adam is commanded. He is not programmed. If he disobeys and eats of the fruit of the tree, his disobedience has a price, but the choice is his. Indeed, Adam and Eve exercise that right of choice, with well-known consequences. Human life and experience as we know it begins with the exercise of our free will.

The story of Cain and Abel is even more explicit in its message of freedom of choice. When Cain's offering to God is rejected, he is greatly distressed. God then speaks to him and says, "Why are you distressed, and why is your face fallen? Surely, if you do right, there is uplift. But if you do not do right, sin crouches at the door; its urge is toward you, yet you can rule over it" (Gen. 4:6–7). Sin is depicted as a monster that waits in secret to pounce and cause evil, but the important message is "you can rule over it." Nothing automatically forces us to do wrong. Ours is the choice. It is not accidental that the word "sin" makes its first appearance in the Torah in this context. Freedom of choice and sin are two sides of the same coin. The one implies the possibility of the other. We cannot sin if our actions are not the result of free choice. That was Einstein's ethical dilemma.

An ancient midrash based on the verse "Fear not, for God has heeded the cry of the boy where he is" (Gen. 21:17) relates that when God decides to save Ishmael from death by revealing the location of a well to his mother, Hagar, the angels ask the Holy One, "Why should you save the life of a man whose descendants will kill Your children?" God replies, "What is he now—at this moment?" They answered, "He is righteous." God then replied, "I judge a person solely by what he is at this moment—'where he is.'" Therefore, Ishmael is saved.[14] The story implies that regardless of how it appears, and regardless of what may be foreseen, at any moment the individual stands at the crossroads and can choose in which direction to go. Until the action has been taken, the die is not cast.

Indeed, the early stories of Genesis—Adam and Eve, Cain and Abel, the flood, the Tower of Babel—are all predicated on the concept of free will and the freedom given to human beings to disobey and to rebel against the express will of God. "In place of myth Israelite religion conceived the historical drama of human rebellion and sin," notes Kaufmann.[15] Sin brings consequences in its wake, but the choice of rebellion or obedience is ours. No force or fate compels us one way or the other.

The Inclination toward Evil

What, then, seems to cause humans to make the wrong choice so often? From this question emerges the idea of the *yetzer*, the human inclination or urge, sometimes called the *yetzer ha-ra*, the evil inclination (discussed in chapter 2). After the story of the flood, God pledges never to destroy all humanity again because "the inclination of a person's heart is evil from his youth" (Gen. 8:21). Humans can be expected to sin because there are impulses and urges built into the human psyche that lead them in that direction. "To err is human." Yet, as Cain was told, these urges can be controlled. Furthermore, the same impulse that leads to evil can also lead to good. Thus, Rabbi Samuel ben Nachman taught that the evil impulse was actually very good because "were it not for the evil impulse, no one would build a house, marry, beget children, or engage in trade."[16]

Modern psychoanalysis might well identify the *yetzer* with the id, impulses that need to be controlled. Judaism teaches that the solution to this dilemma of the *yetzer* is the life of discipline under the commandments, the *mitzvot*, which teach human beings control. This was the meaning of the teaching of the Babylonian *Amora* Raba, "If God created the evil inclination, He also created the Torah with which to temper it" (Talmud, *Baba Batra* 16a). Urges need not be suppressed. Rather, they can be channeled and thus controlled. "You can rule over it"; it need not rule over you. Neither the Torah nor the teachings of the Rabbis underestimate the power of the evil inclination. It plays a major role in human life. Humans are not automatically good. They have to work at it—but neither are they automatically evil.[17]

As Yehezkel Kaufmann writes, "Sin is not a tragic necessity; it is always the fruit of will, and its guilt is always deserved.... The important point is that the ultimate causes of sin and punishment lie always in the will and act of man. Because man can choose to do good, he is answerable for his evil-doing. Hence the unparalleled moral passion of the Bible."[18]

Free Will and God's Omniscience

Theological speculation in Judaism—and in other religions as well—has often dwelt on the problem of free will and God's omniscience. How is it possible for God to be all-knowing yet for free will to exist? If God knows everything that will happen and knows all the choices that a person will make, there seems to be no room for personal choice. Such knowledge implies predestination; personal choice becomes a delusion. We think we are free to choose, but in reality, we are only doing what has already been determined we will do!

As contemporary Jewish thinker Louis Jacobs puts it:

> To deny God's foreknowledge seems to suggest ignorance and limitation of God and hence appears to be incompatible with God's utter perfection. To deny human freedom, on the other

hand, seems to make nonsense of the Jewish religion, which contains innumerable appeals to man to choose the good and which informs him that he will be rewarded for so doing, but punished if he does evil.[19]

Although this dilemma presented a problem, medieval Jewish thinkers could not conceive of humanity's being deprived of freedom of choice. The exception to this view is Jewish pholosopher Hisdai Crescas (1340–1410), who denied free will to uphold God's omniscience.[20]

For the most part, the medieval philosophers who discussed this problem found a way of keeping both ends of the conundrum, not being willing to give up either God's perfection or human free will, which was and remains so important and so precious within Jewish thinking. Generally, they posit that God's knowledge is not the same as that of human beings and we cannot grasp it, or that time is not the same for God as for us, or, as Lurianic Kabbalah put it, God has withdrawn, has limited Himself, to give humans the ability to make choices.

In truth, this theological dilemma never existed prior to the Middle Ages, when Jewish philosophers, Saadia and Maimonides prominent among them, began to deal with Jewish belief in categories, largely borrowed from Greek philosophical speculation, that were unknown previously in Judaism.[21] Neither the Torah nor the Rabbis were ever concerned with this problem. Their concept of God was not based on the Greek idea of perfection, to wit, that God was perfect and therefore all-knowing and that if one said God did not know what choice a person might make, God was not perfect. The God of the Torah is a living being who can even change His mind and is not depicted as knowing all things in advance.[22]

Many translators have interpreted a statement of Rabbi Akiba in *Pirkei Avot* 3:15 as if it dealt with this conundrum and have translated it as "All is foreseen, but freedom of choice is given." The correct translation, however, is more likely "All is seen, and freedom is given."[23] If anything, Akiba actually emphasizes freedom of choice while stating that God beholds and is aware of everything that we do. There is no contradiction between these statements.

In a sense, the idea of free will is implied in the Torah's concept of divinity, which, as we have seen, denies the existence of any power other than God, of any "fate" that controls God, or of any magic or ritual that can coerce God. God is free; so too humans, made in God's image, are free. Even God cannot or will not force His creatures to act one way or another. Without denying that God has a plan for humanity—such as the plan for Israel's descent into Egypt and its redemption from slavery—this does not mean that individuals are destined to do one thing or the other and do not have freedom of choice and action. In the words of biblical scholar Moshe Greenberg, "Events unfold under the providence of God, yet their unfolding is always according to the motives of their human actors through whom God's will is done without their realizing it."[24]

Abraham Lincoln, who often wrestled with questions of religious belief, left a scrap of paper that has come to be known as the "Meditation on Divine Will":

> The will of God prevails. In great contests each party claims to act in accordance with the will of God. Both *may* be, and one *must* be, wrong. God cannot be *for* and *against* the same thing at the same time. In the present civil war, it is quite possible that God's purpose is something different from the purpose of either party—and yet the human instrumentalities, working just as they do, are of the best adaptation to effect His purpose. I am almost ready to say that this is probably true—that God wills this contest, and wills that it shall not end yet. By His mere great power, on the minds of the now contestants, He could have either saved or destroyed the Union without a human contest. Yet the contest began. And having begun He could give the final victory to either side any day. Yet the contest proceeds.[25]

Hardening the Heart

According to the Torah, fate does not control human life, nor does God determine our actions. The one contradictory instance in the Torah is the story of the hardening of Pharaoh's heart. Beginning with the sixth plague, boils, the Torah uses the expression "YHVH stiffened the heart of Pharaoh, and he would not heed them" (Exod. 9:12). This idea is repeated in Exodus 10:1, 10:20, and 11:10. Prior to that, although God had told Moses earlier that He would stiffen Pharaoh's heart (Exod. 4:21), each time Pharaoh refuses to let the Israelites go the Torah says that Pharaoh's "heart was stiffened" (Exod. 8:15) or Pharaoh became stubborn (Exod. 8:28). Biblical commentator Nahum Sarna explains it this way:

> The "hardening of the heart" thus expresses a state of arrogant moral degeneracy, unresponsive to reason and incapable of compassion. Pharaoh's personal culpability is beyond question. It is to be noted that in the first five plagues Pharaoh's obduracy is self-willed. It is only thereafter that it is attributed to divine causality. This is the biblical way of asserting that the king's intransigence has by then become habitual and irreversible; his character has become his destiny. He is deprived of the possibility of relenting and is irresistibly impelled to his self-wrought doom.[26]

"God made it so, but Pharaoh had only to be himself to do God's will," notes Moshe Greenberg.[27] Freedom of will remains the overriding concept of the Torah regarding human action.[28]

Human Responsibility

From free will, we arrive inevitably at human responsibility and the possibility of repentance and forgiveness. God's words to Cain before he commits the ultimate sin of fratricide—*v'ata timshal-bo*, "yet you can rule over it"—are the rock on which the doctrine of human responsibility is built. While understanding all of the psychological and sociological factors that are involved in antisocial activity, from the petty to the most grave, ultimately people are held responsible for their actions because there comes a moment of choice when "yet you can rule over it." If an individual fails to do so and thereby sins, Judaism still holds out the possibility of change, of repentance. To quote Viktor Frankl again, "Man ...

may well change himself, otherwise he would not be man. It is a prerogative of being human, and a constituent of human existence, to be capable of shaping and reshaping oneself. In other words, it is the privilege of man to become guilty, and his responsibility to overcome guilt."[29]

The origin of the concept of repentance—*teshuvah*, literally "returning"—is found in the book of Deuteronomy. Moses, at the end of his life, foresees that in the future Israel will sin against YHVH and be punished by exile, but "you will return [*v'shavta*] to YHVH your God" (Deut. 30:2). Therefore, he says, God will "return your captivity and return and gather you from all the nations" (30:3), "for you will return to YHVH your God with all your heart and all your soul" (30:10). The full meaning of *teshuvah* is ultimately revealed in the speeches of the prophets and in the book of Jonah. Hosea pleads with Israel, "Return, O Israel, to YHVH your God, for you have fallen because of your sin" (14:2). Jeremiah tells them "Return, rebellious children—declares YHVH" (3:14) and pictures them turning again to God: "Here we are, we are come to You" (3:22). The book of Jonah depicts the entire people of Nineveh heeding the word of their king: "Let everyone turn back from his evil ways and from the injustice of which he is guilty. Who knows but that God may turn and relent? He may turn back from His wrath so that we do not perish" (3:8–9).

The idea that God is forgiving was well established by the story of God's revealing His qualities of mercy to Moses, as related in Exodus 34:6–7. Later, Rabbinic Judaism developed the entire concept of the Days of Awe, Rosh Hashanah through Yom Kippur, as a time for confessing sin, admitting guilt, and returning to God in repentance, after which we attain forgiveness and atonement.[30] The Days of Awe celebrate our free will and the responsibility that comes with it. No wonder they became the most sacred time of the Jewish year and the most important of the holy days of Israel. They represent a basic pillar of our belief: humans have free will and freedom of choice.

The Torah begins with free will and ends with free will. It begins with the choices given first to Adam and Eve and later to Cain, to obey God's commands or not to obey. They choose not to. It ends with Moses's speeches to all the Israelites before they enter Canaan, the main burden of which is the choice they now face to be faithful to the covenant and the commandments or not (Deut.11:26–28, 27:11–30:20). Moses painstakingly points out the choices: between blessing and curse, between life and death. He urges the Israelites to make the right choice. He repeatedly tells them what will happen "if." He speaks to them in terms of "if you will obey" or if you will not. Moses has the Israelites go through an elaborate ceremony at Mount Gerizim, where they hear the curses and the blessings pronounced and answer "Amen" to each. The Hebrew word *im*, "if," is constantly repeated in his exhortations because the choice is theirs. Nothing is determined. Everything is up to the Israelites. They have free will and cannot be forced to follow God. They must make the choice. Nothing is predestined.

Part III
SOCIETY

9
Human Sovereignty
Is Limited

Revolutionary Truth #9: God is the only true Sovereign. Human sovereigns are subordinate to the laws of God.

> Then He became Sovereign in Jeshurun, when the heads of the people assembled, the tribes of Israel together.
>
> *Deuteronomy 33:5*

> And YHVH shall be Sovereign over all the earth: on that day there shall be one YHVH with one name.
>
> *Zechariah 14:9*

> YHVH, enthroned on cherubim, is Sovereign, peoples tremble, the earth quakes.... Mighty Sovereign who loves justice....
>
> *Psalm 99:1, 99:4*

Among the problems that the newly freed slaves had to deal with was the question of polity—who would lead the people now and in the future? How would they be governed? The environment from which they had emerged, the ancient Near East, was a realm in which sovereigns, petty and great, ruled supreme. In Egypt, the sovereigns were more than rulers; they also claimed to be the incarnation of gods. In Mesopotamia, they were divinely appointed and were the source of all law. There is no question that the Torah could never accept the claim of divinity by any human ruler because the boundary between God and human beings was absolute. There might have been room, however, for a human being to rule as the absolute sovereign. That was the common way of the world and, indeed, continued to be so until the twentieth century, when whatever monarchies remained became limited, constitutional monarchies, with the exception of those in the Middle East. But that was not the reality envisioned by the Torah. The concept of rulership taught by Moses was that there was only one Sovereign over Israel—YHVH.

The possibility of appointing a human sovereign is envisioned briefly in only one book of the Torah, Deuteronomy,[1] and even there it is presented only as an option, not as a divine command, and most important, with severe limitations. In general, it would seem that limitation of power was an important component of the new polity that emerged among the Israelites.

The Decentralization of Power

When taking the Israelites out of Egypt and preparing them for independence in their own land, Moses makes no attempt to proclaim himself the sovereign or to propose a system of government in which one man would be sovereign. The Torah recognizes elders as a kind of supreme council as well as n'si'im, heads of clans and tribes (Lev. 4:22), who might come together for important decisions.[2] The leader is Moses, a prophet directly inspired by God and chosen by God to lead the people. The decisions Moses makes, however, are not his own. They come from the Divine Sovereign with whom Moses consults on every issue. For example, when the daughters of Zelophehad come to Moses to ask that they inherit because their father had no sons, "Moses brought their case before YHVH" and conveyed God's decision (Num. 27:5). Moses's successor, Joshua, is similarly considered to have been chosen by YHVH. Moses's children play no role. No dynasty of leadership is established. Michael Walzer points out that the description of Moses's unknown burial place—"and no one knows his burial place to this day" (Deut. 34:6)—is a deliberate contrast to the Egyptian pharaohs, who began to plan their elaborate burial monuments the moment they assumed office.[3] The pyramids and the magnificent tombs in the Valley of the Kings testify to the centralization of power and the absolute authority of the monarch. The absence of a tomb for Moses attests to a completely opposite approach to monarchy and power.

When he is about to die, Joshua calls an assembly of the people and its leaders and urges them again to give their total loyalty to God, and as at Sinai, they affirm their willingness to do so. "We will serve YHVH," they proclaim (Josh. 24:21); and again, "We will serve none but YHVH our God, and we will obey none but Him" (Judg. 24:24). As if to emphasize the exclusive Sovereignty of God, when Joshua dies the people choose no successor, and God proclaims none. None is needed. The leaders who had assembled at Joshua's command are sufficient— "elders and commanders, magistrates and officers" (Josh. 24:1). Human leadership was decentralized and often shared among these groups.[4]

Judges arose, not on a regular basis, but called by God as the situation required. God remained the only Sovereign. This is seen most clearly in the story of Gideon, who is told by God that he has been chosen to deliver Israel from the hands of the Midianites (Judg. 6:11–16). When he does so, the Israelites—anticipating what is to happen later at the time of Samuel—beg him to become their sovereign and establish a hereditary sovereignty. "Rule over us—you, your son, and your grandson as well," they plead. Gideon replies, "I will not rule over you myself, nor shall my son rule over you; YHVH shall rule over you!" (Judg. 8:22–23). As Martin Buber characterizes it, "His No, born out of the situation, is intended to count as an unconditional No for all times and historical conditions. For it leads to an unconditional Yes, that of a kingly proclamation *in aeternum*.... 'YHVH, who is God Himself, He it is who is to rule over you.'"[5]

Moses proposed a revolution in the form of governance, deliberately rejecting the forms known to him and preferring one in which no man could aspire to the absolute control that could lead so easily to a divine or semidivine status. As Moshe Greenberg puts it:

In the divinely ordained polity provided for Israel, power is dispersed among the members of society and many devices prevent its accumulation and concentration. The society envisioned in the Torah lacks a strong, prestigious focus of power; on the contrary, dignity and authority are distributed…. In its aversion to the concentration of power and its tendency to equalize resources among the citizenry, the system of biblical law resembles democracy.[6]

Israel's New Doctrine of God's Sovereignty

The idea of presenting a pagan god as a sovereign was prevalent in the ancient world, but it was always as a reflection of the human sovereign who actually ruled. In Israel, on the other hand, the doctrine of the Sovereignty of God originated at a time when they did not have a human sovereign and did not desire one, and when none was envisioned for the future.[7] In the Song at the Sea, which may have been composed during or after the time of Solomon as a protest against the excesses and hubris of that sovereign,[8] the poet has Israel proclaim, "YHVH shall reign for ever and ever!" (Exod. 15:18). This is the first time that sovereignty is ascribed to God in the Torah. It serves beautifully as a prelude to the ceremony held at Sinai that is the true acceptance by Israel of God as their eternal Sovereign. That God is to become their Sovereign is implied in Exodus 19:6, when Israel is told that they are to be "a kingdom of priests" to YHVH.[9] A "kingdom" implies a king, a sovereign—in this case YHVH. Their reply—"All that YHVH has spoken we will do!" (Exod. 19:8)—is their acceptance of God's Sovereignty, which is emphasized again in the demand of the first commandment that "You shall have no other gods besides Me" (Exod. 20:3). Throughout the Torah, the relationship to God is couched in terms that are used elsewhere for the relationship between a human sovereign and his nation.[10] Just as a human sovereign demands exclusivity, so too the Divine Sovereign requires that there be one and only one ruler over Israel, which in itself excludes the possibility of a human sovereign.

This is recognized throughout the Torah. Even the pagan prophet Balaam proclaims, "YHVH their God is with them, and their Sovereign's acclaim in their midst" (Num. 23:21). In his final blessing to Israel, Moses says, "Then He became Sovereign in Jeshurun, when the heads of the people assembled, the tribes of Israel together" (Deut. 33:5).

Even centuries later, when the Davidic dynasty was already in existence and was considered divinely ordained, the idea of God's ultimate Sovereignty remained. In the book of Psalms, God's Sovereignty is often celebrated: "YHVH is Sovereign, He is robed in grandeur" (Ps. 93:1).[11] Much later the prophets, envisioning apocalyptic events leading to the ultimate goal of one humanity living in peace, saw it as the time when God's Sovereignty would be recognized and proclaimed by all: "And YHVH shall be Sovereign over all the earth: on that day there shall be one YHVH with one name" (Zech. 14:9). "For liberators shall march up on Mount Zion to wreak judgment on Mount Esau, and the Sovereignty shall be YHVH's" (Obad. 1:21). In later Judaism this concept of the Sovereignty of God was made the subject of the well-known *Aleinu* prayer that concludes every worship service: "You will perfect the world by Your Sovereignty."

According to Deuteronomy, in one of his orations to the nation before it is to enter Canaan, Moses says:

> If, after you have entered the land that YHVH your God has assigned to you, and taken possession of it and settled in it, you decide, 'I will set a sovereign over me, as do all the nations about me,' you may set a sovereign over yourself whom YHVH your God will choose; set over you a sovereign from among your own people; you must not set a foreigner over you, one who is not your kinsman.
>
> *(Deut. 17:14–15)*

In other books of the Torah, there is not even a hint that a sovereign would be chosen.[12]

In all likelihood, by the time Deuteronomy was composed both Judah and Israel had long-established monarchies that ruled.[13] The wording of this pericope echoes and was undoubtedly influenced by the tradition recorded in 1 Samuel 8, in which the elders of Israel come to the elderly Samuel to complain that his sons, whom he had appointed in his place, were not worthy. "Therefore appoint a sovereign for us, to govern us *like all the nations*" (1 Sam. 8:5).[14]

The story has an aura of truth. It must have been an embarrassment to the sovereigns of Israel because it speaks so negatively about sovereigns and what they will do and because God considers this request to be a rejection not of Samuel but of God's own rulership, a continuation of the acts of rebellion that had taken place ever since the Exodus from Egypt. "It is not you that they have rejected; it is Me they have rejected as their Sovereign" (1 Sam. 8:7). God permits Samuel to accede to the elders' demands but instructs him to warn the people about what a sovereign is likely to do. He will conscript their sons and make them tend to his fields and his weaponry. He will take their daughters and make them domestic servants. He will confiscate their property and give it to his own courtiers, tax them so that "you shall become his slaves." God concludes with a dire warning that "the day will come when you cry out because of the sovereign whom you yourselves have chosen; and YHVH will not answer you on that day" (1 Sam. 8:11–18). Never has there been a more negative assessment of the monarchy, one that proved to be too true not only about Israelite sovereigns but also about tyrannical sovereigns throughout human history. They nevertheless insist on a sovereign because they want to "be like all the other nations: Let our sovereign rule over us and go out at our head and fight our battles" (1 Sam. 8:20). Samuel then receives final permission from God to appoint a sovereign. The very fact that Samuel does not seem to know that Deuteronomy had already given the green light to the appointment of a sovereign is proof enough that such a law was not known at that time.

Unlike Samuel, who warns the people against a sovereign, realistically listing what a sovereign would do, Deuteronomy takes a softer approach. It gives permission in advance, although not recommending it, but then sets certain conditions and limitations on the powers of the sovereign. Deuteronomy grudgingly accepts the reality of a monarchy but wants to make certain that its authority is limited. The sovereign is not allowed to have large numbers of horses or to send people back to Egypt to attain them. He is not to have many wives. He is not to amass silver and gold (Deut. 17:16–17). All of these limitations sound suspiciously as if they were aimed at the notorious actions of Solomon, as described in 1 Kings 11: 9: "YHVH was angry with Solomon, because his heart turned away from YHVH, the God of Israel, who had appeared to him twice and had commanded him about this matter, not to follow other gods; he did not obey what YHVH had commanded."

Limitations of Human Sovereignty

The sovereign of Israel was by no means absolute and resembled the kind of constitutional monarchy that became common much later in the Western world.

These limitations were "unparalleled in antiquity," according to Moshe Greenberg.[15] As if to emphasize them, the sovereign is required to have with him at all times a scroll of God's word written especially for him, which he is to read and observe "so that he will not act haughtily toward his fellows" (Deut. 17:18–20). He is to be something that is almost unheard of—a humble monarch. Deuteronomy does not spell out any powers he may have or any duties other than observing faithfully every word of "this Teaching" (17:18). The absence of any job description for the sovereign is very strange. We know what the priests and Levites are to do. We know what judges and officers do. We have no idea what the duties and the rights of the sovereign are, only the prohibitions. At the most, Deuteronomy offers a halfhearted endorsement of the monarchy, behind which is hidden the feeling that this is at best unnecessary and at worst harmful.[16] In truth, as God's words to Samuel make clear, the monarchy is a betrayal of the original concept of the Torah: the Sovereign of Israel is God and God alone.

The monarchy came into being in the tenth century BCE as a response to the dangerous situation that existed, the threat of the powerful Philistine cities to conquer the Israelites and their land. The people felt, and perhaps with a measure of justification, that they needed a reliable system of leadership, with no gaps in between rulers. They saw the system of monarchy in the surrounding nations as an example of the structure that they required. They did not see it, as did both God and

Samuel, as a rejection of God's sovereignty. Seeking to have both a human sovereign and a Divine Sovereign, the Israelites developed the doctrine that the house of David was itself chosen by God and therefore legitimate. Generations later, when the Davidic dynasty no longer ruled, they envisioned it as the source of the Messiah, the anointed sovereign, who would lead the Jews back to sovereignty and the whole world to an unprecedented time of peace.

The Accumulation of Power

The establishment of a human monarchy had all the negative consequences that Samuel had envisioned and more. Perhaps it was inevitable; a monarchy by its very nature requires a concentration of power and of wealth. It establishes a bureaucracy of officials, some of whom—hopefully not all—will be corrupt and will use their power to enhance their own wealth and property. Even if the sovereign himself is well intentioned, which was not always the case, others may not be. Greenberg notes, "The policy of the monarchy subordinated the ideal of becoming a holy nation to the achievement of national prestige and security. It was concerned with building up the military and establishing alliances with powerful neighbors. In the end, it subverted the institutions of religion into instruments of royal policy."[17]

The limitations that Deuteronomy sought to place on the sovereign may not have eliminated all the problems of a human monarchy, but they did have the effect of making the sovereign subordinate to God and to God's teaching, at least in theory if not always in practice. These limitations also gave unprecedented rights to those who spoke in the name of God to criticize and chastise the sovereign for moral wrongs and for disobeying God's command. In that way, at least, God remained Sovereign. Samuel removes Saul as sovereign on that basis (1 Sam. 15:22–31), and Saul's successor, David, is castigated by Nathan for a terrible sin (2 Sam. 12:1–14). Although Hittite sovereigns had limited authority—there is even a document from Babylon between 1000 and 700 BCE in which a prince is warned of dire consequences if he does not uphold certain treaties and rights[18]—it is difficult to imagine another nation in which one could with impunity stand up to the sovereign with an accusing finger and say, "That man is you!" as Nathan does to David (2 Sam. 12:7), to which the sovereign replies, "I stand guilty before YHVH!" (2 Sam. 12:13).

That this tradition was a reality in ancient Israel can be seen in the story of Elijah and King Ahab, where Elijah proclaims Ahab's guilt and his death in the matter of Naboth's vineyard (1 Kings 21:17–24). Like David, Ahab reacts by doing penance for what he has done (1 Kings 21:27). The classical prophets Amos and Jeremiah are similarly courageous in both their criticism of the entire society and their predictions of doom and destruction, although they do not specifically single out the sovereign. The priest of the temple at Bethel calls on King Jeroboam to punish Amos, accusing the prophet of treason (Amos 7:10–11). Jeroboam's reaction is not recorded, but Amaziah banishes Amos and forbids him from prophesying at Bethel (Amos 7:12). At least Amos is not executed, which is a tribute to the freedom of speech accorded prophets, even if in this instance it may have been curtailed.

Some two centuries later, Jeremiah follows Amos's pattern and predicts the destruction of both Jerusalem and the Kingdom of Judah, and the exile of the people. He declares that the Temple has been turned into a "den of thieves" (Jer. 7:11). Nothing is done to stop him from speaking in God's name. Later, King Jehoiakim attempts to have Jeremiah imprisoned but does not succeed (Jer. 36:26). Toward the end of the siege of Jerusalem, King Zedekiah imprisons Jeremiah in the palace compound but does not dare to execute him. The king permits palace officials to place Jeremiah in a mud pit, with no water, to die of hunger—Zedekiah does not dare execute Jeremiah outright—but is then persuaded to release the prophet once again. Jeremiah remains in the prison until the capture of Jerusalem (Jeremiah 37–38). Considering the total power that sovereigns had, the restraint of these monarchs of Israel and Judah can only be attributed to the way in which the passage in Deuteronomy limited their authority and placed God and God's word above the power of the monarchy.

Moses's original plan of a nation ruled by God alone proved too utopian and too impractical to survive the reality of a world of rival kingdoms and empires, but the ideal presented had its lasting effects by limiting the power of sovereigns and elevating the law above the will of any ruler. If these ideas had any effect on human civilization, and I believe they did, it came through the doctrines taught in the Torah that became the heritage of the civilized world.

10

The Priesthood Is Divorced from Magic

Revolutionary Truth #10: Priests and Levites have no special powers and no secret knowledge. They are to teach God's instruction to all the people.

> Advance the tribe of Levi and place them in attendance on Aaron the priest to serve him. They shall perform duties for him and for the whole community before the Tent of Meeting, doing the work of the Tabernacle.
>
> *Numbers 3:6–7*

> You must teach the Israelites all the laws which YHVH has imparted to them through Moses.
>
> *Leviticus 10:11*

> Proper rulings were in his mouth, and nothing perverse was on his lips; he served Me with complete loyalty and held many back from iniquity. For the lips of a priest guard knowledge, and men seek rulings from his mouth; for he is a messenger of YHVH of Hosts.
>
> *Malachi 2:6–7*

The roles assigned to the *kohanim*, the priests, by the codes of the Torah are important and honorable, but they carry none of the supernatural powers that were ascribed to pagan priests. Perhaps the main task of the priest was the offering of sacrifices. Chapter after chapter of the book of Leviticus, known in Hebrew as *Torah HaKohanim*, "The Instruction of the Priests," is devoted to exactly what the sacrifices were, when to bring them, and how to do so (Leviticus 1–7). As representatives of the entire people of Israel, the priests alone performed the sacrifices, including all the preparation, the slaughter, the offering up, and the work of cleaning the altar—tasks that were sometimes physically demanding and perhaps unpleasant but that nevertheless marked the highest degree of ritual service to God. We have already seen that the rituals in the sanctuary, primarily the offering of sacrifices, were divested of any meaning other than human needs and that the priests performed them in silence, uttering no incantations, as was done in pagan ritual.

Aside from conducting the rites in the sanctuary, the main tasks of the Israelite priests were determining ritual purity and impurity, blessing the people, and teaching the laws of the Torah. The *kohanim* are indeed "holy unto YHVH"—the phrase was inscribed on the metal plate the high priest wore on his forehead when officiating (Exod. 28:36)—but all Israel was also holy to God (Num. 15:40). "Holy," in this instance, indicates belonging to God, being dedicated to God's service. God had said to the Israelites at Sinai, "You shall be to Me a kingdom of priests and a holy nation" (Exod. 19:6). Israel is the priesthood for the nations of the world; the descendants of Aaron are the priesthood for Israel. Neither is endowed with magical powers above those of any other human beings.

Any organized religion needs a cadre of people who will lead its worship and give guidance in belief and practice. The Israelite religion as an organized religion did not really exist before the time of Moses. The patriarchs had broken decisively with the religion of Mesopotamia and followed their new beliefs and practices, but they did this as individuals and as a family, not as an organized group. As a matter of fact, we know very little about their religious practices. They were devoted to one God, El Shaddai (Gen. 17:1), the meaning of which remains a matter of speculation.[1] Abraham also identified his God as El Elyon (Most High God) and as YHVH[2] (Gen. 14:22), the source of all being. The family and followers of Abraham practiced circumcision on the eighth day as a sign of their covenant with that God (Gen. 17:9–14), and from time to time they dedicated altars to God "and invoked YHVH by name" (Gen. 12:8, 13:4, and 26:25). Abraham also planted a tamarisk "and invoked there the name of YHVH, the Everlasting God" (Gen. 21:33). We know that at least once, Abraham brought an animal sacrifice to YHVH (Gen. 15:9–10). He also offered a ram "in place of his son" when Isaac was spared from being sacrificed (Gen. 22:13). Jacob offered a sacrifice after erecting a pillar as a witness of his agreement with Laban (Gen. 31:54). Jacob also set up a sacred stone at Bethel and pledged to give God a tithe (Gen. 28:18–22), and he later built an altar at Bethel (Gen. 35:7) and erected there a sacred pillar and offered a libation (Gen. 35:14). We know from reading the story of Joseph that the patriarchs observed certain mourning rites, tearing their garments and putting on sackcloth (Gen. 37:34). A practice similar to the later rule of marrying your brother's childless widow was also part of their lifestyle (Gen. 38:8). Such is the extent of our knowledge of the patriarchal religion. No provision seems to have existed for specific religious officiants. Each individual took care of his own ritual needs.

The Appointment of Priests and Levites

When Moses assumed the leadership of the people of Israel, they were no longer a small family but a people that had "multiplied and increased very greatly" (Exod. 1:7), so much so that the new king considered them a threat to Egypt (Exod. 1:9). There is no indication of what religious structure, if any, they had during those four hundred years in Egypt. Certainly, by the time Moses succeeded in freeing them and was taking them out of Egypt, preparing them for sovereignty in their own land, the Israelites required religious leadership. They needed those who would serve both God and the people in their worship and in fulfilling their religious obligations. Aaron and his sons were appointed priests to serve in the Tabernacle and to offer the sacrifices (Exod. 28:1). We can assume there were priests even before the giving of the Ten Commandments from Exodus 19:24, "Go down, and come back together with Aaron, but let not the priests or the people break through to come up to YHVH." Sacrifices were also offered before the theophany; Moses "designated some young men among the Israelites, and they offered burnt offerings and sacrificed bulls as offerings of well-being to YHVH" (Exod. 24:5). Moses himself took on the role of a priest, dashing the blood on the altar and on the people (Exod. 24:6–8). Psalm 99:6 recalls that "Moses and Aaron were among His priests."

Later, the entire tribe of Levi became religious functionaries, charged with the care of the Tabernacle. This may have been a reward for their actions after the sin of the Golden Calf, when Moses said, "Whoever is for YHVH, come here!" and "all the Levites rallied to him" (Exod. 32:26). Furthermore, the Levites were the ones who actually did the work of drawing up the inventory of the materials used in creating the Tabernacle (Exod. 38:21). Because of their loyalty, inspired perhaps by the fact that they were the tribe of Moses, the Levites were given the task of "being in attendance upon Aaron the priest to serve him. They shall perform duties for him and for the whole community before the Tent of Meeting, doing the work of the Tabernacle" (Num. 3:6–7). According to Numbers 3:9, the Levites were formally assigned to Aaron "from among the Israelites" and replaced the firstborn who had been consecrated to God when the firstborn of Egypt were slain in the last plague (Num. 3:12–13; Exod. 13:11–15). It is most likely that the "young men" referred to, who had officiated as priests before the appointment of Aaron and his family, were the firstborn.

Levitical Tasks

The actual work done by the Levites at first involved taking down and setting up the Tabernacle (Num. 4:47)[3] and, more important, guarding it. "They shall perform your guard duty and the guarding of the Tent of Meeting, all the service of the Tent," while the priests alone performed "the duties connected with the Shrine and the altar" (Num. 18:4). Guarding a sacred precinct was common practice both in Mesopotamia and in Egypt[4] to prevent unauthorized persons from approaching and to ensure its sanctity. This vital function continued as long as a Temple existed, when Levites guarded twenty-four hours around the clock, as testified by both the Mishnah (*Middot* 1; *Tamid* 1:1) and Josephus.[5] When the Jerusalem Temple came into being, the Levites attended the priests, stood guard, and served as a choir that chanted psalms.[6]

Functions of the Priest

As important as the functions of the Levites may have been, they paled beside the tasks and the status that was given to the priests, a specific group within the tribe of Levi, the family of Aaron. What the priests did *not* do is as important as what they did do. As Yehezkel Kaufmann writes, "Aaron performs technical wonders in Egyptian style, but it is of utmost significance that he did not bequeath this function to his descendants. The Israelite priest, unlike the pagan, does not perform wonders, heal, utter incantations, or interpret omens."[7] He never combats evil powers or performs any acts that would depict or impact on the life of God, feats that were vital to pagan religion. After dwelling in Egypt for all of those centuries and being exposed to the magnificent rituals of Egyptian worship, it is inconceivable that Moses and the Israelites would not have been familiar with Egyptian priestly functions. The Torah deliberately rejects these practices and many others. "You shall not copy the practices of the land of Egypt where you dwelt, or of the land of Canaan to which I am taking you; you shall not follow their laws" (Lev. 18:3).

Furthermore, it is important to note that the priesthood was severely limited in its powers. Aaron is not the head of the people. At all times he—high priest that he may be—is always subservient to Moses, the prophet. Aaron's functions seem to be restricted to the realm of rituals, to the cult. He is not a political leader or a lawgiver.[8] Only in the book of Deuteronomy is the priest given a role as a judge in civil matters as well as cultic affairs. It is difficult if not impossible to accurately reconstruct what the actual role of priests was in the life of the wilderness wanderers and later in that of the community within the land of Canaan, but one thing is certain: they were not in political command. In ancient Israel, the priesthood was exalted in holiness but demoted in power and authority.[9] In postexilic times, however, until the rise of Herod in the first century BCE, the political leadership of the nation was in the hands of the priests, but such a reality was neither based on nor foreseen by the Torah.[10]

Oracles

Priests in pagan religions were constantly occupied with oracles, the reading of signs that predicted future events and made crucial decisions. The Mesopotamian chronicles make it very clear that divination, especially the configuration of the entrails and liver of sacrificial animals, was central to all of their religious activity. The religious functionaries had to be experts at this, because every important decision of national policy, war and peace, was made on the basis of these omens.[11]

In Israel, there was no reading of animal entrails, as was so common elsewhere. The use of portents was restricted to the use of the Urim and Thummim alone. The Urim and Thummim were small objects kept in the breastplate worn by the high priest (Exod. 28:30; Lev. 8:8). The meaning of these words is not clear but may well indicate "cursed" (Urim, from *arrur*) and "faultless" (Thummim, from *tammim*), that is, either rejected or accepted. These dicelike objects would be cast to answer a question—yes or no, accepted or rejected by God. Thus, unlike complicated signs and oracles, there was nothing to see or read aside from the yes or no answer. The casting was not to be done by all the priests, but was restricted to the high priest alone. Use of the Urim and Thummim did not survive the exile and was not revived after the return to Zion.[12] Having the use of this oracular device gave importance and authority to the high priest, but even here it was limited. His role was to assist the political and military leader, not to lead himself.

When Joshua is to be invested as the successor to Moses, for example, God tells Moses to place his hands on Joshua while the latter stands before Eleazar, the high priest, "who shall on his behalf seek the decision of the Urim before YHVH. By such instruction they shall go out and by such instruction they shall come in, he and all the Israelites, the whole community" (Num. 27:20–21). The consultation of the Urim, according to this, is used principally in questions concerning warfare—to go to battle or not. The decision is not that of the high priest, but of the oracle that is controlled by God. It is interesting to note, as does Jacob Milgrom, that "the Bible never states explicitly that Joshua consults the Urim."[13]

Diagnosis and Purgation of Impurity

With respect to healing, the Torah is very careful to differentiate between diagnosis and healing. Whereas a pagan priest would be called on to heal through magical incantations and other actions, nothing of the sort is found in the rules of the biblical priests. Interestingly enough, the instances of healing that are found in the Torah and other biblical books are all connected to prophets, not priests. These prophets are able to effect healing through prayer to God, not by means of incantations or sacrificial rites. In the Torah's briefest prayer, Moses calls on God to heal Miriam: "O God, pray heal her!" (Num. 12:13). Elijah heals a sick child (1 Kings 17:17–24), calling on YHVH to "let this child's life return to his body" (v. 21). His disciple Elisha brings a "dead" child of the Shunamite woman back to life after praying to YHVH (2 Kings 4:33–35). Elisha also tells the pagan Naaman how to be healed in a story that demonstrates the gulf between pagan expectations of magical rites and Israel's ideas (2 Kings 5:9–15). There is no instance in which priests are ever called on to heal.[14]

Chapters 13 and 14 of Leviticus deal with serious skin diseases and infections of cloth and of buildings. The priest has two important functions to fulfill in these circumstances, which were considered dangerous to the community and rendered the affected person or object impure: to diagnose the infection and pronounce it either pure or impure, and when the signs of impurity were gone, to conduct the rather complicated rituals of purification. The Torah gives exact criteria by which the priest was to judge when something is impure and when it has become pure again. He need only follow the instructions in the Torah itself to make that determination. The priest performs no ritual, utters no prayer or incantation when performing the diagnosis. He does absolutely nothing to bring about purification other than isolating the impure individual from the community. There is no ritual act that he performs until the healing has already taken place. Therefore, the priest is not a healer in any sense. His task of purification and all the rituals it entails are performed after the growths and discolorations have already disappeared. So, in Baruch Levine's phrase, the priest is "the purificatory priest."[15] There is no magic or healing in anything that he does.[16]

No Contact with the Dead

Another important task of the pagan priest concerned the realm of the dead and the many rituals that had to do with death, the afterlife, and the rites of mummification. Perhaps the most important book of Egyptian religion was the Book of the Dead. Yet the Israelite priest had nothing to do with any such cult, since none existed in the religion that Moses taught. On the contrary, the priest was forbidden to even come into contact with the dead, but for a few specific exceptions. Leviticus is very strict on that point. "None shall defile himself for any [dead] person among his kin, except for the relatives that are closest to him: his mother, his father, his son, his daughter, and his brother; also for a virgin sister, close to him because she has not married" (Lev. 21:1–3). The rules for the high priest, who has a higher degree of sanctity and may perform rituals that no other priest may carry out, are even more restrictive. "He shall not go in where there is any dead body; he shall not defile himself even for his father or mother" (Lev. 21:11). Thus, the Israelite priest is totally removed from the realm that was most central to the pagan cults of Egypt. The Israelite priest deals only with the living, never with the dead.

Teaching Torah

In his final blessing as stated in Deuteronomy, Moses speaks about the tribe of Levi, referring to the priesthood. "They shall teach Your laws to Jacob and Your instructions to Israel. They shall offer You incense to savor and whole-offerings on Your altar" (Deut. 33:10). Moses sees the task of the priest as twofold: performing the sacrificial rites, in which they present gifts to God on behalf of Israel, and teaching God's instruction to the people of Israel. This latter task had been outlined previously in

Leviticus 10:10–11, when Aaron was told by God that he must be the one to "teach the Israelites all the laws which YHVH had imparted to them through Moses," distinguishing between the pure and the impure, the sacred and the profane. Unlike the prophet, however, the priest does not receive instruction from God. He only passes on that which has been recorded in the Torah from the words imparted to the prophet Moses by God.

Deuteronomy 17:8–13 includes in this teaching not only matters of ritual purity but also civil laws and gives the priests the authority to teach and also to judge cases between individuals. The Israelites are warned in dire terms that they must then "act in accordance with the instructions given you and the ruling handed down to you," not deviating in any way "either to the right or to the left" (v. 11). Every lawsuit was subject to the priests' ruling (Deut. 21:5). The right to act as civil judges, however, is never mentioned in the other books, only in Deuteronomy, and may have been an innovation of that code.

The role of the priests as teachers, however, was accepted by all. This was crucial to the new and revolutionary concepts taught by the Torah. In paganism, the knowledge of the ways of the gods and the instructions for the cult were esoteric and remained the exclusive realm of the priests. They did not share their knowledge with the common people. The religion of Israel opened this knowledge to everyone: "Surely, this Instruction which I enjoin upon you this day is not too baffling for you, nor is it beyond reach. It is not in the heavens, that you should say, 'Who among us can go up to the heavens and get it for us and impart it to us, that we may observe it?' Neither is it beyond the sea" (Deut. 30:11–13). The Torah and its instructions are to be accessible to everyone, and the priests are assigned the task of teaching it openly. Certainly, the priests were the ones turned to on all ritual matters because only they possessed the expertise to make such decisions. Did they actually serve as religious instructors in a general way, teaching Torah to all Israel? According to 2 Kings 17:28, when the northern kingdom Israel was exiled to Assyria, one of the priests "taught them how to worship YHVH."[17] As Jeffrey Tigay remarks, however, "We do not know what further institutional form their instruction took, such as teaching in schools or at festivals or other gatherings."[18] On this, the sources are silent.

The Priestly Blessing

In recalling the incident of the Golden Calf, Moses remarks that "at that time YHVH set apart the tribe of Levi to carry the Ark of YHVH's Covenant, to stand in attendance upon YHVH, and to bless in His name, as is still the case" (Deut. 10:8). At the conclusion of the dedication of the sanctuary, after offering sacrifices, "Aaron lifted his hands toward the people and blessed them" (Lev. 9:22). Although there are very few tasks that priests have continued to perform throughout the ages to this very day, blessing the people in the name of YHVH remains one of them.

The blessing itself is well known. There are three stanzas, with each successive verse two words longer than the one preceding it—going from three to five to the sacred number seven—and the name of God, YHVH, is the second word in each. The blessing is addressed to the individual in the second person singular. God is called on to "bless and guard you," to "make His countenance shine on you and be gracious to you," to "lift up His countenance to you and grant you peace" (Num. 6:24–26). The antiquity and the popularity of the blessing were demonstrated by the fact that two silver amulets with versions of this blessing on them, dating from the seventh or sixth century BCE, were found in an ancient burial ground in Jerusalem.[19] This blessing was pronounced whenever people came to the Temple in Jerusalem. They brought their offering, and they received God's blessing. In the words of the psalm, one who comes to the sanctuary "will carry away a blessing from YHVH" (Ps. 24:5).

We might think that the priests therefore had the capability of bestowing blessings with automatic efficacy, but this is not the case. This blessing is no more than the priest turning in prayer to God, asking God to bless the assembled people. The Torah makes this very clear by stating, "Thus they shall link My name with the people of Israel and I will bless them" (Num. 6:27). If the pagan priest had powers of blessing and cursing, the Israelite priest had only the right to invoke God by name and ask for God's beneficence.

Priestly Powers

By removing the magical powers from the priesthood, the Torah revolutionized the concept of the servants of God. No longer were they endowed with special powers. Rather, they had special tasks: to teach the word of God, to decide what was pure and what was impure, to adjudicate disputes, to call upon God to bless the people, and to conduct the sacrifices and rituals held in the sanctuary.

Over the years, the role of the priests was greatly reduced. Following the return from exile and the promulgation of the Torah, priests lost whatever role they had had as teachers and deciders of what the Torah and its laws meant. Gradually, this role was taken over by sages, later called rabbis, who traced their authority not to the priests, but to Moses and the prophets.[20] Furthermore, the sages were not part of a hereditary group but, like the prophets, could come from any sector of the populace.[21] Religious leadership underwent a process of democratization and became open to anyone who could attain the requisite knowledge.

The religious leadership of later Judaism or of Islam would not have been possible without this new concept. Christianity also patterned itself after the Israelite priest, even with respect to the garments of their priests, but until the Protestant Reformation also gave their officiants certain esoteric powers that set them apart from others and that no Israelite priest had ever possessed.

The Torah created a revolutionary new type of religious authority, one who had no magical powers and who was not in possession of secrets or esoteric knowledge. The priest was rather a person who related to the masses and who imparted knowledge to them, opening the Torah to wider and wider audiences. This represented a major step forward in the development of rational and humanistic religion and paved the way for the democratization of religious leadership.

11

Land and Wealth Are to Be Distributed Equally

Revolutionary Truth #11: There should be an equitable distribution of land and wealth, including the return of the land and the forgiveness of debts. The Sabbatical and Jubilee years represented an attempt at achieving equity if not equality.

> But the land must not be sold beyond reclaim, for the land is Mine; you are but strangers resident with Me.
>
> *Leviticus 25:23*

> Six years you shall sow your land and gather in its yield; but in the seventh you shall let it rest and lie fallow. Let the needy among your people eat of it.
>
> *Exodus 23:10–11*

> Every seventh year you shall practice remission of debts. This shall be the nature of the remission: every creditor shall remit the due that he claims from his fellow; he shall not dun his fellow or kinsman, for the remission proclaimed is of YHVH.
>
> *Deuteronomy 15:1–2*

The task facing Moses was enormous. It was nothing less than creating a nation out of a group of former slaves, members of twelve family-based clans, united only by a common memory of ancestors who had wandered from Mesopotamia to Canaan. His challenge was not only to take them back to their old-new land, where they would settle, but also to create a new society politically and economically from scratch. This was also an enormous opportunity. With no legacy of how that society was to function, Moses could write on this tabula rasa whatever he envisioned. What he envisioned was a radical and revolutionary concept: a society in which the distribution of wealth would be as equal and equitable as humanly possible. It was a utopian vision of courageous and daring dimensions, requiring a set of laws dealing with economic matters.

The Sources of Wealth

The society Moses envisioned was basically agricultural, although some provision would have to be made for cities and villages as well. In such a society, there were two sources of wealth: land, which was primary, and money, which was secondary.

The central role played by the land in agrarian societies is stated clearly by the biblical scholar Baruch Levine in his commentary to Leviticus 25:

> Virtually all indebtedness was associated with the land. One borrowed for the purpose of securing seed, implements, or work animals and to defray the cost of hiring laborers. The loan was to be repaid after the harvest. If the crop failed, or if the borrower … found himself unable to repay his debt, the next step was mortgaging or selling land. And, as a consequence, one who no longer had land to pledge or sell was often forced to indenture himself or his children to work off the debt.[1]

Land Ownership

The laws that Moses promulgated concerning land, which have come down to us in various formulations and interpretations of his original teachings by different groups as part of the Teaching of Moses, are based on one primary concept: the land belongs to God alone. "The foundation of ancient economy being ownership of land, God grants the Israelites a land for their possession, but He conditions their continued tenancy on obedience to His laws."[2] Leviticus 25:38, unique in the Torah, specifies the connection between God, the land of Canaan, and the people Israel, "I YHVH am your God, who brought you out of the land of Egypt, to give you the land of Canaan, to be your God."

Just as the Israelites belonged to God and therefore could not be the slaves of any human being, so too did the land belong to God. Since the land is YHVH's, it can never be truly possessed by any individual. "But the land must not be sold beyond reclaim, for the land is Mine: you are but strangers resident with Me" (Lev. 25:23). Eventually this concept was translated into practice in three ways:

1. Equal distribution of the land
2. Letting the land remain fallow each seventh year
3. Returning land to the original owners each Jubilee (fiftieth) year

Distribution of the Land

Equal distribution of the land in Canaan after the forthcoming conquest is discussed in Numbers 33. The Israelites are standing at the Jordan River opposite Jericho shortly before the death of Moses. God instructs Moses to tell the Israelites that after conquering Canaan, "you shall apportion the land among yourselves by lot, clan by clan: with larger groups increase the share, with smaller groups reduce the share. Wherever the lot falls for anyone, that shall be his" (v. 54). Although we do not know the details of exactly how the lots were to be cast, it is obvious that the intent was to see to it that each tribe and each clan would receive an equitable amount according to its size. In this way, all family units would be equal, and with the exception of the tribe of Levi, no one would be landless.

The text in Numbers 33 continues by delineating the borders of the land and listing the names of the men through whom the land will be apportioned to the various tribes. According to the detailed description in chapters 14–21 of the book of Joshua, the actual division of the land was carried out by Joshua and Eleazar, the high priest. "As YHVH commanded Moses, so the children of Israel did, and they divided the land" (Josh. 14:5).

What compelled Moses to devise this system? Could he have done it any other way? There was always the possibility of simply letting the Israelites all enter the land, conquer whatever they could, and occupy whatever they laid their hands on, following the well-known principle "Whoever is most powerful will prevail." But Moses did not allow this to happen. That would have broken the fragile unity that prevailed among the tribes, setting one group against another, and it would have violated the concept of being tenants in a land that God was allotting to the entire people. The very fact that the two and a half tribes that were not settling in the land but remaining in Transjordan also had to participate in the conquest of the land—land they would never occupy—demonstrates the length to which Moses went to preserve the unity and the equality of all.

At that moment on the banks of the Jordan, Israel was by its very nature a classless society, a gathering of the children of former slaves. There was no aristocracy and no difference between one and another in regard to wealth and possessions because they had none to speak of. This was a perfect moment to perpetuate that situation and make it the norm. The plan was actually an attempt to approach equality in dividing the land among them, first by tribes, then by clans and families, and finally by individuals. Each began with an even slate. In any case, the land did not truly belong to anyone, not even to Israel. It belonged exclusively to God: "For the land is Mine" (Lev. 25:23). All Israel and each person is a resident alien, living on the land that is leased to him by God but never owning it.

The Sabbatical Year

One way of emphasizing the fact that no one had absolute ownership of the land was through the command to let the land remain fallow and unworked every seventh year, the sabbatical year. As owner of the land, God could command the resident aliens to leave it untouched for a year. The fact that this practice had an agricultural advantage is never mentioned in the Torah. Without fertilizer or the rotation of crops, land that never rests soon uses up all it resources and becomes barren. This happened to the Neo-Sumerian economy in Mesopotamia in the second millennium BCE, where crops failed as the alkaline content of the soil increased year by year, causing economic disaster.[3]

The ancient law code of Exodus, *Sefer HaBerit*, or the Book of the Covenant, that immediately follows the proclamation of the Decalogue and has the same status as the Ten Commandments, having been revealed to Moses at Sinai at the same time, contains the germ of the sabbatical year law: "Six years you shall sow your land and gather its yield; but in the seventh you shall let it rest and lie fallow" (Exod. 23:10–11). The year is given no specific name, nor is there any specific reason given for this practice. It is presented, however, as one of the ways in which the needy—those without land—would be helped: "Let the needy among your people eat of it" (Exod. 23:11). Having this entire year free from agricultural work and thus being dependent on the crops harvested previously certainly made the Israelites conscious of dependency on God and of their place as tenants rather than owners of this land. Allowing the poor to eat from the produce was another powerful indication that the individual owner was not really in control of the land.

The Levitical code of law found in chapter 25 is based on the verses of Exodus but also expands on them. Letting the land remain fallow in the sabbatical year is given a prominent role: "The land shall observe a Sabbath of YHVH" (25:2). Leviticus, unlike Exodus, calls it a Sabbath and goes so far as to use the same terminology for the sabbatical year as it uses for the seventh day. That, too, is a Sabbath "of YHVH" (Exod. 20:10). On the seventh day, humans and beasts must rest (Exod. 20:10). In the seventh year, "the land shall have a Sabbath of complete rest, a Sabbath of YHVH" (Lev. 25:4).

Leviticus does not mention the poor. On the contrary, only those living on the landowner's property were allowed to eat what grows by itself that year, "you, your male and female slaves, the hired and bound laborers who live with you, and your cattle and the beasts in your land may eat all its yield" (Lev. 25:6–7). Jacob Milgrom, in his monumental three-volume commentary on Leviticus, suggests that the poor are not mentioned here because they did not need this aftergrowth; the Levitical code gives them other benefits not found in Exodus, namely the gleanings of the fields at every harvest (Lev. 19:9–10, 23:22).[4] The emphasis in Leviticus, rather, is on the land itself, which is personified: "It shall be a year of complete rest for the land" (Lev. 25:5). Again, agricultural benefit plays no role; rather, Israel is to ponder the land and the land's relationship to God. The land belongs to God and is therefore observing a Sabbath "of YHVH." The individual residing on the land must permit the land to rest, just as he must permit his family and his servants and cattle to rest on the seventh day.

The emphasis on the land is based on the ancient concept that the land—meaning the land of Canaan—belongs to God, as was stated in Exodus 15:17. This was taken for granted by the prophets and in the book of Psalms. Isaiah calls it "the soil of YHVH" (14:2), "My land," and "My mountain" (14:25). Jeremiah refers to it as "My land" as well (2:7). Psalm 10:16 says that "the nations will perish from His land," and Psalm 85:2 asks God to "favor Your land." Leviticus puts great stress on the idea of holiness—"You shall be holy, for I, YHVH your God, am holy" (Lev. 19:2). Anything belonging to God is holy. God owns the land and gave it to the people of Israel on condition that it be distributed equitably, and God has the right to demand that they observe these Sabbatical and Jubilee laws. As Milgrom wrote, "It stresses that the land is God's, and in ceding it to Israel, God makes it incumbent on all the people to obey all the laws relating to the land, especially the Sabbatical and Jubilee."[5]

It is probable that the sabbatical year was only rarely observed in preexilic times,[6] which may explain the severity of God's threat of dire punishment, including exile, if they do not obey.[7] The land will become a desolate ruin. "Then shall the land make up for its Sabbath years throughout the time that it is desolate and you are in the land of your enemies; then shall the land rest and make up for its Sabbath years" (Lev. 26:34). Long after the exile, when writing the history of Israel, the chronicler paraphrased that verse, citing the lack of permitting the land to rest on the Sabbath year as the reason for the exile. They were exiled to Babylon "until the land paid back its Sabbaths; as long as it lay desolate it kept Sabbath, till seventy years were completed" (2 Chron. 36:21). Perhaps as a result of this belief, in postexilic Judea the sabbatical year was observed, even after the destruction of the Second Temple in 70 CE.[8] Today, too, it is observed in Israel, although it is considered to be merely a Rabbinic injunction (Talmud, *Gittin* 36a–b) rather than a biblical command, and most follow a ruling of the early twentieth-century chief rabbi Harav Abraham Isaac Kook that permitted the land to be worked after being "sold" for the year to a non-Jew. Ultra-Orthodox kibbutzim, however, do not accept this and use hydroponics as a substitute for regular agriculture that seventh year.

The Jubilee Year

The third, and perhaps most daring and revolutionary of the Torah's regulations concerning land, is the redemption of land that takes place during the Jubilee year, the fiftieth year following seven cycles of sabbatical years. "Redemption denoted the restoration of the status quo."[9] Restoration of land to its original owners without their having to pay for it was the key provision of this rule: "In this year of Jubilee, each of you shall return to his holding" (Lev. 25:13). The situation of land ownership in which each Israelite was given a plot of land, remarkable in itself, was not allowed to become perverted. During the years, as one landholder prospered and another went into debt, a situation of inequality would arise, the extreme being that one would sell or lease his property to another and become landless, having to find work on someone else's land. Since the Jubilee occurs only once in fifty years, it would certainly be possible that the individual might not live to be restored to his rightful inheritance, but at least he would always know that his heirs would return. The emphasis, then, was less on the individual than on the family and the clan. The result of the Jubilee year's return of land was, as Neal M. Soss puts it, that the "Culture of Poverty … arising when successive generations are economically disenfranchised cannot arise in the Torah."[10] Such a socially progressive concept has never been attempted before or since.

This concept had its built-in problems. Obviously, if an individual had to sell (or better, lease) his land, the fewer years remaining until the

Jubilee, the lower the price. The real danger was that the buyer would take advantage of the seller's dire straits and give less than was fair. Therefore, the Torah admonishes, "Do not wrong one another, but fear your God; for I YHVH am your God" (Lev. 25:17). Fear of YHVH indicates there is no way this injunction can be enforced by human courts; therefore, it is left to the conscience of the individual and his sense of morality and righteous conduct.

The return of land at the Jubilee was actually seen as the last resort. A better solution would be for a near relative to redeem the land as soon as possible or for the seller to acquire it again as soon as he had the means at hand (Lev. 25:25–26). The purchaser did not have the right to refuse to sell it back at the appropriate price (Lev. 25:27). If neither of these methods of redemption was possible, the land would remain in the possession of the purchaser until the Jubilee year, when it would automatically be redeemed and returned to the original landholder (Lev. 25:28). If the redeemer cannot act, explains Milgrom, "God intervenes by the unilateral action of his Jubilee, which automatically cancels the debt and restores the land to its original possessor."[11]

Leviticus makes a distinction between agricultural land and houses in a walled city, thus taking into account an urban situation in addition to an agricultural society. Such homes could only be redeemed or reclaimed within a year of the sale. After that, the sale was permanent. Such a law would be more appropriate to a later time rather than to the years before the actual conquest and could have been added when the conditions of life changed.[12] Milgrom notes, "Since the Jubilee was intended to preserve the viability of the peasant farmer, there was no need to protect urban property from alienation."[13]

Although it is impossible to know with any certainty the exact dating or even the exact chronology of these texts, there is good reason to assume that the Jubilee laws were promulgated sometime in the eighth or ninth century BCE, when urbanization and the use of money as opposed to agricultural produce transformed society, making the role of the peasant farmer ever more precarious. This is the situation that confronted the classical prophets, who were attempting to bring society back to the norms of a simpler time.[14]

The end result of all of these laws is an entire philosophy of the ownership of land, one that gives the Israelites only tenancy and not ownership, that indicates that no one person has the right to more land than another, and that takes steps to make everyone aware of this (the sabbatical year) and, either through the process of redemption or the release of the Jubilee year, to remedy the situation bound to arise in which an individual loses his land. Exactly how much of this originated with Moses and how much was extrapolated later on the basis of Moses's original insight concerning equality and divine ownership of the land cannot be ascertained, but his vision certainly underlies all of this legislation.

In the fifth century BCE, at the time of Nehemiah, after the return from Babylonia, a situation arose in which people had been forced to sell their land and had even been pressed into servitude because of their debts. This was exactly what the Torah had warned against. They complained to Nehemiah the governor, and following the spirit of the Torah's legislation, if not exactly the details of it, he ordered those who had taken the land to return it: "Give back at once their fields, their vineyards, their olive trees, and their homes and abandon the claims for the hundred pieces of silver, the grain, the wine, and the oil that you have been pressing against them" (Neh. 5:11). To their credit, people immediately agreed and took an oath to do so; they "answered, 'Amen,' and praised YHVH" (Neh. 5:12–13). The spirit of Moses's teaching had prevailed.

Money Regulations

Although there is no attempt in the Torah to achieve total equality of wealth, there is a plan to mitigate the dependency of the poor on the wealthy and to close the gap between rich and poor through a series of laws. One of the most important is the law concerning the remission of debts, a truly revolutionary concept found in Deuteronomy 15, as well as the laws of gleaning (Lev. 19:9–10, 23:22) and the "poor tithe" (Deut. 14:22). Taken together, these four regulations formed, as Soss puts it, "the nucleus of an income maintenance program."[15]

A taking of interest is also forbidden in Leviticus 25:35–38. The situation described there does not concern loans being taken to further commercial affairs, but loans needed by one who "in dire straits comes under your authority" (Lev. 25:35). Interest is also forbidden according to the law code of Deuteronomy, "so that YHVH your God may bless you in all your undertakings" (Deut. 23:21).

The release of debt, a most radical social idea, is found in Deuteronomy 15:1–11. It is associated there with the sabbatical year. Unlike the laws in Exodus and Leviticus, the only provision mentioned in Deuteronomy for the sabbatical year is the release of debts. There is no mention of leaving the land fallow. "Every seventh year you shall practice remission of debts. This shall be the nature of the remission: every creditor shall remit the due that he claims from his fellow; he shall not dun his fellow or kinsman, for the remission proclaimed is of YHVH" (Deut. 15:1–2). It is unclear whether Deuteronomy accepts the idea of the land lying fallow as a given and therefore does not mention it or whether it does not recognize the validity of that law. The former is quite likely, because the term that is used for "remission"—*shemitah*—is also used in Exodus 23:10–11 with respect to leaving fields and vineyards uncultivated in the seventh year.[16] The remission of debts, however, is most likely an innovation of Deuteronomy, which was composed in the days of the kingdom when monetary debts became a more critical problem.

Jacob Milgrom, on the other hand, takes the opposite point of view. Although in Leviticus the release of debts is not mentioned, Milgrom believes that Leviticus takes debt release for granted, while Deuteronomy knows only about debts.[17] In any case, at a later time, after the exile, both practices were considered to be valid.[18] As we read in Nehemiah 10:32, "We will forgo [the produce of] the seventh year, and every outstanding debt."

The Torah warns against hesitating to loan money to someone in need because "the seventh year, the year of remission, is approaching" (Deut. 15:9). In the same verse, Israelites are warned that if they do so, "he will cry out to YHVH against you, and you will incur guilt." "I command you: open your hand to the poor and needy kinsman in your land" (Deut. 15:11). During late Second Temple times, however, such a law became a hindrance rather than a help because people refrained from lending money before the seventh year—exactly what the Torah warns against. In the first century BCE, the great sage Hillel introduced a legal document called the prosbul (Talmud, *Gittin* 36a) by which the borrower waived the cancellation of his debt and turned the collection of debts over to the courts, effectively negating that part of the law. The legal fiction of the prosbul enabled the poor to obtain needed loans.

Whereas the return of land occurred only once in fifty years, Deuteronomy requires the remission of debts every seventh year! Solon in sixth-century Athens once cancelled debts, and there are many instances in which kings or rulers in ancient Near Eastern societies, including Ptolemaic Egypt, proclaimed a *misharum*, cancelling all debts when the social situation became desperate or to gain favor at the beginning of a reign.[19] The Torah, however, is unique in requiring this not as a goodwill dispensation of the ruler but because it is "of YHVH," and not on a ruler's whim but as a requirement every seventh year on a regular basis.

Although these various laws relating to wealth—both land and money—may have reflected differing methods of achieving the common goal, that goal remained the same: a society in which there were no unbridgeable gaps between rich and poor, no people landless while others accumulated huge allocations. This was an attempt to alleviate, if not eliminate, gross poverty. Which codes were followed and how strictly during the days before the exile is impossible to know. Regardless, by the time of Ezra and Nehemiah, the Torah as we know it had been compiled and accepted by the returnees as the official, God-given constitution of the people Israel, and every attempt was made to live by it as it was interpreted by the scribes and teachers. This is described in great detail in chapters 8–10 of the book of Nehemiah.

The Torah's utopian program could never be totally sustained. After the exile, the return of land to its original owners was not even possible, but the concept of a society in which ownership was not without limits always remained. In the twentieth century, the original kibbutz experiment was an expression of that, as was the Israeli law by which property is only leased from the state to individuals for a period of either forty-nine or ninety-eight years.

Taxes

Taxes are another way of expressing the desire for equity and of creating a more equitable distribution of wealth. The Torah has only one fiscal tax, the half-shekel that was to be collected from each adult aged twenty years and up (Exod. 30:14–16). This was a method of taking a census without actually counting the people. The money collected was then to be used "to the service of the Tent of Meeting; it shall serve the Israelites as a reminder before YHVH, as expiation for your persons" (Exod. 30:16). Exodus 30:15 emphasizes that "the rich shall not pay more and the poor shall not pay less than half a shekel." The silver collected was then used to cast the sockets and other silver pieces used in creating the sanctuary (Exod. 38:27–28). The insistence that every individual contribute exactly the same amount indicated that each Israelite had an equal share in the creation of the sanctuary, the place where God's presence dwelt in the midst of the people. Wealth was not a factor in the relationship between the individual and God; all Israelites were thus equal.

Although this collection was a onetime affair, it became a yearly contribution to the Temple made by Jews wherever they lived and was used to purchase the daily communal sacrifice, again emphasizing that each Jew had an equal part in the Temple rites.[20] Later, an entire tractate of the Mishnah, *Shekalim*, was created that dealt with the laws and usage of the half-shekel.

The other taxation legislated by the Torah is the system of tithes, the collection of one-tenth of the agricultural produce raised that year, as well as animals. In complete contrast to the half-shekel, this tax takes a different amount from each household based on the amount of their produce. Equity is attained because those with less will not be overburdened by having to pay an excessive proportion, while the wealthy will give more, because they have more. Like an income tax, it casts a fair and equitable share of the burden on each household.

The idea of a tithe is not new to the Torah legislation, as we see from the fact that both Abraham and Jacob give tithes (Gen. 14:20 and 28:22). These, however, are voluntary, onetime contributions, while at least some of the Torah texts require a mandatory yearly sum.[21] There are different sets of laws concerning tithes in the various sources in the Torah, reflecting different points of view and different periods of development. Leviticus 27:30–32 requires that all tithes, agricultural and animal, become "holy to YHVH" without explaining exactly what that means. The assumption is that they are used to support the worship of God. In Numbers 18:21–25, the tithes are all given to the Levites, who have no land and therefore no other source of income. They, in turn, must give a portion to the priests. Deuteronomy 14:22–29, reflecting the later situation in which there is to be only one sanctuary, requires the tithe to be brought there and consumed there every first, second, fourth, and fifth year of the seven-year cycle. This strengthened the ties to the central sanctuary and benefitted it economically as well. It seems that the tithe was shared by the family, the Levite, the stranger, the fatherless, and the widow (Deut. 14:29).[22] Every third and sixth year the tithe was left in the home settlements for the Levite and the poor. We have no way of knowing how these tithes were actually observed in the early days; during the time of the Second Temple, the different laws underwent a process of interpretation and were harmonized to permit an orderly observance.[23]

It is striking that nowhere in the Torah is there provision for taxation to support any form of governmental structure. When the people ask Samuel for a king, one of the things he warns them is that "he will take a tenth part of your grain and vintage and give it to his eunuchs and courtiers" (1 Sam. 8:15). Indeed kings did, and much more as well.

Although the Torah makes no provisions for fiscal support of kings or any other rulers, it does ask the people to support those who are appointed to serve as religious leaders and to share their wealth equitably with the poorer elements of society in need of help. Soss notes:

> We have characterized this society by its stability and its guarantee of economic stability to the individual.... No family should be permanently debarred from full participation in economic life through some temporary aberration or misfortune.... The individual is protected by an incomes maintenance program, which also tends the distribution of disposable income toward equality.[24]

This concept, this revolutionary truth of the Torah, was unique in human thinking at its time and can serve today as an inspiration for humane living.

In a world of haves and have-nots, these ideas of the Torah regarding economic rights, especially as expressed in the Jubilee laws, can serve as a beacon for economically oppressed peoples and nations, much as the idea of the Exodus served as a rallying point for politically oppressed peoples throughout the centuries. It is "a realistic blueprint for bridging the economic gap between the have and have-not nations."[25]

12

Slavery Must Be Mitigated

Revolutionary Truth #12: Human beings are not chattel. Israelites must not be enslaved, and slavery for others should be mitigated.

I am YHVH. I will free you from the labors of the Egyptians and deliver you from their enslavement.

Exodus 6:6

Bear in mind that you were slaves in the land of Egypt, and the Lord your God redeemed you; therefore I enjoin this commandment upon you today.

Deuteronomy 15:15

I made a covenant with your fathers when I brought them out of the land of Egypt, the house of enslavement, saying, "In the seventh year each of you must let go any fellow Hebrew who may be sold to you; when he has served you six years, you must set him free." But your fathers would not obey Me or give ear.

Jeremiah 34:13–14

"Proclaim liberty throughout the land for all its inhabitants" (Lev. 25:10). This dramatic verse, inscribed on the American Liberty Bell, introduces the laws of the Jubilee year, the fiftieth year. Among those laws is one concerning the Israelite who, because of poverty, has no choice but to sell himself to his fellow Israelite: "Do not subject him to the treatment of a slave. He shall remain with you as a hired or bound laborer; he shall serve with you only until the Jubilee year. Then he and his children with him shall be free of your authority" (Lev. 25:39–41). With one bold stroke, Israelite slavery was forbidden. The Israelite could be an indentured servant, but not a slave. An Israelite could not become chattel, subject to the total rule of his master.

The evil of slavery is so obvious, it seems superfluous even to mention it. Yet, we should not forget that even today, there are places in the world where slavery still exists. Slavery was abolished in the United States of America less than 150 years ago, a brief moment in the vast history of civilization. How was it possible, we might well ask, for men who were slaveholders to write, "We hold these truths to be self-evident, that all men are created equal, that they are endowed by their Creator with certain unalienable Rights, that among these are Life, Liberty and the pursuit of Happiness"? Did they not understand the import of what they wrote? They seem not to have seen the irony in these words. Moses took a more active role against slavery than did Jefferson.

Considering the prevalence of slavery until our own times, it would indeed be surprising if the Torah, created for a society that existed more than three thousand years ago, had abolished all slavery. It had not, nor had any contemporary society done so. Twenty percent of the populations of ancient Athens and Imperial Rome were slaves.[1] The wonder, therefore, is that the Torah outlawed slavery among Israelites and mitigated it among non-Israelites.

The institution of slavery for non-Jews continued to exist among Jews well into the Common Era, as is attested both by codes of Jewish law and by other writings and inscriptions.[2] Jews in the Confederate South felt comfortable defending the institution by pointing to the biblical laws of slavery. Although there was little involvement of Jews in the Atlantic slave trade and few Jewish plantation owners, Jews living in Southern cities had slaves, as did their Gentile neighbors.[3] The paradox is that abolitionists also based themselves on the Bible, and with justification. Just as the Torah details laws of slavery, so, too, it lays the foundation for the abolition of that evil institution. With its admonition to "proclaim liberty," the Torah planted the seeds of the antislavery revolution.

The basic narrative of the Torah is the powerful story of a slave rebellion, one initiated and sanctioned by God. The words of God in Exodus 5:1, spoken by God's representative, Moses, to Pharaoh form the first recorded slogan of freedom from slavery: "Let My people go!" No wonder it became a powerful slave spiritual and later the slogan for the free Soviet Jewry movement. There are few stronger antislavery statements than God's words to Moses: "I have now heard the moaning of the Israelites because the Egyptians are holding them in slavery, and I have remembered My covenant. Say, therefore, to the Israelite people: I am YHVH. I will free you from the labors of the Egyptians and deliver you from their slavery" (Exod. 6:5–6).

Once Israel attained its freedom, Israelites were commanded to observe the Passover holiday, which enshrined the concept of freedom from bondage, each year on the anniversary of leaving Egypt: "And Moses said to the people, 'Remember this day, on which you went free from Egypt, the house of slavery.... And you shall explain to your son on that day, "It is because of what YHVH did for me when I went free from Egypt"'" (Exod. 13:3, 13:8). At this stage, the command to the Israelites to observe Passover and remember their freedom comes directly from Moses, their leader, not, as was usually the case, from God through Moses. As leader of the slave rebellion, Moses understood the consequences of it and wanted it to be engraved on the people's consciousness and that of all subsequent generations. The Sages later officially designated Passover as "the season of our freedom" and, after the destruction of the Temple in 70 CE, created the home seder ritual and the Haggadah, the book read at the seder, as a narrative and reenactment of the experience of attaining freedom from slavery.

Nevertheless, in the very laws concerning the Passover lamb eaten on this holiday of freedom, we read, "Any slave a man has bought may eat of it once he has been circumcised" (Exod. 12:44). Obviously, this refers to a Gentile slave. What might such a slave have thought as he participated in the seder? Scholar Catherine Hezser suggests that such participation "would have given them hope, even if only for the brief time of the ritual, that they might eventually obtain freedom themselves."[4] Might it not also have made them wonder how their owners could be celebrating freedom and equality and yet still be holding them in bondage?

Transforming Slavery

Laws of slavery are the very first laws given to the newly freed Israelites following the Ten Commandments. They are found in the collection of laws in Exodus 21–23. Those who have just left slavery themselves are told by God what to do when acquiring a slave. The Hebrew word for "slave," *eved*, comes from the root meaning "to work" or "to serve." When it is used in regard to an Israelite, the phrase is *eved ivri*, usually translated a "Hebrew slave." However, if by "slave" we mean one who has no rights, is totally subject to his master's will, and may be punished in case of disobedience,[5] the term "slave" would seem to be inappropriate. Talmudic scholar Jacob Lauterbach remarks, "The Jewish law does not allow an Israelite to become or to be made a slave in the real sense of the word. The term *eved*, 'slave,' then, when applied to a Hebrew or an Israelite, can only mean one who has to serve for a certain definite period."[6] As the midrash says, "Perhaps he should not be called 'slave' at all, since it is a shameful term? But the text says 'If you buy a Hebrew slave.' Against his will the Torah designates him a slave."[7] As we have seen, Leviticus 25:35–43 clearly defines the Hebrew "slave" as "a hired or bound laborer" (v. 40).

It is not accidental that the very first law concerning slavery limits the term of slavery: "When you acquire a Hebrew slave, he shall serve six years; in the seventh year he shall go free, without payment" (Exod. 21:2). Only if he decides of his own free will that he wishes to remain a slave may his master take him before judges and then make him a slave for life (Exod. 21:5–6). Rabbinic law went further and declared that even then, the slave went free in the Jubilee year.

The revolutionary idea that no Israelite could be a slave stemmed from the Israelites' experience of slavery during their sojourn in Egypt. That terrible ordeal sensitized the people Israel and is used by the Torah to help them understand why they should not treat others as they had been treated. This is spelled out in the law code of the book of Deuteronomy, which also explains the reason for it. When a slave is freed, he must be given provisions "out of the flock, threshing floor, and vat, with which YHVH your God has blessed you" (Deut. 15:14). This is followed by the injunction "Bear in mind that you were slaves in the land of Egypt and YHVH your God redeemed you; therefore I enjoin this commandment upon you today" (15:15).

As Nahum Sarna points out, the laws of slavery found in Exodus 21:2–11 deal specifically with "the imposition of legal restraints on the power of a master over his Hebrew male and female slaves, and the establishment of the legal rights of slaves."[8] In other words, the Torah does not command us to take Hebrew slaves. It simply takes it for granted that there will be slaves because the poor are likely to find themselves in a position in which they have no choice but to sell themselves into a form of slavery, better termed "indentured servitude." Furthermore, the Torah attempts to regulate that "slavery" and to limit the rights of the owner. It emphasizes that slaves must be treated as human beings, not as chattel, and puts legal limitations on the rights of the so-called owner. This is why Israel is immediately commanded that after six years the so-called slave must go free.[9]

Although there are significant differences in the laws of slavery found in all three legal codes of the Torah—Exodus, Leviticus, and Deuteronomy—in all of them, the Torah places severe limitations on Israelite slavery. Greenberg states that "the laws mitigate the harshness that accompanies the status of chattel, and they enhance the recognition of the slave as a human being."[10]

Thus, the Torah's laws concerning slavery go a long way toward modifying slavery for Israelites, either changing it into indentured servitude or, according to Leviticus 25:39–40, something even less problematic that in no way can be regarded as slavery, designating the person "a hired or bound laborer."

Israelites Belong to God

The Torah explains the abolishment of true Hebrew slavery by mentioning the unique relationship of God to the Israelites. "For they are My slaves, whom I freed from the land of Egypt; they may not give themselves over into slavery" (Lev. 25:42). By freeing them from their Egyptian masters, God acquired the right to be their master; that right precludes any human being from acquiring Israelites as slaves. The Rabbis in the midrash made this very clear:

> "These are the laws ... when you acquire a Hebrew slave" (Exod. 21:1–2)—Since God had freed them from slavery and granted them freedom, God commanded them first of all not to enslave their brothers by force and not to enslave them in perpetuity but only until the seventh year, as it is said, "For they are My slaves" (Lev. 25:42).[11]

The *Sifra*, the early tannaitic midrash to Leviticus, concludes from the words "they are My slaves" in that verse that God acquired them prior to anyone else and that the mention of freeing them "from the land of Egypt" indicates that God freed them "on condition that one not be sold as a slave is sold ... nor is one to be made to stand on a trading platform in the street."[12]

The use of the word *eved*, "slave," in regard to the Israelites' relationship to God does not carry the harshness slavery usually implies, which is why the usual translations prefer the word "servants." Moses is called *eved Adonai*, "the slave of God" (Deut. 34:5), but the implication is of a beloved servant. Based on this, centuries later Second Isaiah referred to Israel as God's *eved*: "But you, Israel, My slave, Jacob, whom I have chosen, seed of Abraham My friend ... to whom I said, 'You are My slave'; I chose you, I have not rejected you" (Isa. 41:8–9). This *eved* is a beloved, devoted servant, not a lowly slave.

It is sometimes difficult to know whether in a particular law the Torah is referring to all slaves, including the non-Israelite, or only to the Hebrew slave. Exodus 21:26–27, for example, states, "When a man strikes the eyes of his slave, male or female, and destroys it, he shall let him go free on account of his eye. If he knocks out the tooth of his slave, male or female, he shall let him go free on account of his tooth." A *baraita*, an early teaching of the *Tannaim*, in the Talmud uses these verses as proof that a heathen slave goes free "through the loss of his eye, tooth, and projecting limbs that do not return" (*Kiddushin* 24a). The Ten Commandments specify that "your male or female slave" shall not work on the Sabbath (Exod. 20:10), and in total contradiction to all other codes at that time, Deuteronomy 23:16–17 decrees that a runaway slave is not to be returned to his master.[13] There is no reason to believe that this law applied only to Hebrew slaves.[14] As Daniela Piattelli has pointed out in a recent study, this law "differs most significantly from all the others in antiquity," because Sumerian and Akkadian sources specify penalties against those who help fugitive slaves.[15] Ironically, it was ignored in pre–Civil War American laws of slavery.

We do not know whether these laws of the Torah were actually followed in total in the early days or remained in the realm of theory.[16] A passage in the book of Jeremiah would indicate that they were not always followed. When Nebuchadnezzar was waging war against Jerusalem during the reign of King Zedekiah, the righteous king decreed "that everyone should set free his Hebrew slaves, both male and female, and that no one should keep his fellow Judean enslaved" (Jer. 34:9). Everyone did so, but the owners soon forced their slaves back into bondage. Jeremiah then delivered a message to the slaveholders, reminding them that God had commanded them when they were freed from Egyptian bondage that they had to set their Hebrew slaves free after six years: "But your fathers would not obey Me or give ear" (Jer. 34:14); because they also had reneged on the freeing of their slaves, they would be handed over to their enemies.[17] This passage indicates that although these rules were not obeyed, they remained in the consciousness of at least some of the political and religious leaders of Israel.[18]

The Canaanite Slave

The abolition of slavery was limited to Israelites, to the *eved ivri*, the "Hebrew slave," mentioned in Exodus 21:2. Although the laws of slavery concerning others—the term coined by the Sages was *eved K'na-ani*, literally "a Canaanite slave"—were also sensitive and went a long way to limiting the rights of the owner, they did not abolish slavery. They did, however, prevent the return of runaways. The non-Israelite slave was a slave forever, as indicated by Leviticus 25:44–46, which says specifically that "you may keep them as a possession for your children after you, for them to inherit as property for all time" (v. 46). The Talmud cites this verse as proof that the Canaanite slave does not go free or revert to a previous owner even at the Jubilee (*Kiddushin* 22b). He does go free, however, if his master injures him so that he loses a limb. Maimonides limits this manumission to those slaves who have been circumcised and undergone ritual immersion, thus attaining a status of being "partially observant of mitzvot."[19]

That there existed a feeling in biblical times that all slavery was wrong may be inferred from a verse in the book of the prophet Joel. Speaking of a time in the future when God will "pour out [His] spirit on all flesh," the prophet concludes, "I will even pour out My spirit upon male and female slaves in those days" (Joel 3:1–2). Similarly, as pointed out in chapter 6, Job—who was not a Hebrew, nor were his slaves—speaks of his good treatment of his male and female slaves and declares, "Did not He who made me in my mother's belly make him? Did not One form us both in the womb?" (Job 31:15). All human beings, including slaves, are the creations of the same God and are not inferior by birth because of race or nationality.

Rabbinic Laws of Slavery

The development of Jewish law in the Rabbinic period went even further in mitigating the severity of the Hebrew slave. Basing itself on the verse in Leviticus 25:39, "You shall not make him serve as a slave," the early midrash the *Mekhilta* rules that the slave is not to "wash the feet of his master, nor put his shoes on him, nor carry his things before him when going to the bath house, nor support him by the hips when ascending steps, nor carry him in a litter or a chair or a sedan chair as slaves do." Ironically, it adds that a son or a pupil may do these things. Then, based on Leviticus 25:40, "as a hired man," the *Mekhilta* goes on to rule that just as a hired man cannot be made to do work that is not in his trade, so too the Hebrew slave cannot and may not be put to work in any trade, such as barbering, tailoring, or baking, in which he must serve the public. He cannot be made to work at night but only during the day.[20] The early midrash to Leviticus, the *Sifra*,[21] also states that a master is not to give the Hebrew slave unnecessary work such as telling him to heat or cool a drink when he does not really want it. Since no one else can know what is in the master's mind, this is left to the owner's conscience and his reverence for God.

Rabban Yochanan ben Zakkai interprets the verse in Exodus 21:6 that if a slave decides not to go free after six years as is his right, "his master shall pierce his ear with an awl, and he shall then remain his slave for life," thus: "The ear, which heard at Sinai, 'For it is to Me that the Israelites are slaves: they are My slaves whom I freed from the land of Egypt, I YHVH your God' (Lev. 25:55) but nevertheless preferred subjection to men rather than to God, deserves to be pierced!"[22] Whereas the Torah simply states that if the man decides to remain a slave, he may do so and then have his ear pierced as a sign of this status, Ben Zakkai sees this as a shameful act. Slavery, even if freely accepted, is a disgraceful matter.[23]

Similarly, Rabbi Simeon ben Rabbi teaches that the reason the door and the doorpost were used when the ear was bored was because the door and the doorpost

> were witnesses in Egypt when I passed over the lintel and the doorposts and proclaimed "For it is to Me that the Israelites are slaves: they are My slaves whom I freed from the land of Egypt" (Lev. 25:55), and not the slaves of slaves. Nevertheless this slave preferred subjection to men rather than to God and [the ear that heard this proclamation] deserves to be pierced!"
>
> (*Talmud*, Kiddushin 22b)

The Sages also interpret the word "forever" to mean only until the Jubilee year. "When the Jubilee arrives he goes free. If his master dies sooner, he also goes free."[24] Even if there is a son who inherits, the slave goes free immediately.[25] The *Tannaim* also dispute whether the person who sells himself into slavery may forfeit his freedom and have his ear bored, thereby selling himself into perpetual service (Talmud, *Kiddushin* 14b).

Rabbinic law limits the service of a Hebrew slave to the master and, if he dies, to his son, but not to a daughter or anyone else. A female Hebrew slave serves only the master and no one else.[26]

According to a *baraita*, the verse "he [the slave] is happy with you" (Deut. 15:16) indicates that the slave must have whatever you have. That is the meaning of the words "with you"—"He must be 'with you' in food and drink. You cannot eat white bread and he black bread, you cannot drink old wine and he new wine, you cannot sleep on a feather bed and he on straw. Thus the popular saying: if one acquires a Hebrew slave, one acquires a master."[27] Note that this interpretation of Deuteronomy 15:16 applies specifically only to the Hebrew slave and not to others. According to the Talmud, the institution of the Hebrew slave was totally abolished when the Jubilee year fell out of practice, that is, after the destruction of the First Temple in 586 BCE.[28] In view of this, the extensive discussions of Hebrew slavery in the Mishnah, the various tannaitic midrashim, the Talmud, and later codes would seem to be theoretical. The assumption may be that the time will come when the Jubilee is again in force, and therefore these laws too could become relevant. It is questionable, however, whether that was actually the case, and it is possible that Jews may indeed have continued to be slaves to other Jews throughout that period.[29] In any case, slavery of others was never officially suspended or abolished even in theory.

Slavery in Later Codes

After devoting an entire chapter to the laws of the Hebrew slave, Maimonides reiterates that these apply "only when the laws of the Jubilee are in force"[30] but then devotes an additional four chapters to the Hebrew slave. Nevertheless, Rabbi Yehiel Epstein (1829–1908), the author of the code of Jewish law *Arukh HaShulchan*, introduces the section on laws of slavery with the statement, "The laws of slavery were followed in ancient times, but now the laws of slavery are not in force at all, for there are no slaves in our communities."[31]

Because the Torah states, "You shall not rule over him ruthlessly" (Lev. 25:43) specifically in reference to the Hebrew slave, it was inferred that it was permitted to do so with the non-Hebrew slave. Thus Maimonides ruled, "It is permitted to make a Canaanite slave work ruthlessly."[32] He then continues:

> Even though this is the law, the quality of mercy and the ways of wisdom teach that one should be merciful and pursue righteousness and not act unjustly toward his slave or work hardship on him. Rather he should give him all kinds of food and drink…. Nor should one scream at or be angry overmuch with his slave, but speak with him kindly and listen to his complaints…. Cruelty and harshness are the ways of idolaters, while the seed of our father Abraham, Israel, who were taught by the Holy One through the beneficence of the Torah laws and statutes of righteousness, are merciful toward all.[33]

Although the Torah never called for a similar downgrading of slavery among non-Jews to indentured servitude, it did mitigate some of the severity of slavery, recognizing the humanity of even the Gentile slave. This influenced Rabbinic law as well as the early philosophers and medieval codifiers. Whereas Aristotle believed that some people are slaves by nature, virtually subhuman, Philo denies that and makes it clear that slaves are not like animals.[34] Rabbinic law was also careful to include slaves among those "who have understanding" and not to categorize them together with animals.[35] Unlike Roman law, Jewish law, both biblical and Rabbinic, did not grant the master unlimited power of life and death over his slave.[36] Thus, Philo taught that by nature all men are free and that masters should treat their slaves with brotherly love.[37]

Biblical scholar Jeffrey Tigay sums up the matter well:

> Servitude was an accepted fact of life in Israel as it was everywhere in the ancient world. Biblical law and ethical teachings aimed at securing humane treatment for servants. These aims are based on the Bible's recognition of the shared humanity of

master and servant and on the special empathy the Bible expects of Israelites because their ancestors were slaves in Egypt. The Torah, unique among ancient law codes, insists that servants be given rest on the Sabbath, be included in the festivities of holidays, and be protected from physical abuse and harm by their masters.[38]

The ideal that true slavery, in which a human being becomes no more than a tool of another human being,[39] was forbidden within the community of Israel remained alive if sometimes latent and could be invoked as representing the true will of God.

Although the Torah specifies laws to regulate slavery, these laws must be regarded as a compromise for their day and not as laws valid for all time. The basic truth revealed by the Torah's story of freedom and by the radical legislation that completely eliminated actual slavery among Israelites and mitigated it for Gentiles as well is that freedom and not slavery is the will of the Almighty and the goal toward which humankind must strive.

13

The Needy Must Be Cared For

Revolutionary Truth #13: Concern for the weaker elements of society, the impoverished, the needy, the widow, the orphan, and the stranger.

> For YHVH your God … shows no favor and takes no bribe, but upholds the cause of the fatherless and the widow, and befriends the stranger, providing him with food and clothing. You too must befriend the stranger, for you were strangers in the land of Egypt.
>
> *Deuteronomy 10:17–19*

> Ah, you who trample the heads of the poor into the dust of the ground, And make the humble walk a twisted course!
>
> *Amos 2:7*

What is the responsibility of a society toward its neediest members, toward those who are poverty stricken or cannot care for themselves?

The Torah's answer is unequivocal: society must provide them with protection and help them in their time of need. Every one of the legal codes of the Torah speaks of the need to care for the poor and the stranger. Furthermore, according to the Torah, those unfortunates in need of help are under the direct protection of God. Caring for them is not an act of charity but an act of righteousness, fulfilling God's demands.

Even more striking is the fact that this revolutionary idea is based on the conception of a society of equals, a society without class divisions in which even the neediest is termed "your brother," your kinsman. Moses, the leader of this group of former slaves, has a remarkable vision of a society in which the needs of all will be met and in which each individual will feel responsibility toward others. This is made crystal clear in Leviticus in a command addressed to each Israelite individually in the singular: "If your brother, being in straits, comes under your authority, and you hold him as though a resident alien, let him live with you. Do not exact from him advance or accrued interest, but fear your God and let your brother live with you"[1] (Lev. 25:35–36). The following section (25:39ff.), dealing with one who has to sell himself into indentured servitude because of poverty, begins the same way: "If your brother, being in straits...." Three times the term "your brother" is repeated. Each Israelite is "your brother," your kin, even when not related specifically to your family. For the sensitive reader, the use of that term cannot help but recall the story of Cain and Abel, where Cain replies to God's cry, "Where is your brother Abel?" with the words, "Am I my brother's keeper?" (Gen. 4:9). The answer, unequivocally, is "Yes!" Whatever you would feel obligated to do for your brother or your sister, you must do for any member of the nation. The Torah strives to create a society of equals, of brothers and sisters, a revolutionary idea unknown elsewhere in the ancient Near East.

Of course, it would be an exaggeration to contend that ancient Israel was a completely classless society. The Levites and the *kohanim* (priests) were special groups having a singular status, with certain rights but also with special responsibilities.[2] Nevertheless, the society envisioned in the Torah and that existed until the establishment of the kingship was—again with the exception of the Levites and *kohanim*—a society with no class divisions. As for the Levites and priests, unlike all other Israelites, they had no land. Therefore, as we have seen, they were granted tithes to enable them to live, but the laws gave them no other special privileges, and there was no intention of creating in them a class of nobility or an attempt at making them wealthy at the expense of others. Contrast this to the way in which Joseph saw to it that Pharaoh owned all the land in Egypt and received one-fifth of all the harvests. Only the Egyptian priests continued to hold their own land (Gen. 47:22–26). There were no nobles and, as we have seen earlier, no slaves among the Israelites, only indentured servitude.

In translating the famous Babylonian Code of Hammurabi (1728–1686 BCE), Theophile J. Meek constantly translates the word *awelum* as "seignior"—"If a seignior...." He explains that the word literally means "man" but in the legal literature "sometimes indicates a man of the higher class, a noble." Therefore, he uses the term *seignior* from Italian and Spanish, where it indicates "a free man of standing, and not in the strict feudal sense, although the ancient Near East did have something approximating the feudal system and that is another reason for using 'seignior.'"[3] The Babylonian system had different laws for different classes. In laws 196–208 in the code,[4] for example, the laws and penalties for offenses against aristocracy are different from those for offenses against commoners. The Torah has nothing of that sort, nor does it have an equivalent term, because there was no such feudal system or group of nobles in ancient Israel. Most important, the laws of the Torah were the same for all Israelites, rich and poor alike, and showed great sensitivity to the helpless and downtrodden in Israeli society.[5] It constantly singled out four different groups for special protection and care: the poor, the widow, the orphan, and the "stranger," that is, the non-Israelite who resided in the land.

It was not until the American Revolution that the Western world had a society free of class distinctions, something the Torah had envisioned nearly three thousand years before, and even then there was the notorious exception of black slaves.

The words spoken by the Statue of Liberty in Emma Lazarus's poem "The New Colossus" express the spirit of America, rejecting the class system of Europe:

> "Keep, ancient lands, your storied pomp!" cries she
> With silent lips. "Give me your tired, your poor,

Your huddled masses yearning to breathe free,
The wretched refuse of your teeming shore,
Send these, the homeless, tempest-tossed to me,
I lift my lamp beside the golden door!"

Unfortunately, America has not always lived up to these words, as seen in selective immigration laws in the 1920s and in the dark days of the Second World War when it rejected Jewish refugees. The poem has always served as an inspiration and a hope rather than a description of reality.

Provisions for the Needy

Concern for these needy groups, those "wretched masses," if you will, appears first in the legal code of Exodus. Within a few consecutive verses the four groups needing protection are mentioned:

> You shall not wrong a stranger or oppress him, for you were strangers in the land of Egypt. You shall not ill-treat any widow or orphan. If you do mistreat them, I will heed their outcry as soon as they cry out to Me, and My anger shall blaze forth and I will put you to the sword, and your own wives shall become widows and your children orphans. If you lend money to My people, to the poor among you, do not act toward them as a creditor; exact no interest from them. If you take your neighbor's garment in pledge, you must return it to him before the sun sets; it is his only clothing, the sole covering for his skin. In what else shall he sleep? Therefore, if he cries out to Me, I will pay heed, for I am compassionate.
>
> (Exod. 22:20–26)

In their interpretations of these verses, the Sages defined "wrong" as verbal and emotional abuse and "oppress" as defrauding in monetary matters: You shall not wrong the stranger with words. Neither shall you oppress him—in money matters.[6]

These seven verses compose an unparalleled credo of concern for the wretched and the needy, a compassionate call expressing God's care for those who cannot care for themselves. To further emphasize the concern for the stranger, a similar idea is found in the very next chapter: "You shall not oppress a stranger, for you know the feelings of the stranger, having yourselves been strangers in the land of Egypt" (Exod. 23:9).

The *ger*—the resident alien—benefits from the regulations of the community, sharing, for example, in the gleanings left for the poor (Lev. 19:10, 23:22). Deuteronomy also classifies the *ger* together with other defenseless members of society, the fatherless, and the widow, who are entitled to receive the tithe of the third and sixth year of each cycle (Deut. 14:29).

In general, the Torah classifies the stranger, that is, the resident alien, together with those who are needy, as in Deuteronomy 24:14–15: "You shall not abuse a needy and destitute laborer, whether a fellow countryman or a stranger.... You must pay him his wages on the same day, before the sun sets, for he is needy and urgently depends on it; else he will cry to YHVH against you and you will incur guilt." YHVH will hear the cry of the stranger equally with that of the Israelite. There is also the possibility that the stranger may prosper, even to the extent of being able to purchase a native Israelite as an indentured servant (Lev. 25:47).

The Holiness Code in Leviticus equates the stranger to the native: "When a stranger resides with you in your land, you shall not wrong him. The stranger who resides with you shall be to you as one of your citizens; you shall love him as yourself, for you were strangers in the land of Egypt: I YHVH am your God" (Lev. 19:33–34).[7]

Leviticus, which commands us to love our fellow, makes a special provision for the stranger—who is really *not* our fellow. He is "the other." The "stranger" in the Torah is someone who lives in the land as a resident, not merely someone passing through. As an alien, not a citizen, his rights were not always identical with the native Israelite. Abraham identifies himself as being such a stranger when he attempts to buy a burial place for Sarah: "I am a resident alien among you; sell me a burial site among you," says Abraham (Gen. 23:4). As a resident alien, a *ger v'toshav*, he has no right to purchase land. Therefore, he must implore the Hittites to make an exception for him.

Leviticus also bestows on the stranger and the poor, connecting two of the downtrodden groups, the rights to portions of the harvest. In an agricultural society, such rights were the difference between life and starvation. These laws are found first in Leviticus 19:9–10 and then repeated in 23:22. Four different products are to be left for the poor and the stranger: *pe'ah*—the corners of the grain field; *leket*—the gleanings that fall to the ground when the grain is harvested; *olelot*—grape clusters not fully grown; and *peret*—fruit that falls to the ground. "You shall leave them for the poor and the stranger: I YHVH am your God" (Lev. 19:10, 23:22). The book of Ruth describes exactly this situation. Ruth, who is destitute and helping to provide for her mother-in-law, Naomi, goes into the fields of the wealthy Boaz to glean in the field behind the reapers (Ruth 2:3). The result is well known.

These laws concerning the harvest are repeated again in Deuteronomy 24:19–22. Here, too, these portions belong "to the stranger, the fatherless, and the widow" because we were slaves "in the land of Egypt." Later, Rabbinic law delineated exactly how much should be left for them and considered it a most important commandment that everyone should be anxious to fulfill.[8]

When the theme of the stranger is taken up by Deuteronomy, it requires the judicial system to protect the rights of the stranger and "decide justly between any man and a fellow Israelite or a stranger" (Deut. 1:16). "For YHVH your God … upholds the cause of the fatherless and the widow, and befriends the stranger, providing him with food and clothing. You too must befriend the stranger, for you were strangers in the land of Egypt" (Deut. 10:17–19).

As Sarna points out, "Because [the stranger] could not fall back upon local family and clan ties, he lacked the social and legal protection that these ordinarily afforded. Being dependent on the goodwill of others, he could easily fall victim to discrimination and exploitation."[9] They were easy victims of economic exploitation, the deprivation of property, or denial of legal rights. Therefore, the Torah provides for their protection.

Tigay, noting the many times this idea is expressed in the Torah, states, "Concern for the protection of strangers was not nearly so common elsewhere in the ancient Near East. The only passages I have noted are in the Egyptian wisdom text Amenemopet, chap. 28."[10]

The Torah prohibits the stranger from doing things that would render the land unclean, including the worship of idols. It permits him to participate in some acts of worship of YHVH if he so desires but does not require him to do so. Above all, it protects him and helps him when needy.[11] As mentioned above, the Torah itself ascribes this sensitivity to the alien to the fact that the Israelites themselves had been aliens in Egypt and therefore know from bitter experience what it means to be a stranger: "When a stranger resides with you in your land, you shall not wrong him. The stranger who resides with you shall be to you as one of your citizens; you shall love him as yourself, for you were strangers in the land of Egypt: I YHVH am your God" (Lev. 19:33–34). This remarkable passage goes beyond law in requiring the Israelite to refrain from any wrong, that is, economic exploitation, to the stranger, by also demanding that just as you must act lovingly to your fellow (Lev. 19:18), so you must act lovingly to the stranger—both because you have experienced exactly the opposite in Egypt and because God commands it. The experience of Egypt served to sensitize Israelites to the plight of the stranger and taught them not to treat the stranger as they had been treated. But the ideological basis that made this possible was the teaching embodied in the story of creation— that all human beings are brothers, the children of one human father and mother as well as the children of one God.

Israel's Humble Origins

These vulnerable groups—the stranger, the widow, the orphan, the poor— are all under God's special protection. The reasons for their care were also summed up in these verses as well as elsewhere: the experience of being a helpless stranger in Egypt should cause you to care for the stranger in your midst. Israel was not ashamed of its humble origins as wanderers and slaves. On the contrary, each person bringing his first fruits to God had to declare:

> My father was a fugitive Aramean. He went down to Egypt with meager numbers and sojourned there; but there he became a

great and very populous nation. The Egyptians dealt harshly with us and oppressed us; they imposed heavy labor upon us. We cried to YHVH, the God of our fathers, and YHVH heard our plea and saw our plight, our misery, and our oppression. YHVH freed us from Egypt by a mighty hand.

(*Deut. 26:5–8*)

These verses later were incorporated into the Passover Haggadah as well. This experience of misery and oppression as strangers in a strange land form the very basis for sensitive treatment of strangers and those in need. Israel's ethical treatment of others is a direct result of its own suffering.

In matters of justice, Exodus similarly warns Israel, "Do not subvert the rights of your needy in their disputes" (Exod. 23:6). The Torah also emphasizes that God heeds the cry of the widow and the orphan as well as the cry of the poor; God is compassionate and has no tolerance for injustice. In the words of Nahum Sarna, "Social evil is thus a sin against humanity and God."[12]

As the philosopher of post-Holocaust Judaism Emil Fackenheim writes, "But who except Jews (and following them, Christians) has ever heard of a God loving widows and orphans? A God (or gods) loving heroes, sages, and martyrs one has heard of. All these, however—the martyrs included—are winners. Widows and orphans, in contrast, are losers ... the stranger is the third in the trinity of losers, beloved of the God of Israel."[13]

In Deuteronomy, beginning with chapter 19, Moses presents the people of Israel with a lengthy series of laws that they are to follow when they enter the Land of Canaan. Some reiterate laws previously stated; some are new. Several concern proper treatment of the needy and are phrased with more than simple legal terminology. Rather, they demonstrate a deep and passionate concern for the underprivileged in society. Because Deuteronomy is generally considered to be a work that was basically edited during the latter days of the kingdom, in the seventh century BCE or even later,[14] when society had become much more complex and polarized into haves and have-nots, the rhetoric of the book very likely reflects this prophetic concern.

The Prohibition Against Taking Interest

The Torah makes a differentiation concerning foreigners in regard to taking interest on loans. Taking interest from "your brother" is prohibited in Leviticus 25:36 and in Deuteronomy 23:20, where the law specifies that "you may deduct interest from loans to foreigners" (Deut. 23:21). Here, the word for "foreigner" is not *ger* but *nochri*. The distinction between the two is that the *ger* is a resident, dwelling in the land, while the *nochri* is a foreigner who is only temporarily there. Because the *ger* is not specifically mentioned, we can assume that interest was not to be taken from him. The *nochri*-foreigner, on the other hand, is not part of the society and therefore does not benefit from the general financial and welfare regulations of the Israelite way of life. Ezekiel, in proposing laws for the postexilic community, seems to have condemned taking interest from anyone (Ezek. 18:8,18:13,18:17).[15]

The prohibition against taking interest first found in Exodus 22:24 is repeated in Deuteronomy 23:20, "You shall not require interest from loans to your countrymen." The rule concludes, "so that YHVH may bless you in all your undertakings in the land that you are about to enter and possess" (Deut. 23:21). Though it may seem difficult to lend money and not receive anything back except the original sum, God will compensate you for that by giving you a great blessing.

Although Greek philosophers opposed interest and in early Rome it was sometimes forbidden,[16] this complete prohibition against taking interest "whether in money or food or anything else that can be deducted as interest" (Deut. 23:20) is unique to the Torah. Mesopotamian law specifies interest with rates as high as 33 percent.[17] Taking a pledge was permitted; however, even there sensitivity was to be shown: "If he is a needy man, you shall not go to sleep in his pledge; you must return the pledge to him at sundown, that he may sleep in his cloth and bless you" (Deut. 24:12–13). Again, a blessing will come to those who treat the needy well. That taking a garment actually occurred is seen in the references to it in Proverbs 20:16 and 27:13 and in Job 22:6, as well as in the prophet Amos's denunciation of the activity: "They recline by every altar in garments taken in pledge" (2:8).

The prohibition against taking interest was suitable for an agricultural society, but less so for one that reflected the commerce of an urban society. Nevertheless, Deuteronomy makes no concessions on this matter, something that later Jewish law had to take into account.

Deuteronomy repeats a labor regulation appearing in Leviticus 19:13 that requires payment of wages on the very same day that the work takes place and adds that it must be done before sunset, applying it specifically to "a needy and destitute laborer." In this regulation, as in many others on similar subjects in Deuteronomy, God's passionate concern for the underprivileged breaks out of the legal formulation in startling force: "You shall not abuse a needy and destitute laborer, whether a fellow countryman or a stranger in one of the communities of your land … for he is needy and urgently depends on it; else he will cry to YHVH against you and you will incur guilt!" (Deut. 24:14–15).

Deuteronomy requires the judicial system to protect the rights of the stranger. Moses relates that when he appointed heads for the groups of Israelites in the desert, he specifically commanded them to "decide justly between any man and a fellow Israelite or a stranger" (Deut. 1:16). Deuteronomy 24:17 teaches, "You shall not subvert the rights of the stranger or the fatherless; you shall not take a widow's garment in pawn"—and again gives the experience of Egyptian slavery as the reason for care for these unfortunate people: "Remember that you were a slave in Egypt and that YHVH your God redeemed you from there; therefore do I enjoin you to observe this commandment" (Deut. 24:18).

Deuteronomy also requires that every third year of the seven-year cycle of sabbatical years, tithes be given for the benefit of "the Levite, who has no hereditary portion as you have, and the stranger, the fatherless; and the widow," who will then "come and eat their fill, so that YHVH your God may bless you in all the enterprises you undertake" (Deut. 14:29). This command is repeated in Deuteronomy 26:12, together with a declaration that the giver is to make a declaration "before YHVH your God," probably meaning at the Temple in Jerusalem, although the tithe itself will already have been offered at his hometown. The declaration attests that he has followed all the commandments and has given the tithe "to the Levite, the stranger, the fatherless, and the widow, just as You commanded me" (Deut. 26:13). As discussed in chapter 11, these tithes were a kind of tax paid by each landowning farmer for the welfare of those in need, those without their own land. In addition to receiving these tithes, the needy were specifically granted the right to eat produce that grew freely during the seventh year, the sabbatical year (Exod. 23:10–11).

Deuteronomy also warns Israel not to refrain from lending money to the needy when the seventh year is near, given that in the seventh year all debts were forgiven. In an exhortation that cannot be legally enforced but appeals to the conscience of each person, Moses says to the Israelites, "Do not harden your heart and shut your hand against your needy kinsman. Rather, you must open your hand and lend him sufficient for whatever he needs.... Give to him readily and have no regrets when you do so, for in return YHVH your God will bless you.... For there will never cease to be needy ones in your land, which is why I command you: open your hand to the poor and needy kinsman in your land" (Deut. 15:7–11).

Concern for the Needy in Biblical Books

The Torah's profound concern for the needy—those Victor Hugo called *les misérables*—made an indelible impact on Israelite society and was echoed repeatedly in later books of the Bible as well. In the psalms, many of which were recited in the Temple itself, God is described as one who "secures justice for those who are wronged, gives food to the hungry ... makes those who are bent stand upright ... watches over the stranger, gives courage to the orphan and widow" (Ps. 146:7–9). In Psalm 35:10, God is the one who saves "the poor from one stronger than he, the poor and needy from his despoiler." A wicked man is described there as someone who "was not minded to act kindly, and hounded to death the poor and needy man, one crushed in spirit" (Ps. 109:16). Similarly, in Psalm 82:3–4 we read, "Judge the wretched and the orphan, vindicate the lowly and the poor, rescue the wretched and the needy; save them from the hand of the wicked." Of particular significance is Psalm 94, in which the psalmist, sounding more like a prophet than a poet, addresses God directly, asking how long God will suffer the wicked to flaunt their arrogant ways (vv. 1–4). "They crush Your people, O YHVH, they afflict Your very own; they kill the widow and the stranger; they murder the fatherless" (vv. 5–6). The widow, the orphan, and the stranger are once again singled out as those needing God's protection; here, however, the enemy is not some foreign nation but the wicked within the community of Israel itself! The psalm concludes with an assertion of faith that "YHVH our God will annihilate them" (v. 23).

Another book of wisdom literature, Proverbs, reiterates these same themes, repeating the Torah's assertion that God takes a special interest in the needy and will defend them against their oppressors: "Do not rob the wretched because he is wretched; do not crush the poor man in the gate; for YHVH will take up their cause and despoil those who despoil them of life (Prov. 22:22–23). Similarly, in Proverbs 23:10–11, we are warned, "Do not encroach upon the field of orphans, for they have a mighty Kinsman, and He will surely take up their cause with you."

Did the people of Israel and the aristocracy of the monarchy and the wealthy that arose in the kingdoms of Israel and Judah from the time of David onward observe the Torah's laws and adjurations to protect the needy and weak in their societies? Did the rise of a more urbanized and sophisticated society also bring with it the disintegration of the morality that Moses had taught, the dream of a classless society in which the care of the needy was a central pillar of its morality? It would seem so. The proof is found in the words of the classical prophets, who warned of the fall of Israel and Judah because of their sins. As we have seen, they emphasized moral transgressions over ritual ones, and among those moral transgressions they singled out oppression of the poor, the widow and orphan, and the stranger as a primary cause of the coming calamity.

In the eighth century BCE, Amos, prophesying the doom of the northern kingdom, Israel, castigated the society and its rulers "because they have sold for silver those whose cause was just, and the needy for a pair of sandals. Ah! You who trample the heads of the poor into the dust of the ground and make the humble walk a twisted course" (Amos 2:6–7): "You who devour the needy, annihilating the poor of the land" (Amos 8:4); those who say, "We will buy the poor for silver, the needy for a pair of sandals" (Amos 8:6). Another one of their sins was to "impose a tax on the poor and exact from him a levy of grain" (Amos 5:11). As Yehezkel Kaufmann remarks, Amos is the first prophet to point to these everyday social sins as the decisive factor in national destiny and to make it clear that it was the ruling class that was involved.[18]

Amos describes an all too distressingly familiar society of wealth and decadence in which the upper classes indulge themselves in luxurious homes, drinking, and carousing, all the while oppressing the poor. The gap between the rich and the poor is enormous, a situation that is one of today's greatest social problems, particularly acute in both America and Israel. This gap is also found today between nations—the haves and the have-nots, creating a situation that in the long run is no more sustainable today than it was when Amos described it.

Other prophets followed Amos's path. Second Isaiah also blamed the ruling classes for their corruption and their oppression of the downtrodden. What must be done to regain God's favor is "to share your bread with the hungry, and to take the wretched poor into your home; when you see the naked, to clothe them, and not to ignore your own flesh" (Isa. 58:5–7).

Jeremiah, living at the time of the Babylonian conquest, denounced Judean society as a whole for lack of justice. The people will be saved only "if you execute justice between one man and another; if you do not oppress the stranger, the orphan, and the widow; if you do not shed the blood of the innocent in this place; if you do not follow other gods" (Jer. 7:5–6).

Ezekiel, living among the exiles in Babylonia, blamed the destruction on the fact that they "did not support the poor and the needy" (Ezek. 16:49). His definition of a righteous man includes "if he has given bread to the hungry and clothed the naked; if he has not lent at advance interest or exacted accrued interest" (Ezek. 18:7–8); the wicked, Ezekiel admonishes, "has wronged the poor and the needy ... has lent at advance interest, or exacted accrued interest" (Ezek. 18:12–13).

Zechariah, who prophesied to the returnees to Zion, warned them not to act as their ancestors had, conduct that brought about the exile: "Do not defraud the widow, the orphan, the stranger, and the poor" (Zech. 7:10).

Exactly how corrupt were the ancient societies in which the prophets spoke? It may be, as Kaufmann contends, that there was a certain amount of exaggeration in these accusations and that Israel and Judah were no worse in their treatment of the poor than were other societies, including Babylon. "Nothing suggests that the extent of Judah's corruption was abnormal; it was surely no more than its conqueror."[19] Yet for the prophets, Israel's existence was not to be measured by what others did, but by how faithful Israel was to the terms of its covenant with God, the first and foremost measure of which was social justice. "The things that horrified the prophets are even now daily occurrences all over the world.... Prophecy is the voice that God has lent to the silent agony, a voice to the plundered poor.... In the prophet's message nothing that has bearing upon good and evil is small or trite in the eyes of God."[20]

The Torah's concern with the weaker members of society has left an abiding mark on Jewish life and the formulation of the Jewish community to this day. It is not accidental that at the Sabbath table, Proverbs 31, praising the woman of valor, is read aloud. It includes the words "She gives generously to the poor; her hands are stretched out to the needy" (v. 20). During the time of the Mishnah, the Jewish community made provisions for the poor such as the *tamchuy*, a kind of soup kitchen where food was distributed daily to the needy. In *Mishnah Pesachim* 10:1, we read that for Passover everyone must have four cups of wine for the seder, "even if he receives it from the *tamchuy*." No one would starve in a Jewish community unless the community was completely without resources. No one would have to steal a piece of bread to avoid starvation, as did Victor Hugo's Jean Valjean in *Les Misérables*. No one would spend years in a debtors' prison for nonpayment of debt, as Charles Dickens described in his work of social protest, *Little Dorrit*.

In the Middle Ages, Maimonides, or Rambam, taught that there are eight degrees of charity. They range from one who gives grudgingly to one who "assists a poor Jew by providing him with a gift or loan or by accepting him into a business partnership or by helping him find employment—in a word, by putting him where he can dispense with other people's aid."

In their book about life in the European shtetl—the Eastern European little town that existed until the Holocaust—anthropologists

Mark Zborowski and Elizabeth Herzog describe the way in which charity played a major role:

> Life in the shtetl begins and ends with tsdokeh [charity]. When a child is born, the father pledges a certain amount of money for distribution to the poor. At a funeral the mourners distribute coins to the beggars who swarm the cemetery, chanting "Tsdokeh will save from death."
>
> At every turn during one's life, the reminder to give is present. At the circumcision ceremony, the boy consecrated to the Covenant is specifically dedicated to good deeds. Each celebration, every holiday is accompanied by gifts to the needy. Each house has its round tin box into which coins are dropped for the support of various good works.... Before lighting the Sabbath candles, the housewife drops a coin into one of the boxes.... Children are trained to the habit of giving.... The "social justice" of the shtetl is not wholly voluntary and not wholly individual ... it is firmly woven into the organization of the community.[21]

In one of Moses's discourses mentioned above (Deut. 15:4–11), there is the strange anomaly of his beginning with the assertion that "there shall be no needy among you" because YHVH will bless the Israelites in their land *if*—and what a big "if" it is—they will follow God's ways; he concludes by telling them how to help the needy, "for there will never cease to be needy ones in your land." The utopia that Moses would like to create, where "there shall be no needy among you," is unattainable. It gives way to the reality of a world in which "there will never cease to be needy ones in your land." Realistically speaking, we can hope for the elimination of poverty but must do everything possible to deal with the reality of it. In this manner, we can at least say that we have not ignored those in need but have provided for them and, following the Rambam, have done what we can to make them able to sustain themselves.

In the end, every nation and every people will be judged by the way in which it treats those who are in need of help and protection.

Does it throw them away onto the dust heap, or does it help them to raise themselves, "lifting up those who are cast down"?

The Torah's position is very clear. A society that does not care for those who are in need violates the will of God, who hears their cry and whose special care and protection are extended to them.

14

A Day of Rest for All

Revolutionary Truth #14: The Sabbath day, the institution of a day of rest for all—servants and animals included—is a radical social concept. Everyone is entitled to that most elementary thing—time off.

> And God blessed the seventh day and declared it holy, because on it God ceased from all the work of creation that He had done.
>
> *Genesis 2:3*

> Remember the Sabbath day and keep it holy. Six days you shall labor and do all your work, but the seventh day is a Sabbath of YHVH your God: you shall not do any work—you, your son and daughter, your male and female slave, or your cattle, or the stranger who is within your settlements.
>
> *Exodus 20:8–10*

> After the six days of creation, what did the universe still lack? Rest. Came the Sabbath, came rest and the universe was complete.
>
> *Rashi,* Megillah *9a*

The institution of the Sabbath, the weekly seventh day of cessation from labor, a day of rest for all humans, free or slave, and for animals as well, is one of the most radical and revolutionary institutions initiated by the Torah. Never had such a day existed before. Many societies had special days for religious rituals, or market days when most other activities ceased, but none had a regularly scheduled weekly day of rest for all—not merely for the ruling classes or the wealthy. The Israelite seventh day was certainly not connected to market times; on the contrary, buying and selling are totally forbidden on that day.

The Seven-Day Week

The very division of the year into a series of seven-day weeks, not tied to any natural sign such as the phases of the moon, was in itself a radical innovation. Coming from the city that was the center of the worship of the moon-god, Abraham must have been familiar with various practices of setting aside the phases of the moon, especially the new moon and the full moon, for worship. This eventually found its way into the religion of Israel in the celebration of each new moon as a holy day and of the first and seventh full moons as the beginning of seven-day festivals, Passover and Sukkot. Furthermore, Abraham would also have known of seven-day periods corresponding to the phases of the moon that were regarded as unlucky because they were controlled by evil spirits.[1] But he was certainly not familiar with a seven-day rotation with no connection to the phases of the moon. Perhaps that very innovation was a part of the revolt of Israel against the deification of nature and its elements.

The Sabbath—although still unnamed—appears first in the story of creation: "On the seventh day God finished the work that He had been doing, and He rested on the seventh day from all the work that He had done. And God blessed the seventh day and declared it holy, because on it God rested from all the work of creation that He had done" (Gen. 2:2–3). As Yehezkel Kaufmann writes, "The Sabbath is the only Israelite holy day that possesses a kind of myth,"[2] in the sense of relating an event in the "life" of God. Yet, this "myth" at the same time negates the myths in other creation stories. Here God freely creates all of nature, including the moon; but nature is not God, and in so doing, God also creates a holy time, a palace in time rather than in space, to use Abraham J. Heschel's famous phrase, free of all connection to natural phenomenon.[3] There is no inherent sanctity in the day. The sanctity comes from the act of God in blessing the day. Once again myth is repudiated, and in its place comes moral considerations, a day of rest for all God's creatures.[4] In Heschel's words, "This is a radical departure from accustomed religious thinking. The mythical mind would expect that, after heaven and earth have been established, God would create a holy place—a holy mountain or a holy spring—whereupon a sanctuary is to be established. Yet it seems as if to the Bible it is holiness in time, the Sabbath, which comes first."[5]

In their interpretation of these Genesis verses, the Sages negate the mythic elements altogether:

> Is God ever weary? Does it not say, "He never grows faint and weary" (Isa. 40:28)? Rather, it is as if God had written of Himself that He created His world in six days and rested on the seventh to permit the logical inference that if God, who is never weary, had it written of Himself that He created the world in six days and rested on the seventh, how much more must human beings rest thereon![6]

Notice how this Rabbinic teaching has reinterpreted the biblical passage and turned it on its head. From the Torah, one would think that because God rested on the seventh day, humans must rest then as well. The midrash puts it the other way around: God rested—or rather was portrayed as if resting—to make certain that humans would rest on that day!

Many nations had days that they considered unlucky. The Roman ides, the middle of the month, the time of the full moon, is well known. "Beware the ides of March," the soothsayer calls to Julius Caesar in Shakespeare's play, and Caesar's wife, Calpurnia, pleads with him in vain to stay at home on that day, having seen terrible signs and portents on the eve of the ides of March. Attention has often been called to the Babylonian *shapattu*, the ides of the month, considered a day of calamity.

The name certainly suggests the Hebrew *Shabbat*, or Sabbath, but many scholars today feel that any connection is tenuous at best because that day occurred only once a month, and the seven-day phases of the moon that were taboo days were never called *shapattu*.[7] If anything, the Sabbath is the very opposite of the *shapattu* in its meaning and method of observance, indeed a repudiation of it. The notion of days of bad luck when one must refrain from doing anything was completely negated by turning this day into one of blessing and sanctity. The Sabbath is a day of rest and relaxation, a day of joy and freedom from worries, a time of positive association for the Creator and the creation. In the word of the folklore scholar Theodore Gaster, "However it may have begun, the Sabbath was developed by Judaism along entirely original lines."[8]

The Observance of the Sabbath

As we have seen, the first mention of the Sabbath occurs in the creation story (Gen. 2:1–3), where the name Shabbat does not occur, although the same Hebrew root is used in its verb form: *shavat*, meaning "to rest" or "to cease." God invests the seventh day with sanctity from the very beginning of creation, but it is not until the creation of Israel as a covenant people that its significance for human life is mentioned, nor is any observance of the day decreed until then. If it was known or observed by the patriarchs, that fact is never mentioned in the book of Genesis.[9] The first command of observance comes rather obliquely after the Exodus from Egypt in connection with the manna. The Israelites are told that "on the sixth day, when they apportion what they have brought in, it shall prove to be double the amount they gather each day" (Exod. 16:5). Only when that day actually comes does Moses reveal to them the meaning of the double portion: "This is what YHVH meant: tomorrow is a day of rest, a holy Sabbath of YHVH" (Exod. 16:23). This is the first time that the seventh day is given a name. The Israelites are told to prepare their food on the sixth day and put some aside for the Sabbath. On that day they are told, "Eat it today, for today is a Sabbath of YHVH; you will not find it today on the plain" (Exod. 16:25). When some go looking for it anyway, Moses rebukes them and commands them, "Let everyone remain where he is: let no one leave his place on the seventh day" (Exod. 16:29), placing a restriction on movement, a somewhat inauspicious debut for what is to become a day of delight. Strangely enough, the meaning and significance of the day were still not revealed.

Only when they receive the Decalogue at Mount Sinai do the Israelites learn what the Sabbath truly means and how it is to be celebrated: "Remember the Sabbath day and keep it holy. Six days you shall labor and do all your work, but the seventh day is a Sabbath of YHVH your God: you shall not do any work—you, your son or daughter, your male or female slave, or your cattle, or the stranger who is within your settlements" (Exod. 20:8–10). There is no specific definition of "work"; that came later, when the Sages defined it by connecting it to thirty-nine types of activity that were performed in the construction of the sanctuary (*Mishnah Shabbat* 7:2). Although few specifics are given in the Torah concerning what work may not be done on the Sabbath, the kindling of fire is specifically forbidden (Exod. 35:3). Rabbinic Judaism interpreted this to mean that although no fire was to be started, those kindled before the Sabbath began could continue to burn. The Karaites, a Jewish sect that did not accept Rabbinic law, disputed that and insisted on putting out all fires before the beginning of the Sabbath. To combat that, Rabbinic Judaism instituted the kindling of special lamps just before the Sabbath, Sabbath lights, with the recitation of a blessing stating that this was a commandment of God.

No reason is given for the prohibition of making fire. It cannot be that it was considered arduous work; people generally had devices for striking fire or kept a fire burning from which to light others. It may be that because fire is both creative and destructive, changing matter from one form to another, we, commemorating creation, avoid anything that is itself in the nature of creation.

Universal Rest

The free landowner or businessman could always take a day off if he so desired. The truly remarkable thing in the commandment to observe the Sabbath is that the individual is commanded not only to rest himself, but also to let all of the family as well as his slaves rest. Even cattle are to be included. Solomon Goldman remarks that "with the exception of the Jewish code, it does not appear that the useful animal ever obtained the benefit of any legal enactments. The principle of humanity to beasts of labor was never assumed on a basis of legislation in any of the national codes of the ancient world."[10] The social and ethical rationale is introduced immediately into the Sabbath commandment.

In a later reference to the Sabbath, rest for animals and nonfamily members is emphasized as being the very purpose of the day of rest: "But on the seventh day you shall cease from labor, *in order* that your ox and your ass may rest, and that your bondman and the stranger may be refreshed" (Exod. 23:12).[11] According to this verse, "you"—the landowner who controls the lives of bondmen and landless strangers as well as animals—are to cease from all labor so that they too may be refreshed. This idea of being "refreshed" is repeated in a later passage, where it is also said that on the seventh day God "rested and was refreshed" (Exod. 31:17). That idea is an echo of the Decalogue, where the command to permit all to rest is followed by the theological explanation of the day, going back to the creation story: "For in six days YHVH made heaven and earth and sea, and all that is in them, and He rested on the seventh day; therefore YHVH blessed the Sabbath day and hallowed it" (Exod. 20:11). In the Deuteronomic version of the Decalogue, the creation story is replaced with the remembrance of the Exodus: "Remember that you were a slave in the land of Egypt and YHVH your God freed you from there with a mighty hand and an outstretched arm; therefore YHVH your God has commanded you to observe the Sabbath day" (Deut. 5:15).

Jeffrey Tigay suggests that the replacement was made because of Deuteronomy's general humanistic outlook and rejection of anthropomorphisms.[12] Rather than referring to God as "resting," Deuteronomy calls our attention to the suffering of slavery and to the moral responsibility of permitting everyone to rest from slavery. Jewish tradition sees both of these themes as essential to the meaning of the Sabbath. On the one hand, it is a remembrance of creation and directs our minds to God the Creator; on the other, the Sabbath is a remembrance of the Exodus and calls our attention both to God the Redeemer and to our responsibilities to our fellow human beings. Because both the ideas of God as Creator and of God as Redeemer are central to Judaism, later tradition had no difficulty in combining these two themes. Thus, in the *Kiddush* prayer for Friday evening, the following formula is recited: "Freely and in love God has bestowed upon us His sacred Sabbath, a reminder of Creation, for it is the first of the sacred days, in remembrance of the Exodus from Egypt."

A Social Revolution

The Sabbath is both a theological symbol and a moral imperative calling for rest for all. As such, the institution of the Sabbath was an innovation in human life. It defines human beings as more than beasts of burden by outlining a pattern of life: "Six days may work be done, but on the seventh day there shall be a Sabbath of complete rest, holy to YHVH" (Exod. 31:15). Those commanded to rest include everyone—not excepting animals. This was a social revolution without precedent. The Romans considered the Sabbath to be a sign of laziness; taking time off from work and granting such a day to slaves and common laborers seemed against the norms of society.[13] The result of the Sabbath law was no less than a complete reversal of the treatment of workers and even of slaves.

Thousands of years later others followed this path of recognizing that everyone is entitled to a day of rest. Christianity moved it to Sunday (although officially it never removed the designation Sabbath from Saturday, the seventh day), and Muslims observed the rest day on Friday. As a result, even in the heyday of the industrial revolution, in places like England and later America, where workers were practically part of their machines (as Charlie Chaplin depicted them in his brilliant satire *Modern Times*), they still had one day a week to rest. The Torah has many pieces of very advanced social legislation regarding workers and their rights, such as the right to speedy payment of their wages (Lev. 19:13), but this inauguration of the weekly day of rest is undoubtedly the most radical and the most important. Furthermore, the dignity of labor is enshrined in the Sabbath commandment because the phrase "Six days you shall labor"—or, later, "Six days you shall do your work" (Exod. 23:12)—was considered to be a positive command. Labor, too, has its dignity as a part of God's plan and commands.

The Sign of the Covenant

On another level, the Sabbath is considered the sign par excellence of the covenant made between God and Israel:

> Nevertheless, you must keep My Sabbaths, for this is a sign between Me and you throughout the ages, that you may know that I, YHVH, have consecrated you.... The Israelite people shall keep the Sabbath, observing the Sabbath throughout the ages as a covenant for all time: it shall be a sign for all time between Me and the people of Israel.
>
> *(Exod. 31:13, 31:16–17)*

In addition to reminding the people of Israel of God the Creator and God the Redeemer, the Sabbath is a sign of God's revelation on Mount Sinai, where God made a covenant with Israel: they would be God's holy people, and YHVH would be their God (Exod. 19:5–6). Thus, the Sabbath is not only a piece of progressive social legislation but also a statement of Israel's covenantal relationship to God. The covenant must always be signified in some concrete fashion. The first covenant was that made between God and humanity after the flood, and the concrete sign of that covenant is the rainbow: "This is the sign that I set for the covenant between Me and you, and every living creature with you, for all ages to come. I have set My bow in the clouds, and it shall serve as a sign of the covenant between Me and the earth" (Gen. 9:12–13). The second was the covenant made between God and Abraham that his descendants would inherit the land (Gen. 15:17). It too was given a sign, male circumcision: "You shall circumcise the flesh of your foreskin, and that shall be the sign of the covenant between Me and you" (Gen. 17:11). Now the third is the Sabbath, the sign of God's covenant with all Israel.

Because of that covenantal significance, the prophets often singled out the lack of Sabbath observance as a terrible breach of the covenant with YHVH that would bring about destruction. In fact, aside from accusations that Israel worshipped false gods, it was one of the only commandments other than ethical and moral ones to be so mentioned. Jeremiah warns, "But if you do not obey My command to hallow the Sabbath day and to carry in no burdens through the gates of Jerusalem on the Sabbath day, then I will set fire to its gates; it shall consume the fortresses of Jerusalem and it shall not be extinguished" (Jer. 17:27). Ezekiel, too, rails against lack of Sabbath observance: "They grossly desecrated My Sabbaths. Then I thought to pour out My fury upon them in the wilderness and to make an end of them" (Ezek. 20:13); "You have despised My holy things and profaned My Sabbaths" (Ezek. 22:8); and "They have closed their eyes to My Sabbaths. I am profaned in their midst" (Ezek. 22:26). The exilic prophet speaking in Isaiah 58:13, who looked to the time of return, saw observance of the Sabbath as a prerequisite for God's favor: "If you refrain from trampling the Sabbath, from pursuing your affairs on My holy day; if you call the Sabbath 'delight,' YHVH's holy day 'honored'; and if you honor it and go not your ways, nor look to your affairs, nor strike bargains—then you can seek the favor of YHVH."[14]

Commerce on the Sabbath

The main complaint of these prophets has to do with the Israelites' conducting commerce on the Sabbath. The original laws of the seventh day as found in the Torah from an earlier period of time emphasize rest, doing no work, which is appropriate for a rural and agricultural society. As society became more urbanized, the desire to engage in business even on the Sabbath increased, and the beauties of a day of cessation from hard physical labor were forgotten.

In the prophets, we encounter an urban society where commerce—buying, selling, and transporting goods—is central to life and becomes the crux of Sabbath observance or desecration. No wonder, then, that when the Second Commonwealth was established after the return to Zion, observance of the Sabbath again became a matter of grave concern. Nehemiah often expresses his fear that desecration of the Sabbath could bring about another tragedy. The people take an oath that "the peoples of the land who bring their wares and all sorts of foodstuffs for sale on the Sabbath day—we will not buy from them on the Sabbath or a holy day" (Neh. 10:32). In chapter 13, Nehemiah records how he admonished people in Judah who trod on winepresses on the Sabbath or transported grain and sold provisions on it (v. 15). He continues, "What evil thing is this that you are doing, profaning the Sabbath day! This is just what your ancestors did, and for it God brought all the misfortune on this city; and now you give cause for further wrath against Israel by profaning the Sabbath!" (vv. 17–18). Nehemiah subsequently took such severe measures as closing all the gates to Jerusalem on the Sabbath "to preserve the sanctity of the Sabbath" (v. 22).

The Significance of the Sabbath Today

Although the Sabbath originated in a simple, rural society, it has perhaps even more relevance in today's highly technological and highly pressured culture. For most of us, especially city dwellers, hard physical labor is not the problem, but enslavement to possessions, to the pursuit of material ends, and to the pressures of business and competition are obstacles indeed. We have a tremendous need to withdraw from the everyday, to stop the drive toward acquisitiveness, to disengage from technology and reengage with people and with ourselves. The Sabbath provides a way of doing that. The philosopher Abraham Joshua Heschel, toward the beginning of his career, wrote about "the meaning of the Sabbath for modern man" in which he emphasized the difference between space and time: "There is a realm of time where the goal is not to have but to be, not to own but to give, not to control but to share, not to subdue but to be in accord."[15] The Sabbath is the day when we cease to conquer nature and instead appreciate the world that God has created for us, the day when we can withdraw from the daily rat race for greater power and greater wealth and delve deeper into ourselves and the significance of life, friends, and family. "The Sabbath is the day on which we learn the art of surpassing civilization."[16]

Strange as it may be, this ancient institution, which began as a way of freeing human beings from the tyranny of labor, is ideally suited to meet the needs of modern times as well. We have the need "to be refreshed." The word for this in Hebrew, *v'yinafesh*, stems from the Hebrew *nefesh*—"life" or "soul." To give ourselves more life, a reinvigorated soul, is the goal of the Sabbath.

No wonder the Rabbis called the Sabbath "a taste of the world to come."

The Legacy of Moses

Moses emerged from a world of great sophistication; a world rich in artistic achievements, in architecture, literature, and statecraft; a world filled with highly developed religious beliefs and elaborate rites of worship. He also inherited from his Mesopotamian ancestors an appreciation of simplicity, a disdain for cruelty, a love of righteousness and mercy, a dedication to "the God of our fathers," and a rejection of the world of myth. In the conflict between these two worldviews, we can see the raw material from which Moses created his new understanding of the world.

Although brought up in an Egyptian environment as a free man, perhaps even enjoying the privileges and education of the nobility, he was always aware of his brothers, the Hebrew slaves, and of their suffering. He endangered himself on their behalf and had to flee for his life. He returned to Egypt because of an overwhelming conviction that he had been chosen to be their liberator against all odds. When he succeeded, he found himself in the position of being the leader of a loose confederation of clans bound together by common memories and traditions, but lacking the laws and institutions needed for peoplehood or nationhood. His task became to create the foundations for their continued existence. The choices that he made—under divine guidance, if you will—were crucial for the future not only of the Israelites, but of humanity as a whole. Moses chose to believe in one, righteous God, in one humanity with men and women created equal, and in a society based on the principles of equality.

During the years of their wilderness journey, a journey that stretched far beyond what had been expected, Moses developed the codes that would guide the Israelites both in the wilderness and later in their own land. He taught them his view of the world, of God, and of morality, and translated these concepts into rules of conduct that were later expanded and expounded by others to meet the needs of the time. These concepts came to him as flashes of inspiration, as revelations from a divine power, YHVH, the source of all being.

To a large extent, these fundamental beliefs stood in stark opposition to the accepted truths of the ancient civilizations of Egypt and Mesopotamia and must have been difficult for many in his group to accept. These beliefs concern a new understanding of God—above nature and all forces, interacting in human history to bring about freedom and justice—of the proper worship of God, and of the demands and concerns of God. They teach a new conception of the value and purpose of human life, of the unity of humankind, and of the equality of men and women. They include the creation of a society in which there is equity in ownership of land and of wealth, a society in which rich and poor are treated equally by the law, a society free of class distinctions in which there is great care for those who are powerless. They envision a nation in which no human being has ultimate power, for rulership is invested in God alone and even the most powerful person is subject to the laws of God's morality. The concepts taught by Moses did away with magic, myth, and superstition. They invested all humans with the right to know and understand the desires of God. They taught that humans should be free, that slavery was an evil, and that humans have both free will and the responsibility to make choices in life.

Moses was nevertheless a man of his time, bound to some extent by the limited perspectives that constrain all human endeavors and by conventions of society that could not be changed overnight. Therefore the laws promulgated in *Torat Moshe* did not always fully realize the radical ideas that were expressed there. As Maimonides later explained it, even God would have found it impossible to suddenly change from one extreme to the other on many matters. Was Moses himself aware of that, or did he simply accept some of the limitations of the time? These limitations can be seen primarily in three areas:

1. Sacrifices: Sacrifices lost their original function as magical rites and sustenance for the gods, but the outer form of sacrificing animals continued.
2. Slavery: Israelite slavery was eliminated and became indentured servitude. Non-Israelite slavery continued, however, although in a modified and more humane form.
3. Women's equality: In matters of marriage, divorce, and inheritance, women did have not equal rights. This reflected the social reality of the time, in which women were dependent on men for protection and for a livelihood.

In all three areas, attempts to correct these problems have been made through Rabbinic interpretation of the Torah as well as Rabbinic innovation, but more remains to be done. Doing so would mean following the ideals of the Torah to their logical conclusion. God does not need or desire sacrifice. Human beings have the absolute right to freedom. Women are the equal of men and must not be subject to rules that deny them these rights.

To summarize, the absolute truths that formed the basis for Moses's teachings can be grouped into three categories: God, humanity, and society.

God

Moses believed in monotheism, the belief in one God who was the Creator and Sustainer of the universe. This God is the sole divine power that exists and is not subject to nature, fate, or any other outside powers. God has no physical needs, has no beginning and no end, cannot be confined to one place, and cannot be controlled or manipulated by magic or spells. No divine power of evil exists. Any physical representation of God is forbidden as a distraction from God's true being. God is just and merciful and demands that human beings be just and merciful. Ritual and worship of this God are secondary to right conduct and are meaningless without it. God does not require magnificent structures for worship any more than God requires sacrificial offerings. These means of worship are available for the benefit of human beings and to enable them to feel closer to the Divine. Organized worship can be conducted by people who have no divine powers. They merely represent God to the people and the people to God, teaching the people God's ways and blessing them in God's name.

Humanity

Human beings were created by God in the image of God. Therefore, human life is of infinite value and is inviolate. All human beings, men and women, rich and poor, free and slave, from whatever nation and of whatever race and color, are equal. Freedom is the rightful human condition. Slavery is evil, and everything must be done to alleviate and eliminate it.

Society

Society should be organized in such a way that the disparity between rich and poor is reduced as much as possible. The land itself and its resources belong not to individuals but to God and must be shared by all. No one should be allowed to fall into debt and irreversible poverty. Those who are powerless must be protected by the rules of society. Power must be shared and not concentrated in any one individual. All human beings have the right to a day of rest.

These are the self-evident, revolutionary truths that Moses taught. He was a religious reformer and a social reformer. We often picture him breaking the tablets of the Decalogue as a symbol of the broken covenant. But he also broke the tablets on which were written the beliefs of Mesopotamia and tore the pages on which were written the beliefs of Egyptian religion. His truths freed human beings from the shackles of ignorance, magic, and superstition and from the tyranny of human despots. Humans have control over their own minds, their own thoughts, and their own lives.

More than three thousand years have passed since Moses's truths were first formulated. Much has changed during that time. New understandings of science, new developments of technology, new forms of human thought and government have emerged, but human beings and human actions and human needs remain much the same.

Nor have we ever totally achieved the vision that Moses bequeathed to us. It remains as vital today as it ever was, a guide to life and a challenge to humanity. To the instruction of Moses, then, we can apply the words of Proverbs 4:2: "For I have given you good teaching, do not abandon my instruction."

Notes

Introduction: *Torat Moshe*—The Teaching of Moses

1. Solomon Schechter, *Studies in Judaism* (New York: Meridian Books, 1958), 17.
2. Jeffrey H. Tigay, *The JPS Torah Commentary: Deuteronomy* (Philadelphia: Jewish Publication Society, 1996), xxvi.
3. Reuven Hammer, *Entering Torah* (Jerusalem: Geffen Press, 2008), 7.

1. God Is Unique

1. This is translated in the New Jewish Publication Society (NJPS) version as "When God began to create the heavens and the earth," and by Everett Fox as "At the beginning of God's creating."
2. The second story of creation introduces God in a similar fashion: "Such is the story of heaven and earth when they were created. When YHVH God made heaven and earth" (Gen. 2:4).
3. By "mythology" we do not mean any story that is not factual, but stories about the lives of the gods.
4. Yehezkel Kaufmann, *The Religion of Israel*, trans. and abridged by Moshe Greenberg (Chicago: University of Chicago Press, 1960), 17.
5. Other possibilities are "I am who I am" and "I will be what I will be." See NJPS.
6. Moshe Greenberg, *Understanding Exodus* (New York: Behrman House, 1969), 83.
7. Martin Buber, *Moses* (New York: Harper Torchbooks, 1958), 52ff.
8. James B. Pritchard, ed., *The Ancient Near East: An Anthology of Text and Pictures* (Princeton, NJ: Princeton University Press, 1958), 1:31ff.; Nahum M. Sarna, *Understanding Genesis* (New York: Jewish Theological Seminary of America, 1966), 9ff.
9. Yochanan Muffs, *The Personhood of God* (Woodstock, VT: Jewish Lights Publishing, 2005), 9–10.

10. "The Bible nowhere denies the existence of the gods; it ignores them" (Kaufmann, *Religion*, 20). According to Kaufmann, by the time of the biblical age, Israel viewed paganism as no more than fetishism. Any worship of idols in Israel at that time would have been just that, with no understanding of the true nature of polytheism, which by then had been completely obliterated from Israelite religion.

11. This concept may lay behind the references to *adat el*, "the congregation of the divine," although in the religion of Israel this means not gods but angelic beings.

12. E. A. Speiser, *Genesis*, Anchor Bible Series (Garden City, NY: Doubleday and Company, 1964), xlviii.

13. Buber, *Moses*, 52ff.

14. See Kaufmann, *Religion,* 226. Pharaoh Akhenaton also considered himself a god, so it is not certain that this was even monism. In any case, it was the worship of a part of nature and as such was as pagan as any other religious belief.

15. Ibid., 227.

16. Muffs, *Personhood*, 12; Kaufmann, *Religion*, 21ff.

17. Very likely that is why when Moses asks what God's name is, God replies with a description—"I am what I am"—rather than with a name. For pagans, the knowledge of the name was the key to controlling the god by means of magic.

18. See, for example, Genesis 16:7, 19:1; Exodus 3:2.

19. This is the intent of Abraham Joshua Heschel's writings in books such as *God in Search of Man.*

20. Even though Exodus says the opposite: "And they saw the God of Israel" (Exod. 24:10–11).

21. Note that in the Babylonian myth, when the flood is over and the hero offers a sacrifice, the gods, having been deprived of food, swarm down like flies to devour it. The Torah says only that "YHVH smelled the pleasing odor" (Gen. 8:21).

22. See Maimonides, *The Guide for the Perplexed*, pt. 1, chap. 36.

23. See Muffs, *Personhood*, 1–4, 55–60.

24. Jeffrey H. Tigay, *The JPS Torah Commentary: Deuteronomy* (Philadelphia: Jewish Publication Society, 1996), 438ff.

25. Greenberg, *Understanding Exodus,* 133.

26. The Torah does not make this demand, although the story of the Exodus seems to imply it. Deuteronomy 4:19 even states that God created the heavenly bodies for other nations to worship, although forbidding it to Israel.

27. Mordecai M. Kaplan, *Judaism as a Civilization: Toward a Reconstruction of American-Jewish Life* (New York: Reconstructionist Press, 1957), pt. 5, where he discusses the idea of God.
28. Abraham Joshua Heschel, *God in Search of Man* (Philadelphia: Jewish Publication Society of America, 1956), chap. 12.
29. Muffs, *Personhood*, 4.
30. See the discussion in chapters 2 and 8.
31. See Milton Steinberg, *Anatomy of Faith* (New York: Harcourt, Brace, 1960), pt. 1.
32. Ibid., 91.

2. No Divine Power of Evil Exists

1. Yehezkel Kaufmann, *The Religion of Israel,* trans. and abridged by Moshe Greenberg (Chicago: University of Chicago Press, 1960), 23.
2. Ibid., 27.
3. Shalom M. Paul, *Isaiah 40–66* (Jerusalem: Magnes Press, 2008), 219ff.
4. Kaufmann, *Religion*, 64.
5. John Milton, *Paradise Lost*, bk. 1, lines 159ff.
6. Robert Gordis, *The Book of God and Man* (Chicago: University of Chicago Press, 1965), 71. See also pp. 216–17.
7. Archibald MacLeish, *J.B.* (Boston: Houghton Mifflin, 1956).
8. For more on the power of the evil inclination, see George Foot Moore, *Judaism* (Cambridge, MA: Harvard University Press, 1946), 1:468ff.
9. *Genesis Rabbah* 22:9.
10. See Abba Hillel Silver, *Where Judaism Differed* (New York: Macmillan, 1963), 162ff.
11. *Ecclesiastes Rabbah* to 4:13. See a full discussion of this in Milton Steinberg, *Anatomy of Faith* (New York: Harcourt, 1960), 280ff.
12. Translation of Robert Gordis, *Book of God*, 119.
13. Ibid., 133.
14. Moshe Greenberg, *Studies in the Bible and Jewish Thought* (Philadelphia: Jewish Publication Society, 1995), 352.
15. Milton Steinberg, *Anatomy of Faith*, 274ff. "Surd" in mathematics refers to an irrational number, in phonics to an unheard syllable, and in general means something that does not follow expected patterns—therefore, chance.

3. Morality Is God's Supreme Demand

1. *Genesis Rabbah* 49:18.
2. As indicated in Exodus 33:13, "Let me know Your ways, that I may know You."

3. Louis Finkelstein, *Symbols and Values: An Initial Study* (New York: Harper and Brothers, 1954), 93.
4. James B. Pritchard, ed., *Ancient Near Eastern Texts Relating to the Old Testament* (Princeton, NJ: Princeton University Press, 1955), 165.
5. Moshe Greenberg, *Studies in the Bible and Jewish Thought* (Philadelphia: Jewish Publication Society, 1995), 29.
6. Greenberg, *Studies*, 29 and 40n14.
7. Ibid., 30, 40n15.
8. See the discussion of this in chapter 5.
9. See the strict laws of evidence in *Mishnah Sanhedrin* 5.
10. Abraham Joshua Heschel, *God in Search of Man* (Philadelphia: Jewish Publication Society, 1956), 136. The italics are Heschel's.
11. Ibid., 387–88.
12. Pritchard, *Ancient Near Eastern Texts*, 104. See also Nahum M. Sarna, *Understanding Genesis* (New York: Jewish Theological Seminary of America, 1966), 50.
13. Pritchard, *Ancient Near Eastern Texts*, 93.
14. Yehezkel Kaufmann, *The Religion of Israel*, trans. and abridged by Moshe Greenberg (Chicago: University of Chicago Press, 1960), 328.
15. See Baruch A. Levine, "On the Presence of God in Biblical Religion," in *Religions in Antiquity*, ed. Jacob Neusner (Leiden, Netherlands: Brill, 1968), 79.
16. Shalom Spiegel, *Amos versus Amaziah* (New York: Jewish Theological Seminary of America, 1957), 41–43.
17. Abraham J. Heschel, *The Prophets* (Philadelphia: Jewish Publication Society, 1962), 16.
18. Kaufmann, *Religion*, 328–29.
19. *Sifra, Kedoshim* 4.

4. Worship Is for the Benefit of Humans

1. Translation suggested by Jeffrey H. Tigay, *The JPS Torah Commentary: Deuteronomy* (Philadelphia: Jewish Publication Society, 1996), 65.
2. Ibid., 48.
3. Jeroboam says of the calf the same thing the people said of Aaron's calf: "This is your god, O Israel, who brought you up from the land of Egypt!"
4. See also Numbers 11:16.
5. A few exceptions exist, such as Judges 20:27 and 1 Samuel 3.
6. Yehezkel Kaufmann, *The Religion of Israel,* trans. and abridged by Moshe Greenberg (Chicago: University of Chicago Press, 1960), 238.
7. See ibid., 110ff.

8. James B. Pritchard, ed., *Ancient Near Eastern Texts Relating to the Old Testament* (Princeton, NJ: Princeton University Press, 1955), 95.
9. Kaufmann, *Religion*, 111.
10. Maimonides, *Guide for the Perplexed,* pt. 3, chap. 32.
11. Kaufmann, *Religion*, 303.
12. Pritchard, *Ancient Near Eastern Texts*, 325.
13. Kaufmann, *Religion*, 54.
14. Shavuot, the third festival, is actually seen as the continuation and climax of the spring holiday, coming at the conclusion of seven weeks after Pesach, just as Shemini Atzeret comes after seven days of Sukkot. It was not given a historical meaning—the revelation at Sinai—until the post-biblical period.

5. Human Life Is Sacred

1. James B. Pritchard, ed., *Ancient Near Eastern Texts Relating to the Old Testament* (Princeton, NJ: Princeton University Press, 1955), 68. See also E. A. Speiser, *Genesis*, Anchor Bible Series (Garden City, NY: Doubleday, 1964), 9–11, for a detailed comparison of these ancient texts to Genesis.
2. Pritchard, *Ancient Near Eastern Texts*, 99.
3. Speiser, *Genesis*, 8.
4. Or, as Umberto Cassuto suggested, it is the "language of encouragement," prodding oneself to action. See his *Perush al Sefer Bereshit: Me-Adam ad Noach* [A Commentary on the Book of Genesis: From Adam to Noah] (Jerusalem: Magnes Press, 1953), 34.
5. Moshe Greenberg, *Studies in the Bible and Jewish Thought* (Philadelphia: Jewish Publication Society, 1995), 31–34.
6. Ibid., 32.
7. Ibid.
8. *Mekhilta, Bachodesh* 8, ed. Jacob Lauterbach (Philadelphia: Jewish Publication Society, 1949), 2:262.
9. *Leviticus Rabbah* 34:3.
10. Maimonides's *Commentary on the Mishnah, Sanhedrin* 10. These have been popularized in the hymn "Yigdal." Maimonides's ideas, including the denial of any physical form to God, were the subject of great debate.
11. Cassuto, *Perush*, 34–35.
12. Nahum M. Sarna, *Understanding Genesis* (New York: Jewish Theological Seminary of America, 1966), 15–16.
13. Elsewhere the word "image," *tzelem*, is found in reference to idols and images of false gods. Hillel's story is comparing the human being to these images.
14. Speiser, *Genesis*, 15.

15. Ibid., 18–19.
16. The creation of the human serves to explain the name *adam* as coming from the word *adamah*, "earth." This also follows ancient Near Eastern texts in which the human creature is created from clay. See Pritchard, *Ancient Near Eastern Texts*, 99, and Sarna, *Understanding Genesis*, 15.
17. Speiser, *Genesis*, 27; Pritchard, *Ancient Near Eastern Texts*, 75.
18. On the evil urge and human freedom, see chapter 8.
19. Romans 5:19.
20. See Abba Hillel Silver, *Where Judaism Differed* (New York: Macmillan, 1963), chap. 10.
21. Leo Baeck, *Judaism and Christianity* (Philadelphia: Jewish Publication Society, 1958), 244.

6. All Human Beings Are Equal

1. Based on the translation of Everett Fox in *The Five Books of Moses* (New York: Schocken Books, 1995).
2. The Hebrew word *adam* is both the name of the first man and a word that means "a man" or "a person."
3. Moshe Greenberg, *Studies in the Bible and Jewish Thought* (Philadelphia: Jewish Publication Society, 1995), 373.
4. Ibid., 371.
5. See Jacob Lauterbach, "The Attitude of the Jew toward the Non-Jew," in *Central Conference of American Rabbis Yearbook* 31, ed. Isaac E. Maruson (Cincinnati: Central Conference of American Rabbis, 1921), 193.
6. See Louis Ginzberg, *The Legends of the Jews* (Philadelphia: Jewish Publication Society, 1909), 1:54–55, and (1925), 5:15–16.
7. Whether they are Israelites is a matter of dispute among biblical scholars, both ancient and modern.
8. See Nahum M. Sarna, *The JPS Torah Commentary: Genesis* (Philadelphia: Jewish Publication Society, 1989), 66.
9. Greenberg, *Studies*, 388–90.
10. See chapter 13 for a full discussion of the treatment of the stranger.
11. *Beit HaBechirah, Avodah Zarah* 20.
12. Lauterbach, "Attitude," 185.
13. Eliezer Schweid, *Democracy and Halakhah* (Lanham, MD: University Press of America, 2002), 66.
14. Lauterbach, "Attitude," 222.
15. *Tanna d'vei Eliyahu* 9.
16. *Sifra, Kedoshim* 4.
17. *Sefer HaBerit*, cited by Greenberg, *Studies*, 387.

18. Henry Alonzo Myers, *Are Men Equal? An Inquiry into the Meaning of American Democracy* (Ithaca, NY: Cornell University Press, 1945), 35.
19. Ibid., 16.

7. Men and Women Are Equal

1. Translation of Everett Fox in *The Five Books of Moses* (New York: Schocken Books, 1995).
2. *Genesis Rabbah* 8:1. This midrash may be an attempt to unite the two creation stories: the first, saying that male and female were created together, represents the creation of one creature with two facets; the second story, the creation of Eve from Adam, represents the next stage, separation into two creatures.
3. Nahum M. Sarna, *The JPS Torah Commentary: Genesis* (Philadelphia: Jewish Publication Society, 1989), 13.
4. See chapter 5 for a discussion of these two sources.
5. James B. Pritchard, ed., *The Ancient Near East: An Anthology of Text and Pictures* (Princeton, NJ: Princeton University Press, 1958), 99.
6. Martin Luther, *Table-Talk*, no. 727.
7. Italics mine.
8. Or possibly "the woman of torches," that is, the woman who is the torch lighting the way to victory.
9. Tikva Frymer-Kensky, "Virginity in the Bible," in *Gender and Law in the Hebrew Bible and the Ancient Near East*, ed. Victor H. Matthews, Bernard M. Levinson, and Tikva Frymer-Kensky (London: Sheffield Academic Press, 1998), 86ff.
10. For a thorough discussion that concludes Dinah did not consent, see S. David Sperling, "Dinah, 'Innah, and Related Matters," in *Mishneh Torah*, ed. Nili S. Fox, David A. Glatt-Gilad, and Michael J. Williams (Winona Lake, IN: Eisenbrauns, 2008).
11. Hillel I. Millgram, *Four Biblical Heroines and the Case for Female Authorship* (Jefferson, NC: McFarland, 2008).
12. Benjamin Segal, *The Song of Songs: A Woman in Love* (Jerusalem: Gefen, 2009), 166–67.
13. Tikva Frymer-Kensky, *Reading the Women of the Bible* (New York: Schocken Books, 2002), xvi.
14. There is a similar reference to such women in 1 Samuel 2:22.
15. Meyer Gruber, *The Motherhood of God and Other Studies* (Atlanta: Scholars Press, 1992), 62.
16. Ibid., 66.
17. Eckart Otto, "False Weights in the Scales of Biblical Justice?" in Matthews et al., *Gender and Law*, 129, 143.

18. Frymer-Kensky, *Reading the Women*, xv.
19. See, for example, Harold C. Washington, "'Lest He Die in Battle and Another Man Take Her': Violence and the Construction of Gender in the Laws of Deuteronomy 20–22," in Matthews et al., *Gender and Law*, 195.
20. Frymer-Kensky, *Reading the Women*, 79ff.
21. Ibid., 84.
22. Victor H. Matthews, "Honor and Shame in Gender-Related Legal Situations in the Hebrew Bible," in Matthews et al., *Gender and Law*, 108.
23. See Adele Berlin, "Sex and the Single Girl in Deuteronomy 22," in Fox et al., *Mishneh Torah*, 95ff.
24. Frymer-Kensky, *Reading the Women*, 95.
25. Otto, "False Weights," in Matthews et al., *Gender and the Law*, 135.
26. Ibid., 133.
27. Ibid., 139–40.
28. Jeffrey Tigay's position on this is that they may have been discussing different cases and that Exodus may have intended to include women as well. See Jeffrey H. Tigay, *The JPS Torah Commentary: Deuteronomy* (Philadelphia: Jewish Publication Society, 1996), 148.
29. Carolyn Pressler, "Wives and Daughters, Bond and Free," in Matthews et al., *Gender and Law*, 157–161.
30. See Jacob Milgrom, *The JPS Torah Commentary: Numbers* (Philadelphia: Jewish Publication Society, 1990), 347–48.
31. See the discussion in Victor H. Matthews, "Honor and Shame," in Matthews et al., *Gender and Law*, 102ff.
32. Judith Hauptman, *Rereading the Rabbis: A Woman's Voice* (Boulder, CO: Westview Press, 1998), 18.
33. Ibid., 67. See also p. 74, where Hauptman states that marriage underwent a radical change in the Rabbinic period, conferring more rights and benefits upon both women and men, thereby changing marriage from chattel into a negotiated relationship.
34. Tigay, *JPS Torah Commentary: Deuteronomy*, 221.
35. See the discussion in Hauptman, *Rereading the Rabbis*, 116ff.
36. Ibid., 4.
37. Milgrom, *JPS Torah Commentary: Numbers*, 482.
38. Otto, "False Weights," 140.

8. Human Beings Have Free Will

1. Philo, "On the Unchangeableness of God," in *The Works of Philo Judaeus*, trans. from the Greek by Charles Duke Yonge (London: H. G. Bohn, 1854–90), 46–50.

2. William Shakespeare, *Hamlet* (New Haven: Yale University Press, 1947), 159.

3. Sophocles, *Oedipus the King*, in *The Complete Greek Tragedies*, vol. 2, ed. David Grene and Richard Lattimore (Chicago: University of Chicago Press, 1992), 41.

4. Ibid., 45.

5. Ibid., 46.

6. Yehezkel Kaufmann, *The Religion of Israel*, trans. and abridged by Moshe Greenberg (Chicago: University of Chicago Press, 1960), 33.

7. Abraham J. Heschel, *Who Is Man?* (Stanford, CA: Stanford University Press, 1965), 9.

8. Quoted in Walter Isaacson, *Einstein* (New York: Simon and Schuster, 2007), 387.

9. Ibid., 391.

10. Ibid., 392.

11. See Abba Hillel Silver, *Where Judaism Differed* (New York: Macmillan, 1963), 243–53.

12. Viktor Frankl, *The Will to Meaning: Foundations and Applications of Logotherapy* (New York: World Publishing, 1969), 16.

13. Kaufmann, *Religion*, 293.

14. *Genesis Rabbah* 53:18.

15. Kaufmann, *Religion*, 295.

16. *Genesis Rabbah* 9:7.

17. See the discussion in Milton Steinberg's *Anatomy of Faith* (New York: Harcourt, Brace, 1960), 193: "The ancient rabbis ... never minimized the *yezer ha-ra*. It was compared to 'the old, stupid king' of Ecclesiastes, while the *yezer ha-tov*—the good inclination—is but a needy, though wise, child (*Kohelet Rabbah* 4:13)."

18. Kaufmann, *Religion*, 329.

19. Louis Jacobs, *Religion and the Individual* (Cambridge: Cambridge University Press, 1992), 79.

20. Louis Jacobs, *A Jewish Theology* (London: Darton, Longman and Todd, 1973), 78–79. See also Jacob B. Agus, *The Evolution of Jewish Thought* (London: Abelard-Schuman, 1959), 224, 403ff.

21. See George Foot Moore, *Judaism* (Cambridge, MA: Harvard University Press, 1946), 1:454ff.

22. See a full discussion in Jacobs, *A Jewish Theology*, 72–80.

23. See Jacobs, *Religion*, 79–80.

24. Moshe Greenberg, *Understanding Exodus* (New York: Behrman House, 1969), 182.

25. *Collected Works of Abraham Lincoln*, ed. Roy P. Basler (New Brunswick, NJ: Rutgers University Press, 1953), 5:404.
26. Nahum M. Sarna, *The JPS Torah Commentary: Exodus* (Philadelphia: Jewish Publication Society, 1991), 21.
27. Greenberg, *Understanding Exodus*, 182.
28. Brevard S. Childs, in *The Book of Exodus* (Philadelphia: Westminster Press, 1974), 174, comes to the conclusion that "all attempts to relate hardness of heart to a psychological state or derive it from a theology of divine causality miss the mark. The motif of hardening in Exodus stems from a specific interpretation of the functions of signs ... which continued to fail in their purpose. Hardening was the vocabulary used by the biblical writers to describe the resistance which prevented the signs from achieving their assigned task. The motif has been consistently over-interpreted by supposing that it arose from a profoundly theological reflection and seeing it as a problem of free will and predestination."
29. Frankl, *Will to Meaning*, 73.
30. See Reuven Hammer, *Entering the High Holy Days* (Philadelphia: Jewish Publication Society, 1998), for a full discussion of these concepts.

9. Human Sovereignty Is Limited

1. In all likelihood, the monarchical system in both Israel and Judah already existed when Deuteronomy was written, even if it casts itself as being the words of Moses.
2. See Jacob Milgrom, *Leviticus 23–27*, Anchor Bible Series (New York: Doubleday, 1991), 247.
3. Michael Walzer, *Exodus and Revolution* (New York: Basic Books, 1985), 126.
4. Moshe Greenberg, *Studies in the Bible and Jewish Thought* (Philadelphia: Jewish Publication Society, 1995), 54.
5. Martin Buber, *The Kingship of God* (New York: Harper and Row, 1967), 59.
6. Moshe Greenberg, *Studies*, 54, 57.
7. See Moshe Weinfeld, *Deuteronomy and the Deuteronomic School* (Oxford: Clarendon Press, 1972), 82.
8. See Judah Goldin, *The Song at the Sea* (Philadelphia: Jewish Publication Society, 1990), 57.
9. Buber, *Kingship*, 136.
10. Weinfeld, *Deuteronomic School*, 83.
11. See also Psalms 22:29, 95:3, 96:10, 97:1, 99:1, and 99:4.
12. There are two passages in Genesis in which the patriarchs are promised that "sovereigns will emerge from you"—Genesis 17:6 and 35:11. Martin Buber believes these sections to have originated after the Davidic dynasty

was established. See his discussion of this issue in *The Kingship of God*, 40ff. The fact remains that other than in Deuteronomy, there are no laws indicating sovereigns are to be appointed at any time.

13. See Jeffrey H. Tigay, *The JPS Torah Commentary: Deuteronomy* (Philadelphia: Jewish Publication Society, 1996), xxiiff.

14. Italics mine.

15. Greenberg, *Studies*, 54.

16. In his seminal work on Deuteronomy, Moshe Weinfeld takes a different point of view. He believes that the Deuteronomist has a positive attitude toward the monarchy and that his restrictions were directed at Solomon's excesses. Weinfeld points out that the end of the section on sovereigns mentions that if the sovereign is faithful to God's teaching, then "he and his descendants may reign long in the midst of Israel"; see *Deuteronomic School*, 169. Weinfeld accepts, however, that the idea of a human sovereign was not found in the Torah or in reality before the time of Samuel and was in contradiction to the Mosaic ideal of the Sovereignty of God.

17. Greenberg, *Studies*, 59.

18. W. G. Lambert, *Babylonian Wisdom Literature* (Oxford: Clarendon Press, 1967), 112ff. J. J. Finkelstein, "Mesopotamian Historiography," *Proceedings of the American Philosophical Society* 107, no. 6 (1963): 472, points out that this document uses the terminology of omen texts, which are texts that predict what will happen based on omens. Thus, based on what has happened in the past when certain omens appear, the prince knows that these actions will have dire consequences. This seems very different from direct confrontation between a prophet and a monarch over the monarch's immoral action.

10. The Priesthood Is Divorced from Magic

1. "Although this divine Name is usually translated 'God Almighty' there are no convincing traditions as to its meaning" (Nahum Sarna, *The JPS Torah Commentary: Exodus* [Philadelphia: Jewish Publication Society, 1991], 31; see also Excursus 4, 269).

2. See the discussion of this name in chapter 1.

3. Jacob Milgrom, *The JPS Torah Commentary: Numbers* (Philadelphia: Jewish Publication Society, 1990), 343.

4. See the references cited by Milgrom, *JPS Torah Commentary: Numbers*, 341.

5. Josephus, 2.119, 1 Laws 156.

6. The relationship between the priests and the Levites and the historical development of the Levites are complicated and difficult to ascertain. For

a full treatment of the various views of the problem, see Yehezkel Kaufmann, *The Religion of Israel*, trans. and abridged by Moshe Greenberg (Chicago: University of Chicago Press, 1960), 193–200. Kaufmann's own view is that the Aaronides "are the ancient, pagan priesthood of Israel" (197), while the Levite tribe stood at Moses's side against Aaron in the matter of the Golden Calf. The Aaronides were "too venerable to be set aside, but henceforth Levi shares with them the sacred service. The Aaronides demand the exclusive privilege of serving the altar and consent to Levi's being only hierodules" (198).

7. Ibid., 239.
8. Note Aaron's complaint against Moses's exclusive powers in Numbers 12:2.
9. Kaufmann, *Religion*, 185.
10. H. H. Ben-Sasson, ed, *A History of the Jewish People* (Cambridge, MA: Harvard University Press, 1976), 191.
11. J. J. Finkelstein, "Mesopotamian Historiography," *Proceedings of the American Philosophical Society* 107, no. 6 (1963): 464–65.
12. See *Mishnah Sotah* 9:12; Talmud, *Sotah* 48b.
13. Milgrom, *JPS Torah Commentary: Numbers*, 236.
14. The strange story in Exodus 4:24–26 of Zipporah saving the life of either Moses or her son (it is not clear which) through circumcising the son is the only instance in the Torah that resembles healing through a magical rite.
15. Baruch A. Levine, *The JPS Torah Commentary: Leviticus* (Philadelphia: Jewish Publication Society, 1989), 75.
16. The story of Aaron taking incense as an emergency measure to stop a plague in Numbers 17:11–13 is the only recorded incident involving a priest in a lifesaving measure. Even there, it is basically an act of "expiation" similar to that made on behalf of the sins of the people on Yom Kippur.
17. See also 2 Chronicles 19:8–11.
18. Jeffrey H. Tigay, *The JPS Torah Commentary: Deuteronomy* (Philadelphia: Jewish Publication Society, 1996), 325.
19. See Milgrom's discussion of the blessing in *JPS Torah Commentary: Numbers*, 360ff.
20. This is stated in the Mishnah at the beginning of the tractate *Pirkei Avot*: "Moses received Torah from [God] at Sinai and transmitted it to Joshua, Joshua to the elders, the elders to the prophets, and the prophets transmitted it to the members of the Great Assembly" (*Pirkei Avot* 1:1).
21. The exception to this was women, who did not receive rabbinic authority until modern times, and then only in certain circles.

11. Land and Wealth Are to Be Distributed Equally

1. Baruch A. Levine, *The JPS Torah Commentary: Leviticus* (Philadelphia: Jewish Publication Society, 1989), 169. Levine argues that these regulations in Leviticus are later than those in Exodus or Deuteronomy and reflect the situation in Judea after the return from the Babylonian exile (270ff.). Another outstanding scholar, Jeffrey Tigay, seems to take a different approach and states that the Leviticus regulations are incompatible with those of Exodus but that "it is not clear if this system is derived from a geographical or chronological background different from that of Exodus 21 and Deuteronomy, or if it simply reflects the approach of another school of thought" (*The JPS Torah Commentary: Deuteronomy* [Philadelphia: Jewish Publication Society, 1996], 476). Regardless of when it was formulated exactly, a matter of dispute among scholars, my contention is that the basic regulations concerning land were the early work of Moses and those who interpreted his ideas when the settlement took place.
2. Moshe Greenberg, *Studies in the Bible and Jewish Thought* (Philadelphia: Jewish Publication Society, 1995), 54.
3. Levine, *JPS Torah Commentary: Leviticus*, 272.
4. Jacob Milgrom, *Leviticus 23–27*, Anchor Bible Series (New York: Doubleday, 2001), 2154, 2160.
5. Ibid., 2212.
6. Ibid., 2246.
7. Ibid., 2156. Milgrom believes that the sabbatical year of Exodus was not a fixed year. Rather, after any period of six years, the land was left fallow the seventh year, while Leviticus prescribes the same seventh year for the entire land.
8. Ibid.
9. Milgrom, *Leviticus 23–27*, 2189.
10. Neal M. Soss, "Old Testament Law and Economic Society," *Journal of the History of Ideas* 34 (1973): 339.
11. Milgrom, *Leviticus 23–27*, 2191.
12. See Levine's opinion on this, in *JPS Torah Commentary: Leviticus*, 273–74.
13. Milgrom, *Leviticus 23–27*, 2198.
14. Ibid., 2243–45.
15. Soss, "Old Testament Law," 332.
16. Tigay, *JPS Torah Commentary: Deuteronomy*, 145.
17. Milgrom, *Leviticus 23–27*, 2174.
18. See Tigay, *JPS Torah Commentary: Leviticus*, 467–68. The observance of the sabbatical year is mentioned by Josephus in *Antiquities* 11:338 and 14:202 and in the apocryphal book 1 Maccabees 6:49, 53–54.

19. See Tigay, *JPS Torah Commentary: Deuteronomy*, 145; and Milgrom, *Leviticus 23–27*, 2167.
20. See 2 Kings 12:5–17, 22:2–3; 2 Chronicles 25:5–14, 34:8–14; and Nehemiah 10:33–34.
21. See Yehezkel Kaufmann, *The Religion of Israel*, trans. and abridged by Moshe Greenberg (Chicago: University of Chicago Press, 1960), 187–193, on the various laws of tithing.
22. See Tigay, *JPS Torah Commentary: Deuteronomy*, 142–144.
23. See Kaufmann, *Religion*, 192–93.
24. Soss, "Old Testament Law," 343.
25. See Milgrom, *Leviticus 23–27*, 2271. He movingly describes his participation in a conference on the Jubilee attended by representatives of the Third World who made it their "rallying cry."

12. Slavery Must Be Mitigated

1. Catherine Hezser, *Jewish Slavery in Antiquity* (Oxford: Oxford University Press, 2005), 222.
2. Some scholars, such as E. E. Urbach, contend that after the Maccabean era there were no Jewish slaves among Jews, but there is no evidence proving that. See Urbach, "The Laws Regarding Slavery as a Source for Social History of the Period of the Second Temple, the Mishnah and Talmud," in *Papers of the Institute of Jewish Studies*, ed. J. G. Weiss (Jerusalem: Magnes Press, 1964), 1:4.
3. Hezser, *Jewish Slavery*, 2.
4. Ibid., 376.
5. Ibid., 11.
6. In *Mekhilta de-Rabbi Ishmael: A Critical Edition, Based on the Manuscripts and Early Editions, with an English Translation, Introduction, and Notes* (Philadelphia: Jewish Publication Society, 1933), 3:3n3.
7. *Mekhilta, Nezikin* 3:4.
8. Nahum M. Sarna, *Exploring Exodus* (New York: Schocken Books, 1986), 159
9. Although according to the traditional understanding he serves six years and then goes free on the seventh, as found in *Mekhilta, Nezikin* 1, some modern commentators such as Nahum Sarna and Baruch Levine believe that the release was always in the sabbatical year, regardless of when the servitude began. See Baruch A. Levine, *The JPS Torah Commentary: Leviticus* (Philadelphia: Jewish Publication Society, 1989), 271.
10. Moshe Greenberg, *Understanding Exodus* (New York: Behrman House, 1969), 181.

11. *Lekach Tov* to Exodus 21:2.
12. *Sifra, Behar* 6:1.
13. Although the text is not clear on this issue, many biblical scholars believe that this provision deals with non-Israelite slaves who run away from masters elsewhere and seek refuge in Israel. Does it also apply to Israelites? See Jeffrey Tigay, *The JPS Torah Commentary: Deuteronomy* (Philadelphia: Jewish Publication Society, 1996), 215.
14. Catherine Hezser takes this position; see Hezser, *Jewish Slavery*, 268.
15. Daniela Piattelli, "The Enfranchisement Document on behalf of the Fugitive Slave, and as Elaborated in Rabbinic Jurisprudence," in *Jewish Law Association Studies 3: The Oxford Conference Volume*, ed. A. M. Fuss (Atlanta: Scholars Press, 1987), 59.
16. Hezser, *Jewish Slavery*, 29.
17. See also Nehemiah 5:2–13.
18. Similarly, *Sifra, Behar* 2:4–5, indicates that the Jubilee laws of freeing slaves were not always followed in the Rabbinic period as well.
19. Maimonides, *Mishneh Torah, Hilkhot Avadim* 5:5.
20. *Mekhilta, Nezikin* 1. See also Talmud, *Ketubot* 96a; *Sifre, Devarim* 37.
21. *Sifra, Behar* 6:1.
22. *Tosefta, Baba Kamma* 7:5; Talmud, *Kiddushin* 22b. The word *avadim* here is often translated "servants," but the force of the verse is really "slaves."
23. Flesher interprets the original meaning of this piercing as indicating that from now on, the indentured servant "gives up his independent status, enters the purview of the householder, and becomes the latter's dependent" (Paul Virgil McCraken Flesher, *Oxen, Women, or Citizens? Slaves in the System of the Mishnah* [Atlanta: Scholars Press, 1988], 20).
24. *Mekhilta, Nezikin* 2, edition Lauterbach, 3:17.
25. Maimonides, *Mishneh Torah, Hilkhot Avadim* 3:6–7.
26. Talmud, *Kiddushin* 17b; Maimonides, *Mishneh Torah, Hilkhot Avadim* 2:12. If there is no son, the slave goes free immediately.
27. Talmud, *Kiddushin* 20a and 22a; *Sifra, Behar* 7:3.
28. This was based on an interpretation of Leviticus 25:10 in *Sifra, Behar:* "You shall proclaim release throughout the land for all its inhabitants"—"when all its inhabitants are in the land." See Talmud, *Kiddushin* 69a and *Gittin* 65a.
29. Flesher, *Oxen*, 33; Hezser, *Jewish Slavery*, 33.
30. *Mishneh Torah, Hilkhot Avadim* 1:10.
31. *Yoreh Deah, Avadim* 267. This was brought to my attention by Rabbi Charles Kraus.
32. *Mishneh Torah, Hilkhot* 9:8.
33. Ibid.

34. Ibid., 2:69.
35. See Talmud, *Baba Metzia* 7:6; Maimonides, *Mishneh Torah, Hilkhot Avadim,* 4:7.
36. Hezser, *Jewish Slavery,* 211.
37. Philo, "The Special Laws," in *The Works of Philo Judaeus,* trans. from the Greek by Charles Duke Yonge (London: H. G. Bohn, 1854–1890), bk. 2, lines 79ff.
38. Tigay, *JPS Torah Commentary: Deuteronomy,* 148.
39. Flesher, *Oxen,* 167.

13. The Needy Must Be Cared For

1. That is, if he has had to sell or mortgage his land so that he in effect is like the resident alien, a mere tenant in his own home. See Baruch A. Levine, *The JPS Torah Commentary: Leviticus* (Philadelphia: Jewish Publication Society, 1989), 178, where he notes, "It could be taken to mean that the person involved may not be evicted from his land, but must be allowed to continue to reside at your side as a member of the community."
2. See Leviticus 21 for the special regulations of the *kohanim.* See Leviticus 25:32 for laws for Levites.
3. James B. Pritchard, ed., *Ancient Near Eastern Texts Relating to the Old Testament* (Princeton, NJ: Princeton University Press, 1955), 166.
4. Ibid., 175.
5. Hammurabi in the epilogue claims that he promulgated his laws "that the strong might not oppress the weak, that justice might be dealt the orphan (and) the widow," yet the laws themselves—at least those extant—contain nothing that refers to that specifically and certainly does not contain the laws concerning the needy that the Torah does. See Pritchard, *Ancient Near Eastern Texts,* 178.
6. *Mekhilta, Nezikin* 18, iii 137. See also *Midrash HaGadol* to 22:20, which speaks to two types of wrong and two types of oppression, monetary and verbal.
7. See Numbers 9:14, 15:15, 15:29–30; Exodus 12:48–49; Leviticus 7:7, 24:22.
8. See *Mishnah Pe'ah* 1:1–2, which sets no limit to the amount that could be left in the corners.
9. Nahum M. Sarna, *The JPS Torah Commentary: Exodus* (Philadelphia: Jewish Publication Society, 1991), 138. See also Brevard S. Childs, *The Book of Exodus* (Philadelphia: Westminster Press, 1974), 478, 482.
10. Jeffrey H. Tigay, *The JPS Torah Commentary: Deuteronomy* (Philadelphia: Jewish Publication Society, 1996), 346–68.

11. See Excursus 34 in Jacob Milgrom, *The JPS Torah Commentary: Numbers* (Philadelphia: Jewish Publication Society, 1990), 398ff., for a full explanation of the status of the *ger*. See also Sarna, *JPS Torah Commentary: Exodus*, 137.

12. Sarna, *JPS Torah Commentary: Exodus*, 137.

13. Emil Fackenheim, *What Is Judaism?* (New York: Summit Books, 1987), 168.

14. See Tigay, *JPS Torah Commentary: Deuteronomy*, xxiv.

15. For a detailed discussion of usury, see Jacob Lauterbach, "The Attitude of the Jew toward the Non-Jew," in *Central Conference of American Rabbis Yearbook 31*, ed. Isaac E. Maruson (Cincinnati: Central Conference of American Rabbis, 1921), 210.

16. Ibid., 217.

17. See Sarna, *JPS Torah Commentary: Exodus*, 139.

18. Yehezkel Kaufmann, *The Religion of Israel,* trans. and abridged by Moshe Greenberg (Chicago: University of Chicago Press, 1960), 366.

19. Ibid., 402.

20. Abraham J. Heschel, *The Prophets* (Philadelphia: Jewish Publication Society, 1962), 3–5.

21. Mark Zborowski and Elizabeth Herzog, *Life Is with People* (New York: International Universities Press, 1952), 193ff.

14. A Day of Rest for All

1. Nahum M. Sarna, *Understanding Genesis* (New York: Jewish Theological Seminary of America, 1966), 20.

2. Yehezkel Kaufmann, *The Religion of Israel,* trans. and abridged by Moshe Greenberg (Chicago: University of Chicago Press, 1960), 117.

3. Abraham Joshua Heschel, *The Sabbath* (New York: Farrar, Straus and Giroux, 1951), 21.

4. Kaufmann, *Religion*, 117.

5. Heschel, *Sabbath*, 9.

6. *Mekhilta, Bachodesh* 7.

7. See Solomon Goldman, *The Ten Commandments* (Chicago: University of Chicago Press, 1956), 161–65, for a discussion of these various theories.

8. Theodore H. Gaster, *Festivals of the Jewish Year* (New York: William Sloan, 1953), 267.

9. Rabbinic midrash assumes that they observed it, as it anachronistically sees them as observing many of the commandments of the Torah, but this has no historical significance. The midrash even has Adam and Eve observing the Sabbath on their first day of exile from the Garden of Eden (*Avot D'Rabbi Natan A*).

10. Goldman, *Ten Commandments*, 168.

11. Italics mine. See also Deuteronomy 5:14, "so that your male and female slave may rest as you do."

12. See Jeffrey H. Tigay, *The JPS Torah Commentary: Deuteronomy* (Philadelphia: Jewish Publication Society, 1996), xiii, 69.

13. "The Sabbath is a sign of Jewish indolence, was the opinion held by Juvenal, Seneca and others" (Heschel, *Sabbath*, 13).

14. See also Amos 8:5, where they cannot wait for the Sabbath to be over so they can engage in dishonest business practices.

15. Heschel, *Sabbath*, 3.

16. Ibid., 27.

Bibliography

Buber, Martin. *Kingship of God.* New York: Harper and Row, 1967.

———. *Moses: The Revelation and the Covenant.* New York: Harper Torchbooks, 1958.

Cassuto, Umberto. *Perush al Sefer Bereshit: Me-Adam ad Noach* [A Commentary on the Book of Genesis: From Adam to Noah]. Jerusalem: Magnes Press, 1953.

Childs, Brevard S. *The Book of Exodus.* Philadelphia: Westminster Press, 1974.

Fackenheim, Emil. *What Is Judaism?* New York: Summit Books, 1987.

Finkelstein, J. J. "Mesopotamian Historiography." *Proceedings of the American Philosophical Society* 107, no. 6 (1963): 461–72.

Finkelstein, Louis, ed. *Symbols and Values: An Initial Study.* New York: Harper and Brothers, 1954.

Flesher, Paul Virgil McCraken. *Oxen, Women, or Citizens? Slaves in the System of the Mishnah.* Atlanta: Scholars Press, 1988.

Fox, Everett. *The Five Books of Moses.* New York: Schocken Books, 1995.

Fox, Nili S., David A. Glatt-Gilad, and Michael J. Williams. *Mishneh Todah: Studies in Deuteronomy and the Cultural Environment in Honor of Jeffrey H. Tigay.* Winona Lake, IN: Eisenbrauns, 2008.

Frankl, Viktor. *The Will to Meaning: Foundations and Applications of Logotherapy.* New York: World Publishing, 1969.

Frymer-Kensky, Tikva. *Reading the Women of the Bible.* New York: Schocken Books, 2002.

———. "Virginity in the Bible." In *Gender and Law in the Hebrew Bible and the Ancient Near East,* edited by Victor H. Matthews et al. 79–96. Sheffield, England: Sheffield Academic Press, 1998.

Gaster, Theodore H. *Festivals of the Jewish Year.* New York: William Sloan, 1953.

Goldman, Solomon. *The Ten Commandments.* Chicago: University of Chicago Press, 1956.

Gordis, Robert. *The Book of God and Man.* Chicago: University of Chicago Press, 1965.

Greenberg, Moshe. *Studies in the Bible and Jewish Thought.* Philadelphia: Jewish Publication Society, 1995.

———. *Understanding Exodus.* New York: Behrman House, 1969.

Gruber, Meyer. *The Motherhood of God and Other Studies.* Atlanta: Scholars Press, 1992.

Hauptman, Judith. *Rereading the Rabbis: A Woman's Voice.* Boulder, CO: Westview Press, 1998.

Heschel, Abraham Joshua. *God in Search of Man.* Philadelphia: Jewish Publication Society, 1956.

———. *The Prophets.* Philadelphia: Jewish Publication Society, 1962.

———. *The Sabbath.* New York: Farrar, Straus and Giroux, 1951.

———. *Who Is Man?* Stanford, CA: Stanford University Press, 1965.

Hezser, Catherine. *Jewish Slavery in Antiquity.* Oxford: Oxford University Press, 2005.

Jacobs, Louis. *A Jewish Theology.* London: Darton, Longman and Todd, 1973.

———. *Religion and the Individual.* Cambridge: Cambridge University Press, 1992.

Kaplan, Mordecai M. *Judaism as a Civilization: Toward a Reconstruction of American-Jewish Life.* New York: Reconstructionist Press, 1957.

Kaufmann, Yehezkel. *The Religion of Israel.* Translated and abridged by Moshe Greenberg. Chicago: University of Chicago Press, 1960.

Lauterbach, Jacob. "The Attitude of the Jew toward the Non-Jew." In *Central Conference of American Rabbis Yearbook* 31, edited by Isaac E. Maruson, 186–233. Cincinnati: Central Conference of American Rabbis, 1921.

———. *Mekhilta de-Rabbi Ishmael: A Critical Edition, Based on the Manuscripts and Early Editions, with an English Translation, Introduction, and Notes.* Philadelphia: Jewish Publication Society, 1933.

Levine, Baruch A. *The JPS Torah Commentary: Leviticus.* Philadelphia: Jewish Publication Society, 1989.

———. "On the Presence of God in Biblical Religion." In *Religions in Antiquity: Essays in Memory of Erwin Ramsdell Goodenough*, edited by Jacob Neusner, 71–87. Leiden, The Netherlands: Brill, 1968.

MacLeish, Archibald. *J.B.* Boston: Houghton Mifflin, 1956.

Maimonides. *The Guide for the Perplexed*. New York: Dover Publications, 1956.

Matthews, Victor H., Bernard M. Levinson, and Tikva Frymer-Kensky, eds. *Gender and Law in the Hebrew Bible and the Ancient Near East*. Sheffield, England: Sheffield Academic Press, 1998.

Milgrom, Jacob. *The JPS Torah Commentary: Numbers*. Philadelphia: Jewish Publication Society, 1990.

———. *Leviticus 23–27*. The Anchor Bible Series. New York: Doubleday, 2001.

Muffs, Yochanan. *The Personhood of God*. Woodstock, VT: Jewish Lights Publishing, 2005.

Myers, Henry Alonzo. *Are Men Equal? An Inquiry into the Meaning of American Democracy*. Ithaca, NY: Cornell University Press, 1945.

Paul, Shalom M. *Isaiah 40–66*. Jerusalem: Magnes Press, 2008.

Piattelli, Daniela. "The Enfranchisement Document on Behalf of the Fugitive Slave." In *Jewish Law Association Studies 3: The Oxford Conference Volume*, edited by A. M. Fuss. Atlanta: Scholars Press, 1987.

Pritchard, James. B., ed. *The Ancient Near East: An Anthology of Text and Pictures*. Princeton, NJ: Princeton University Press, 1958.

———. *Ancient Near Eastern Texts Relating to the Old Testament*. Princeton, NJ: Princeton University Press, 1955.

Sarna, Nahum M. *Exploring Exodus*. New York: Behrman House, 1969.

———. *The JPS Torah Commentary: Exodus*. Philadelphia: Jewish Publication Society, 1991.

———. *The JPS Torah Commentary: Genesis*. Philadelphia: Jewish Publication Society, 1989.

———. *Understanding Genesis*. New York: Jewish Theological Seminary of America, 1966.

Segal, Benjamin. *The Song of Songs: A Woman in Love*. Jerusalem: Gefen, 2009.

Soss, Neal M. "Old Testament Law and Economic Society." *Journal of the History of Ideas* 34 (1973): 323–44.

Speiser, E. A. *Genesis*. The Anchor Bible Series. Garden City, NY: Doubleday, 1964.

Spiegel, Shalom. *Amos versus Amaziah*. New York: Jewish Theological Seminary of America, 1957.

Steinberg, Milton. *Anatomy of Faith*. New York: Harcourt, Brace and Company, 1960.

Tigay, Jeffrey H. *The JPS Torah Commentary: Deuteronomy*. Philadelphia: Jewish Publication Society, 1996.

Urbach, E. E. "The Laws Regarding Slavery as a Source for Social History of the Period of the Second Temple, the Mishnah and Talmud." In *Papers of the Institute of Jewish Studies London*, vol. 1, edited by J. G. Weiss, 1–94. Jerusalem: Magnes Press, 1964.

Walzer, Michael. *Exodus and Revolution*. New York: Basic Books, 1985.

Weinfeld, Moshe. *Deuteronomy and the Deuteronomic School*. Oxford: Clarendon Press, 1972.

Zborowski, Mark, and Elizabeth Herzog. *Life Is with People*. New York: International Universities Press, 1952.

Index

Bar/Bat Mitzvah

The Mitzvah Project Book
Making Mitzvah Part of Your Bar/Bat Mitzvah ... and Your Life
By Liz Suneby and Diane Heiman; Foreword by Rabbi Jeffrey K. Salkin; Preface by Rabbi Sharon Brous
The go-to source for Jewish young adults and their families looking to make the
world a better place through good deeds—big or small.
6 x 9, 224 pp, Quality PB Original, 978-1-58023-458-0 **$16.99** *For ages 11–13*

The JGirl's Guide: The Young Jewish Woman's Handbook for Coming of Age
By Penina Adelman, Ali Feldman and Shulamit Reinharz
6 x 9, 240 pp, Quality PB, 978-1-58023-215-9 **$14.99** *For ages 11 & up*

The JGirl's Teacher's and Parent's Guide 8½ x 11, 56 pp, PB, 978-1-58023-225-8 **$8.99**

The Bar/Bat Mitzvah Memory Book, 2nd Edition: An Album for Treasuring the
Spiritual Celebration *By Rabbi Jeffrey K. Salkin and Nina Salkin*
8 x 10, 48 pp, 2-color text, Deluxe HC, ribbon marker, 978-1-58023-263-0 **$19.99**

For Kids—Putting God on Your Guest List, 2nd Edition: How to Claim the
Spiritual Meaning of Your Bar or Bat Mitzvah *By Rabbi Jeffrey K. Salkin*
6 x 9, 144 pp, Quality PB, 978-1-58023-308-8 **$15.99** *For ages 11–13*

Putting God on the Guest List, 3rd Edition: How to Reclaim the Spiritual
Meaning of Your Child's Bar or Bat Mitzvah *By Rabbi Jeffrey K. Salkin*
6 x 9, 224 pp, Quality PB, 978-1-58023-222-7 **$16.99**; HC, 978-1-58023-260-9 **$24.99**

Putting God on the Guest List Teacher's Guide
8½ x 11, 48 pp, PB, 978-1-58023-226-5 **$8.99**

Tough Questions Jews Ask, 2nd Edition: A Young Adult's Guide to Building a Jewish Life
By Rabbi Edward Feinstein 6 x 9, 160 pp, Quality PB, 978-1-58023-454-2 **$16.99** *For ages 11 & up*

Tough Questions Jews Ask Teacher's Guide 8½ x 11, 72 pp, PB, 978-1-58023-187-9 **$8.95**

Bible Study/Midrash

Sage Tales: Wisdom and Wonder from the Rabbis of the Talmud
By Rabbi Burton L Visotzky Illustrates how the stories of the Rabbis who lived in the
first generations following the destruction of the Jerusalem Temple illuminate
modern life's most pressing issues. 6 x 9, 256 pp, HC, 978-1-58023-456-6 **$24.99**

The Modern Men's Torah Commentary: New Insights from Jewish Men on the
54 Weekly Torah Portions *Edited by Rabbi Jeffrey K. Salkin*
6 x 9, 368 pp, HC, 978-1-58023-395-8 **$24.99**

The Genesis of Leadership: What the Bible Teaches Us about Vision, Values and
Leading Change *By Rabbi Nathan Laufer; Foreword by Senator Joseph I. Lieberman*
6 x 9, 288 pp, Quality PB, 978-1-58023-352-1 **$18.99**

Hineini in Our Lives: Learning How to Respond to Others through 14 Biblical Texts and
Personal Stories *By Rabbi Norman J. Cohen, PhD* 6 x 9, 240 pp, Quality PB, 978-1-58023-274-6 **$16.99**

A Man's Responsibility: A Jewish Guide to Being a Son, a Partner in Marriage, a Father and a
Community Leader *By Rabbi Joseph B. Meszler* 6 x 9, 192 pp, Quality PB, 978-1-58023-435-1 **$16.99**

Moses and the Journey to Leadership: Timeless Lessons of Effective Management from
the Bible and Today's Leaders *By Rabbi Norman J. Cohen, PhD*
6 x 9, 240 pp, Quality PB, 978-1-58023-351-4 **$18.99**; HC, 978-1-58023-227-2 **$21.99**

Righteous Gentiles in the Hebrew Bible: Ancient Role Models for Sacred Relationships
By Rabbi Jeffrey K. Salkin; Foreword by Rabbi Harold M. Schulweis;
Preface by Phyllis Tickle 6 x 9, 192 pp, Quality PB, 978-1-58023-364-4 **$18.99**

The Wisdom of Judaism: An Introduction to the Values of the Talmud
By Rabbi Dov Peretz Elkins 6 x 9, 192 pp, Quality PB, 978-1-58023-327-9 **$16.99**

Or phone, fax, mail or e-mail to: **JEWISH LIGHTS Publishing**
Sunset Farm Offices, Route 4 • P.O. Box 237 • Woodstock, Vermont 05091
Tel: (802) 457-4000 • Fax: (802) 457-4004 • www.jewishlights.com
Credit card orders: **(800) 962-4544** (8:30AM–5:30PM ET Monday–Friday)
Generous discounts on quantity orders. SATISFACTION GUARANTEED. Prices subject to change.

Congregation Resources

Empowered Judaism: What Independent Minyanim Can Teach Us about Building Vibrant Jewish Communities
By Rabbi Elie Kaunfer; Foreword by Prof. Jonathan D. Sarna
Examines the independent minyan movement and the lessons these grassroots communities can provide. 6 x 9, 224 pp, Quality PB, 978-1-58023-412-2 **$18.99**

Spiritual Boredom: Rediscovering the Wonder of Judaism *By Dr. Erica Brown*
Breaks through the surface of spiritual boredom to find the reservoir of meaning within. 6 x 9, 208 pp, HC, 978-1-58023-405-4 **$21.99**

Building a Successful Volunteer Culture
Finding Meaning in Service in the Jewish Community
By Rabbi Charles Simon; Foreword by Shelley Lindauer; Preface by Dr. Ron Wolfson
Shows you how to develop and maintain the volunteers who are essential to the vitality of your organization and community. 6 x 9, 192 pp, Quality PB, 978-1-58023-408-5 **$16.99**

The Case for Jewish Peoplehood: Can We Be One?
By Dr. Erica Brown and Dr. Misha Galperin; Foreword by Rabbi Joseph Telushkin
6 x 9, 224 pp, HC, 978-1-58023-401-6 **$21.99**

Inspired Jewish Leadership: Practical Approaches to Building Strong Communities
By Dr. Erica Brown 6 x 9, 256 pp, HC, 978-1-58023-361-3 **$27.99**

Jewish Pastoral Care, 2nd Edition: A Practical Handbook from Traditional & Contemporary Sources *Edited by Rabbi Dayle A. Friedman, MSW, MAJCS, BCC*
6 x 9, 528 pp, Quality PB, 978-1-58023-427-6 **$30.00**

Rethinking Synagogues: A New Vocabulary for Congregational Life
By Rabbi Lawrence A. Hoffman, PhD 6 x 9, 240 pp, Quality PB, 978-1-58023-248-7 **$19.99**

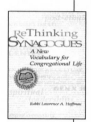

The Spirituality of Welcoming: How to Transform Your Congregation into a Sacred Community *By Dr. Ron Wolfson* 6 x 9, 224 pp, Quality PB, 978-1-58023-244-9 **$19.99**

Children's Books

Around the World in One Shabbat
Jewish People Celebrate the Sabbath Together
By Durga Yael Bernhard
Takes your child on a colorful adventure to share the many ways Jewish people celebrate Shabbat around the world.
11 x 8½, 32 pp, Full-color illus., HC, 978-1-58023-433-7 **$18.99** *For ages 3–6*

What You Will See Inside a Synagogue
By Rabbi Lawrence A. Hoffman, PhD, and Dr. Ron Wolfson; Full-color photos by Bill Aron
A colorful, fun-to-read introduction that explains the ways and whys of Jewish worship and religious life.
8¾ x 10½, 32 pp, Full-color photos, Quality PB, 978-1-59473-256-0 **$8.99** *For ages 6 & up*
(A book from SkyLight Paths, Jewish Lights' sister imprint)

Because Nothing Looks Like God
By Lawrence Kushner and Karen Kushner Introduces children to the possibilities of spiritual life. 11 x 8½, 32 pp, Full-color illus., HC, 978-1-58023-092-6 **$17.99** *For ages 4 & up*

The Book of Miracles: A Young Person's Guide to Jewish Spiritual Awareness
Written and illus. by Lawrence Kushner
6 x 9, 96 pp, 2-color illus., HC, 978-1-879045-78-1 **$16.95** *For ages 9–13*

In God's Hands *By Lawrence Kushner and Gary Schmidt* 9 x 12, 32 pp, Full-color illus., HC, 978-1-58023-224-1 **$16.99** *For ages 5 & up*

In Our Image: God's First Creatures *By Nancy Sohn Swartz*
9 x 12, 32 pp, Full-color illus., HC, 978-1-879045-99-6 **$16.95** *For ages 4 & up*

The Kids' Fun Book of Jewish Time
By Emily Sper 9 x 7½, 24 pp, Full-color illus., HC, 978-1-58023-311-8 **$16.99** *For ages 3–6*

What Makes Someone a Jew? *By Lauren Seidman*
Reflects the changing face of American Judaism.
10 x 8½, 32 pp, Full-color photos, Quality PB, 978-1-58023-321-7 **$8.99** *For ages 3–6*

Children's Books by Sandy Eisenberg Sasso

Adam & Eve's First Sunset: God's New Day
Explores fear and hope, faith and gratitude in ways that will delight kids and adults—inspiring us to bless each of God's days and nights.
9 x 12, 32 pp, Full-color illus., HC, 978-1-58023-177-0 **$17.95** *For ages 4 & up*

Also Available as a Board Book: **Adam and Eve's New Day**
5 x 5, 24 pp, Full-color illus., Board Book, 978-1-59473-205-8 **$7.99** *For ages 0–4*
(A book from SkyLight Paths, Jewish Lights' sister imprint)

But God Remembered: Stories of Women from Creation to the Promised Land
Four different stories of women—Lilith, Serach, Bityah and the Daughters of Z—teach us important values through their faith and actions.
9 x 12, 32 pp, Full-color illus., Quality PB, 978-1-58023-372-9 **$8.99** *For ages 8 & up*

Cain & Abel: Finding the Fruits of Peace
Shows children that we have the power to deal with anger in positive ways. Provides questions for kids and adults to explore together.
9 x 12, 32 pp, Full-color illus., HC, 978-1-58023-123-7 **$16.95** *For ages 5 & up*

For Heaven's Sake
Heaven is often found where you least expect it.
9 x 12, 32 pp, Full-color illus., HC, 978-1-58023-054-4 **$16.95** *For ages 4 & up*

God in Between
If you wanted to find God, where would you look? This magical, mythical tale teaches that God can be found where we are: within all of us and the relationships between us. 9 x 12, 32 pp, Full-color illus., HC, 978-1-879045-86-6 **$16.95** *For ages 4 & up*

God Said Amen
An inspiring story about hearing the answers to our prayers.
9 x 12, 32 pp, Full-color illus., HC, 978-1-58023-080-3 **$16.95** *For ages 4 & up*

God's Paintbrush: Special 10th Anniversary Edition
Wonderfully interactive, invites children of all faiths and backgrounds to encounter God through moments in their own lives. Provides questions adult and child can explore together. 11 x 8½, 32 pp, Full-color illus., HC, 978-1-58023-195-4 **$17.95** *For ages 4 & up*

Also Available as a Board Book: **I Am God's Paintbrush**
5 x 5, 24 pp, Full-color illus., Board Book, 978-1-59473-265-2 **$7.99** *For ages 0–4*
(A book from SkyLight Paths, Jewish Lights' sister imprint)
Also Available: **God's Paintbrush Teacher's Guide**
8½ x 11, 32 pp, PB, 978-1-879045-57-6 **$8.95**
God's Paintbrush Celebration Kit
A Spiritual Activity Kit for Teachers and Students of All Faiths, All Backgrounds
9½ x 12, 40 Full-color Activity Sheets & Teacher Folder w/ complete instructions
HC, 978-1-58023-050-6 **$21.95**
8-Student Activity Sheet Pack (40 sheets/5 sessions), 978-1-58023-058-2 **$19.95**

In God's Name
Like an ancient myth in its poetic text and vibrant illustrations, this award-winning modern fable about the search for God's name celebrates the diversity and, at the same time, the unity of all people.
9 x 12, 32 pp, Full-color illus., HC, 978-1-879045-26-2 **$16.99** *For ages 4 & up*

Also Available as a Board Book: **What Is God's Name?**
5 x 5, 24 pp, Full-color illus., Board Book, 978-1-893361-10-2 **$7.99** *For ages 0–4*
(A book from SkyLight Paths, Jewish Lights' sister imprint)
Also Available in Spanish: **El nombre de Dios**
9 x 12, 32 pp, Full-color illus., HC, 978-1-893361-63-8 **$16.95** *For ages 4 & up*

Noah's Wife: The Story of Naamah
When God tells Noah to bring the animals of the world onto the ark, God also calls on Naamah, Noah's wife, to save each plant on Earth. Based on an ancient text.
9 x 12, 32 pp, Full-color illus., HC, 978-1-58023-134-3 **$16.95** *For ages 4 & up*

Also Available as a Board Book: **Naamah, Noah's Wife**
5 x 5, 24 pp, Full-color illus., Board Book, 978-1-893361-56-0 **$7.95** *For ages 0–4*
(A book from SkyLight Paths, Jewish Lights' sister imprint)

Life Cycle
Marriage/Parenting/Family/Aging

The New Jewish Baby Album: Creating and Celebrating the Beginning of a Spiritual Life—A Jewish Lights Companion
By the Editors at Jewish Lights; Foreword by Anita Diamant; Preface by Rabbi Sandy Eisenberg Sasso
A spiritual keepsake that will be treasured for generations. More than just a memory book, *shows you how—and why it's important*—to create a Jewish home and a Jewish life. 8 x 10, 64 pp, Deluxe Padded HC, Full-color illus., 978-1-58023-138-1 **$19.95**

The Jewish Pregnancy Book: A Resource for the Soul, Body & Mind during Pregnancy, Birth & the First Three Months *By Sandy Falk, MD, and Rabbi Daniel Judson, with Steven A. Rapp* Medical information, prayers and rituals for each stage of pregnancy. 7 x 10, 208 pp, b/w photos, Quality PB, 978-1-58023-178-7 **$16.95**

Celebrating Your New Jewish Daughter: Creating Jewish Ways to Welcome Baby Girls into the Covenant—New and Traditional Ceremonies *By Debra Nussbaum Cohen; Foreword by Rabbi Sandy Eisenberg Sasso* 6 x 9, 272 pp, Quality PB, 978-1-58023-090-2 **$18.95**

The New Jewish Baby Book, 2nd Edition: Names, Ceremonies & Customs—A Guide for Today's Families *By Anita Diamant* 6 x 9, 320 pp, Quality PB, 978-1-58023-251-7 **$19.99**

Parenting as a Spiritual Journey: Deepening Ordinary and Extraordinary Events into Sacred Occasions *By Rabbi Nancy Fuchs-Kreimer, PhD*
6 x 9, 224 pp, Quality PB, 978-1-58023-016-2 **$17.99**

Parenting Jewish Teens: A Guide for the Perplexed
By Joanne Doades Explores the questions and issues that shape the world in which today's Jewish teenagers live and offers constructive advice to parents.
6 x 9, 176 pp, Quality PB, 978-1-58023-305-7 **$16.99**

Judaism for Two: A Spiritual Guide for Strengthening and Celebrating Your Loving Relationship *By Rabbi Nancy Fuchs-Kreimer, PhD, and Rabbi Nancy H. Wiener, DMin; Foreword by Rabbi Elliot N. Dorff, PhD*
Addresses the ways Jewish teachings can enhance and strengthen committed relationships. 6 x 9, 224 pp, Quality PB, 978-1-58023-254-8 **$16.99**

The Creative Jewish Wedding Book, 2nd Edition: A Hands-On Guide to New & Old Traditions, Ceremonies & Celebrations *By Gabrielle Kaplan-Mayer*
9 x 9, 288 pp, b/w photos, Quality PB, 978-1-58023-398-9 **$19.99**

Divorce Is a Mitzvah: A Practical Guide to Finding Wholeness and Holiness When Your Marriage Dies *By Rabbi Perry Netter; Afterword by Rabbi Laura Geller*
6 x 9, 224 pp, Quality PB, 978-1-58023-172-5 **$16.95**

Embracing the Covenant: Converts to Judaism Talk About Why & How
By Rabbi Allan Berkowitz and Patti Moskovitz 6 x 9, 192 pp, Quality PB, 978-1-879045-50-7 **$16.95**

The Guide to Jewish Interfaith Family Life: An InterfaithFamily.com Handbook
Edited by Ronnie Friedland and Edmund Case
6 x 9, 384 pp, Quality PB, 978-1-58023-153-4 **$18.95**

A Heart of Wisdom: Making the Jewish Journey from Midlife through the Elder Years
Edited by Susan Berrin; Foreword by Rabbi Harold Kushner
6 x 9, 384 pp, Quality PB, 978-1-58023-051-3 **$18.95**

Introducing My Faith and My Community: The Jewish Outreach Institute Guide for the Christian in a Jewish Interfaith Relationship
By Rabbi Kerry M. Olitzky 6 x 9, 176 pp, Quality PB, 978-1-58023-192-3 **$16.99**

Making a Successful Jewish Interfaith Marriage: The Jewish Outreach Institute Guide to Opportunities, Challenges and Resources *By Rabbi Kerry M. Olitzky with Joan Peterson Littman*
6 x 9, 176 pp, Quality PB, 978-1-58023-170-1 **$16.95**

A Man's Responsibility: A Jewish Guide to Being a Son, a Partner in Marriage, a Father and a Community Leader *By Rabbi Joseph B. Meszler*
6 x 9, 192 pp, Quality PB, 978-1-58023-435-1 **$16.99**; HC, 978-1-58023-362-0 **$21.99**

So That Your Values Live On: Ethical Wills and How to Prepare Them
Edited by Rabbi Jack Riemer and Rabbi Nathaniel Stampfer
6 x 9, 272 pp, Quality PB, 978-1-879045-34-7 **$18.99**

Holidays/Holy Days

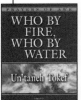

Who by Fire, Who by Water—Un'taneh Tokef
Edited by Rabbi Lawrence A. Hoffman, PhD
Examines the prayer's theology, authorship and poetry through a set of lively essays, all written in accessible language.
6 x 9, 272 pp, HC, 978-1-58023-424-5 **$24.99**

All These Vows—Kol Nidre
Edited by Rabbi Lawrence A. Hoffman, PhD
The most memorable prayer of the Jewish New Year—what it means, why we sing it, and the secret of its magical appeal.
6 x 9, 288 pp, HC, 978-1-58023-430-6 **$24.99**

Rosh Hashanah Readings: Inspiration, Information and Contemplation
Yom Kippur Readings: Inspiration, Information and Contemplation
Edited by Rabbi Dov Peretz Elkins; Section Introductions from Arthur Green's These Are the Words
Rosh Hashanah: 6 x 9, 400 pp, Quality PB, 978-1-58023-437-5 **$19.99**; HC, 978-1-58023-239-5 **$24.99**
Yom Kippur: 6 x 9, 368 pp, Quality PB, 978-1-58023-438-2 **$19.99**; HC, 978-1-58023-271-5 **$24.99**

Jewish Holidays: A Brief Introduction for Christians
By Rabbi Kerry M. Olitzky and Rabbi Daniel Judson
5½ x 8½, 176 pp, Quality PB, 978-1-58023-302-6 **$16.99**

Reclaiming Judaism as a Spiritual Practice: Holy Days and Shabbat
By Rabbi Goldie Milgram 7 x 9, 272 pp, Quality PB, 978-1-58023-205-0 **$19.99**

Shabbat, 2nd Edition: The Family Guide to Preparing for and Celebrating the Sabbath
By Dr. Ron Wolfson 7 x 9, 320 pp, Illus., Quality PB, 978-1-58023-164-0 **$19.99**

Hanukkah, 2nd Edition: The Family Guide to Spiritual Celebration
By Dr. Ron Wolfson 7 x 9, 240 pp, Illus., Quality PB, 978-1-58023-122-0 **$18.95**

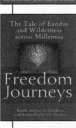

The Jewish Family Fun Book, 2nd Edition
Holiday Projects, Everyday Activities, and Travel Ideas with Jewish Themes
By Danielle Dardashti and Roni Sarig; Illus. by Avi Katz
6 x 9, 304 pp, 70+ b/w illus. & diagrams, Quality PB, 978-1-58023-333-0 **$18.99**

Passover

My People's Passover Haggadah
Traditional Texts, Modern Commentaries
Edited by Rabbi Lawrence A. Hoffman, PhD, and David Arnow, PhD
A diverse and exciting collection of commentaries on the traditional Passover Haggadah—in two volumes!
Vol. 1: 7 x 10, 304 pp, HC, 978-1-58023-354-5 **$24.99**
Vol. 2: 7 x 10, 320 pp, HC, 978-1-58023-346-0 **$24.99**

Freedom Journeys: The Tale of Exodus and Wilderness across Millennia
By Rabbi Arthur O. Waskow and Rabbi Phyllis O. Berman
Explores how the story of Exodus echoes in our own time, calling us to relearn and rethink the Passover story through social-justice, ecological, feminist and interfaith perspectives. 6 x 9, 288 pp, HC, 978-1-58023-445-0 **$24.99**

Leading the Passover Journey: The Seder's Meaning Revealed, the Haggadah's Story Retold
By Rabbi Nathan Laufer
Uncovers the hidden meaning of the Seder's rituals and customs.
6 x 9, 224 pp, Quality PB, 978-1-58023-399-6 **$18.99**; HC, 978-1-58023-211-1 **$24.99**

Creating Lively Passover Seders, 2nd Edition: A Sourcebook of Engaging Tales, Texts & Activities
By David Arnow, PhD 7 x 9, 464 pp, Quality PB, 978-1-58023-444-3 **$24.99**

Passover, 2nd Edition: The Family Guide to Spiritual Celebration
By Dr. Ron Wolfson with Joel Lurie Grishaver 7 x 9, 416 pp, Quality PB, 978-1-58023-174-9 **$19.95**

The Women's Passover Companion: Women's Reflections on the Festival of Freedom
Edited by Rabbi Sharon Cohen Anisfeld, Tara Mohr and Catherine Spector; Foreword by Paula E. Hyman
6 x 9, 352 pp, Quality PB, 978-1-58023-231-9 **$19.99**; HC, 978-1-58023-128-2 **$24.95**

The Women's Seder Sourcebook: Rituals & Readings for Use at the Passover Seder
Edited by Rabbi Sharon Cohen Anisfeld, Tara Mohr and Catherine Spector
6 x 9, 384 pp, Quality PB, 978-1-58023-232-6 **$19.99**

Inspiration

God of Me: Imagining God throughout Your Lifetime
By Rabbi David Lyon Helps you cut through preconceived ideas of God and dogmas that stifle your creativity when thinking about your personal relationship with God. 6 x 9, 176 pp, Quality PB, 978-1-58023-452-8 **$16.99**

The God Upgrade: Finding Your 21st-Century Spirituality in Judaism's 5,000-Year-Old Tradition *By Rabbi Jamie Korngold; Foreword by Rabbi Harold M. Schulweis* A provocative look at how our changing God concepts have shaped every aspect of Judaism. 6 x 9, 176 pp, Quality PB, 978-1-58023-443-6 **$15.99**

The Seven Questions You're Asked in Heaven: Reviewing and Renewing Your Life on Earth *By Dr. Ron Wolfson* An intriguing and entertaining resource for living a life that matters. 6 x 9, 176 pp, Quality PB, 978-1-58023-407-8 **$16.99**

Happiness and the Human Spirit: The Spirituality of Becoming the Best You Can Be *By Rabbi Abraham J. Twerski, MD* Shows you that true happiness is attainable once you stop looking outside yourself for the source. 6 x 9, 176 pp, Quality PB, 978-1-58023-404-7 **$16.99**; HC, 978-1-58023-343-9 **$19.99**

A Formula for Proper Living: Practical Lessons from Life and Torah
By Rabbi Abraham J. Twerski, MD 6 x 9, 144 pp, HC, 978-1-58023-402-3 **$19.99**

The Bridge to Forgiveness: Stories and Prayers for Finding God and Restoring Wholeness *By Rabbi Karyn D. Kedar* 6 x 9, 176 pp, Quality PB, 978-1-58023-451-1 **$16.99**

The Empty Chair: Finding Hope and Joy—Timeless Wisdom from a Hasidic Master, Rebbe Nachman of Breslov *Adapted by Moshe Mykoff and the Breslov Research Institute* 4 x 6, 128 pp, Deluxe PB w/ flaps, 978-1-879045-67-5 **$9.99**

The Gentle Weapon: Prayers for Everyday and Not-So-Everyday Moments—Timeless Wisdom from the Teachings of the Hasidic Master, Rebbe Nachman of Breslov *Adapted by Moshe Mykoff and S. C. Mizrahi, together with the Breslov Research Institute* 4 x 6, 144 pp, Deluxe PB w/ flaps, 978-1-58023-022-3 **$9.99**

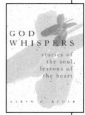

God Whispers: Stories of the Soul, Lessons of the Heart *By Rabbi Karyn D. Kedar* 6 x 9, 176 pp, Quality PB, 978-1-58023-088-9 **$15.95**

God's To-Do List: 103 Ways to Be an Angel and Do God's Work on Earth
By Dr. Ron Wolfson 6 x 9, 144 pp, Quality PB, 978-1-58023-301-9 **$16.99**

Jewish Stories from Heaven and Earth: Inspiring Tales to Nourish the Heart and Soul *Edited by Rabbi Dov Peretz Elkins* 6 x 9, 304 pp, Quality PB, 978-1-58023-363-7 **$16.99**

Life's Daily Blessings: Inspiring Reflections on Gratitude and Joy for Every Day, Based on Jewish Wisdom *By Rabbi Kerry M. Olitzky* 4½ x 6½, 368 pp, Quality PB, 978-1-58023-396-5 **$16.99**

Restful Reflections: Nighttime Inspiration to Calm the Soul, Based on Jewish Wisdom *By Rabbi Kerry M. Olitzky and Rabbi Lori Forman-Jacobi* 4½ x 6½, 448 pp, Quality PB, 978-1-58023-091-9 **$15.95**

Sacred Intentions: Morning Inspiration to Strengthen the Spirit, Based on Jewish Wisdom *By Rabbi Kerry M. Olitzky and Rabbi Lori Forman-Jacobi* 4½ x 6½, 448 pp, Quality PB, 978-1-58023-061-2 **$16.99**

Kabbalah/Mysticism

Jewish Mysticism and the Spiritual Life: Classical Texts, Contemporary Reflections *Edited by Dr. Lawrence Fine, Dr. Eitan Fishbane and Rabbi Or N. Rose* Inspirational and thought-provoking materials for contemplation, discussion and action. 6 x 9, 256 pp, HC, 978-1-58023-434-4 **$24.99**

Ehyeh: A Kabbalah for Tomorrow
By Rabbi Arthur Green, PhD 6 x 9, 224 pp, Quality PB, 978-1-58023-213-5 **$18.99**

The Gift of Kabbalah: Discovering the Secrets of Heaven, Renewing Your Life on Earth
By Tamar Frankiel, PhD 6 x 9, 256 pp, Quality PB, 978-1-58023-141-1 **$16.95**

Seek My Face: A Jewish Mystical Theology *By Rabbi Arthur Green, PhD*
6 x 9, 304 pp, Quality PB, 978-1-58023-130-5 **$19.95**

Zohar: Annotated & Explained *Translation & Annotation by Dr. Daniel C. Matt; Foreword by Andrew Harvey* 5½ x 8½, 176 pp, Quality PB, 978-1-893361-51-5 **$15.99**
(A book from SkyLight Paths, Jewish Lights' sister imprint)

See also *The Way Into Jewish Mystical Tradition* in The Way Into... Series.

Social Justice

Confronting Scandal
How Jews Can Respond When Jews Do Bad Things
By Dr. Erica Brown
A framework to transform our sense of shame over reports of Jews committing crime into actions that inspire and sustain a moral culture.
6 x 9, 192 pp, HC, 978-1-58023-440-5 **$24.99**

There Shall Be No Needy
Pursuing Social Justice through Jewish Law and Tradition
By Rabbi Jill Jacobs; Foreword by Rabbi Elliot N. Dorff, PhD; Preface by Simon Greer
Confronts the most pressing issues of twenty-first-century America from a deeply Jewish perspective. 6 x 9, 288 pp, Quality PB, 978-1-58023-425-2 **$16.99**
There Shall Be No Needy Teacher's Guide 8½ x 11, 56 pp, PB, 978-1-58023-429-0 **$8.99**

Conscience
The Duty to Obey and the Duty to Disobey
By Rabbi Harold M. Schulweis
Examines the idea of conscience and the role conscience plays in our relationships to government, law, ethics, religion, human nature, God—and to each other.
6 x 9, 160 pp, Quality PB, 978-1-58023-419-1 **$16.99**; HC, 978-1-58023-375-0 **$19.99**

Judaism and Justice
The Jewish Passion to Repair the World
By Rabbi Sidney Schwarz; Foreword by Ruth Messinger
Explores the relationship between Judaism, social justice and the Jewish identity of American Jews. 6 x 9, 352 pp, Quality PB, 978-1-58023-353-8 **$19.99**

Spirituality/Women's Interest

New Jewish Feminism
Probing the Past, Forging the Future
Edited by Rabbi Elyse Goldstein; Foreword by Anita Diamant
Looks at the growth and accomplishments of Jewish feminism and what they mean for Jewish women today and tomorrow.
6 x 9, 480 pp, Quality PB, 978-1-58023-448-1 **$19.99**; HC, 978-1-58023-359-0 **$24.99**

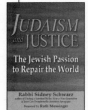

The Divine Feminine in Biblical Wisdom Literature
Selections Annotated & Explained
Translation & Annotation by Rabbi Rami Shapiro
5½ x 8½, 240 pp, Quality PB, 978-1-59473-109-9 **$16.99**
(A book from SkyLight Paths, Jewish Lights' sister imprint)

The Quotable Jewish Woman
Wisdom, Inspiration & Humor from the Mind & Heart
Edited by Elaine Bernstein Partnow
6 x 9, 496 pp, Quality PB, 978-1-58023-236-4 **$19.99**

The Women's Haftarah Commentary
New Insights from Women Rabbis on the 54 Weekly Haftarah Portions, the 5 Megillot & Special Shabbatot
Edited by Rabbi Elyse Goldstein
Illuminates the historical significance of female portrayals in the Haftarah and the Five Megillot. 6 x 9, 560 pp, Quality PB, 978-1-58023-371-2 **$19.99**

The Women's Torah Commentary
New Insights from Women Rabbis on the 54 Weekly Torah Portions
Edited by Rabbi Elyse Goldstein
Over fifty women rabbis offer inspiring insights on the Torah, in a week-by-week format.
6 x 9, 496 pp, Quality PB, 978-1-58023-370-5 **$19.99**; HC, 978-1-58023-076-6 **$34.95**

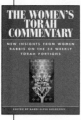

See Passover for *The Women's Passover Companion: Women's Reflections on the Festival of Freedom* and *The Women's Seder Sourcebook: Rituals & Readings for Use at the Passover Seder.*

Spirituality/Prayer

Making Prayer Real: Leading Jewish Spiritual Voices on Why Prayer Is Difficult and What to Do about It *By Rabbi Mike Comins*
A new and different response to the challenges of Jewish prayer, with "best prayer practices" from Jewish spiritual leaders of all denominations.
6 x 9, 320 pp, Quality PB, 978-1-58023-417-7 **$18.99**

Witnesses to the One: The Spiritual History of the *Sh'ma*
By Rabbi Joseph B. Meszler; Foreword by Rabbi Elyse Goldstein
6 x 9, 176 pp, Quality PB, 978-1-58023-400-9 **$16.99**; HC, 978-1-58023-309-5 **$19.99**

My People's Prayer Book Series: Traditional Prayers, Modern Commentaries *Edited by Rabbi Lawrence A. Hoffman, PhD*
Provides diverse and exciting commentary to the traditional liturgy. Will help you find new wisdom in Jewish prayer, and bring liturgy into your life. Each book includes Hebrew text, modern translations and commentaries from all perspectives of the Jewish world.

Vol. 1—The *Sh'ma* and Its Blessings
  7 x 10, 168 pp, HC, 978-1-879045-79-8 **$29.99**
Vol. 2—The *Amidah* 7 x 10, 240 pp, HC, 978-1-879045-80-4 **$24.95**
Vol. 3—*P'sukei D'zimrah* (Morning Psalms)
  7 x 10, 240 pp, HC, 978-1-879045-81-1 **$29.99**
Vol. 4—*Seder K'riat Hatorah* (The Torah Service)
  7 x 10, 264 pp, HC, 978-1-879045-82-8 **$29.99**
Vol. 5—*Birkhot Hashachar* (Morning Blessings)
  7 x 10, 240 pp, HC, 978-1-879045-83-5 **$24.95**
Vol. 6—*Tachanun* and Concluding Prayers
  7 x 10, 240 pp, HC, 978-1-879045-84-2 **$24.95**
Vol. 7—Shabbat at Home 7 x 10, 240 pp, HC, 978-1-879045-85-9 **$24.95**
Vol. 8—*Kabbalat Shabbat* (Welcoming Shabbat in the Synagogue)
  7 x 10, 240 pp, HC, 978-1-58023-121-3 **$24.99**
Vol. 9—Welcoming the Night: *Minchah* and *Ma'ariv* (Afternoon and
  Evening Prayer) 7 x 10, 272 pp, HC, 978-1-58023-262-3 **$24.99**
Vol. 10—Shabbat Morning: *Shacharit* and *Musaf* (Morning and
  Additional Services) 7 x 10, 240 pp, HC, 978-1-58023-240-1 **$29.99**

Spirituality/Lawrence Kushner

I'm God; You're Not: Observations on Organized Religion & Other Disguises of the Ego
6 x 9, 256 pp, HC, 978-1-58023-441-2 **$21.99**

The Book of Letters: A Mystical Hebrew Alphabet
Popular HC Edition, 6 x 9, 80 pp, 2-color text, 978-1-879045-00-2 **$24.95**
Collector's Limited Edition, 9 x 12, 80 pp, gold-foil-embossed pages, w/ limited-edition silkscreened print, 978-1-879045-04-0 **$349.00**

The Book of Miracles: A Young Person's Guide to Jewish Spiritual Awareness
6 x 9, 96 pp, 2-color illus., HC, 978-1-879045-78-1 **$16.95** *For ages 9–13*

The Book of Words: Talking Spiritual Life, Living Spiritual Talk
6 x 9, 160 pp, Quality PB, 978-1-58023-020-9 **$18.99**

Eyes Remade for Wonder: A Lawrence Kushner Reader *Introduction by Thomas Moore*
6 x 9, 240 pp, Quality PB, 978-1-58023-042-1 **$18.95**

God Was in This Place & I, i Did Not Know: Finding Self, Spirituality and
Ultimate Meaning 6 x 9, 192 pp, Quality PB, 978-1-879045-33-0 **$16.95**

Honey from the Rock: An Introduction to Jewish Mysticism
6 x 9, 176 pp, Quality PB, 978-1-58023-073-5 **$16.95**

Invisible Lines of Connection: Sacred Stories of the Ordinary
5½ x 8½, 160 pp, Quality PB, 978-1-879045-98-9 **$15.95**

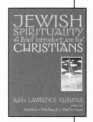

Jewish Spirituality: A Brief Introduction for Christians
5½ x 8½, 112 pp, Quality PB, 978-1-58023-150-3 **$12.95**

The River of Light: Jewish Mystical Awareness
6 x 9, 192 pp, Quality PB, 978-1-58023-096-4 **$16.95**

The Way Into Jewish Mystical Tradition
6 x 9, 224 pp, Quality PB, 978-1-58023-200-5 **$18.99**; HC, 978-1-58023-029-2 **$21.95**

Theology/Philosophy

The God Who Hates Lies: Confronting & Rethinking Jewish Tradition
By Dr. David Hartman with Charlie Buckholtz
The world's leading Modern Orthodox Jewish theologian probes the deepest questions at the heart of what it means to be a human being and a Jew.
6 x 9, 208 pp, HC, 978-1-58023-455-9 **$24.99**

Jewish Theology in Our Time: A New Generation Explores the Foundations and Future of Jewish Belief Edited by Rabbi Elliot J. Cosgrove, PhD; Foreword by Rabbi David J. Wolpe; Preface by Rabbi Carole B. Balin, PhD
A powerful and challenging examination of what Jews can believe—by a new generation's most dynamic and innovative thinkers.
6 x 9, 240 pp, HC, 978-1-58023-413-9 **$24.99**

Maimonides, Spinoza and Us: Toward an Intellectually Vibrant Judaism
By Rabbi Marc D. Angel, PhD A challenging look at two great Jewish philosophers and what their thinking means to our understanding of God, truth, revelation and reason. 6 x 9, 224 pp, HC, 978-1-58023-411-5 **$24.99**

The Death of Death: Resurrection and Immortality in Jewish Thought
By Rabbi Neil Gillman, PhD 6 x 9, 336 pp, Quality PB, 978-1-58023-081-0 **$18.95**

Doing Jewish Theology: God, Torah & Israel in Modern Judaism By Rabbi Neil Gillman, PhD
6 x 9, 304 pp, Quality PB, 978-1-58023-439-9 **$18.99**

Hasidic Tales: Annotated & Explained Translation & Annotation by Rabbi Rami Shapiro
5½ x 8½, 240 pp, Quality PB, 978-1-893361-86-7 **$16.95***

A Heart of Many Rooms: Celebrating the Many Voices within Judaism
By Dr. David Hartman 6 x 9, 352 pp, Quality PB, 978-1-58023-156-5 **$19.95**

The Hebrew Prophets: Selections Annotated & Explained
Translation & Annotation by Rabbi Rami Shapiro; Foreword by Rabbi Zalman M. Schachter-Shalomi
5½ x 8½, 224 pp, Quality PB, 978-1-59473-037-5 **$16.99***

A Jewish Understanding of the New Testament By Rabbi Samuel Sandmel;
Preface by Rabbi David Sandmel 5½ x 8½, 368 pp, Quality PB, 978-1-59473-048-1 **$19.99***

Jews and Judaism in the 21st Century: Human Responsibility, the Presence of God and the Future of the Covenant Edited by Rabbi Edward Feinstein; Foreword by Paula E. Hyman
6 x 9, 192 pp, Quality PB, 978-1-58023-374-3 **$19.99**

A Living Covenant: The Innovative Spirit in Traditional Judaism
By Dr. David Hartman 6 x 9, 368 pp, Quality PB, 978-1-58023-011-7 **$25.00**

Love and Terror in the God Encounter: The Theological Legacy of Rabbi Joseph B. Soloveitchik By Dr. David Hartman 6 x 9, 240 pp, Quality PB, 978-1-58023-176-3 **$19.95**

A Touch of the Sacred: A Theologian's Informal Guide to Jewish Belief
By Dr. Eugene B. Borowitz and Frances W. Schwartz
6 x 9, 256 pp, Quality PB, 978-1-58023-416-0 **$16.99**; HC, 978-1-58023-337-8 **$21.99**

Traces of God: Seeing God in Torah, History and Everyday Life By Rabbi Neil Gillman, PhD
6 x 9, 240 pp, Quality PB, 978-1-58023-369-9 **$16.99**

Your Word Is Fire: The Hasidic Masters on Contemplative Prayer
Edited and translated by Rabbi Arthur Green, PhD, and Barry W. Holtz
6 x 9, 160 pp, Quality PB, 978-1-879045-25-5 **$15.95**

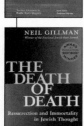

I Am Jewish
Personal Reflections Inspired by the Last Words of Daniel Pearl
Almost 150 Jews—both famous and not—from all walks of life, from all around the world, write about many aspects of their Judaism.
Edited by Judea and Ruth Pearl 6 x 9, 304 pp, Deluxe PB w/ flaps, 978-1-58023-259-3 **$18.99**
Download a free copy of the *I Am Jewish* Teacher's Guide at www.jewishlights.com.

Hannah Senesh: Her Life and Diary, The First Complete Edition
By Hannah Senesh; Foreword by Marge Piercy; Preface by Eitan Senesh; Afterword by Roberta Grossman
6 x 9, 368 pp, b/w photos, Quality PB, 978-1-58023-342-2 **$19.99**

**A book from SkyLight Paths, Jewish Lights' sister imprint*

Theology/Philosophy/The Way Into... Series

The Way Into... series offers an accessible and highly usable "guided tour" of the Jewish faith, people, history and beliefs—in total, an introduction to Judaism that will enable you to understand and interact with the sacred texts of the Jewish tradition. Each volume is written by a leading contemporary scholar and teacher, and explores one key aspect of Judaism. The Way Into... series enables all readers to achieve a real sense of Jewish cultural literacy through guided study.

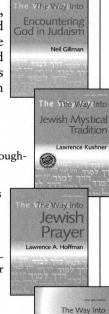

The Way Into Encountering God in Judaism
By Rabbi Neil Gillman, PhD
For everyone who wants to understand how Jews have encountered God throughout history and today.
6 x 9, 240 pp, Quality PB, 978-1-58023-199-2 **$18.99**; HC, 978-1-58023-025-4 **$21.95**
Also Available: **The Jewish Approach to God:** A Brief Introduction for Christians
By Rabbi Neil Gillman, PhD
5½ x 8½, 192 pp, Quality PB, 978-1-58023-190-9 **$16.95**

The Way Into Jewish Mystical Tradition
By Rabbi Lawrence Kushner
Allows readers to interact directly with the sacred mystical texts of the Jewish tradition. An accessible introduction to the concepts of Jewish mysticism, their religious and spiritual significance, and how they relate to life today.
6 x 9, 224 pp, Quality PB, 978-1-58023-200-5 **$18.99**; HC, 978-1-58023-029-2 **$21.95**

The Way Into Jewish Prayer
By Rabbi Lawrence A. Hoffman, PhD
Opens the door to 3,000 years of Jewish prayer, making anyone feel at home in the Jewish way of communicating with God.
6 x 9, 208 pp, Quality PB, 978-1-58023-201-2 **$18.99**

The Way Into Jewish Prayer Teacher's Guide
By Rabbi Jennifer Ossakow Goldsmith
8½ x 11, 42 pp, PB, 978-1-58023-345-3 **$8.99**
Download a free copy at www.jewishlights.com.

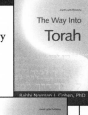

The Way Into Judaism and the Environment
By Jeremy Benstein, PhD
Explores the ways in which Judaism contributes to contemporary social-environmental issues, the extent to which Judaism is part of the problem and how it can be part of the solution.
6 x 9, 288 pp, Quality PB, 978-1-58023-368-2 **$18.99**

The Way Into Tikkun Olam (Repairing the World)
By Rabbi Elliot N. Dorff, PhD
An accessible introduction to the Jewish concept of the individual's responsibility to care for others and repair the world.
6 x 9, 304 pp, Quality PB, 978-1-58023-328-6 **$18.99**

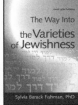

The Way Into Torah
By Rabbi Norman J. Cohen, PhD
Helps guide you in the exploration of the origins and development of Torah, explains why it should be studied and how to do it.
6 x 9, 176 pp, Quality PB, 978-1-58023-198-5 **$16.99**

The Way Into the Varieties of Jewishness
By Sylvia Barack Fishman, PhD
Explores the religious and historical understanding of what it has meant to be Jewish from ancient times to the present controversy over "Who is a Jew?"
6 x 9, 288 pp, Quality PB, 978-1-58023-367-5 **$18.99**; HC, 978-1-58023-030-8 **$24.99**

JEWISH LIGHTS BOOKS ARE AVAILABLE FROM BETTER BOOKSTORES. TRY YOUR BOOKSTORE FIRST.

About Jewish Lights

People of all faiths and backgrounds yearn for books that attract, engage, educate, and spiritually inspire.

Our principal goal is to stimulate thought and help all people learn about who the Jewish People are, where they come from, and what the future can be made to hold. While people of our diverse Jewish heritage are the primary audience, our books speak to people in the Christian world as well and will broaden their understanding of Judaism and the roots of their own faith.

We bring to you authors who are at the forefront of spiritual thought and experience. While each has something different to say, they all say it in a voice that you can hear.

Our books are designed to welcome you and then to engage, stimulate, and inspire. We judge our success not only by whether or not our books are beautiful and commercially successful, but by whether or not they make a difference in your life.

For your information and convenience, at the back of this book we have provided a list of other Jewish Lights books you might find interesting and useful. They cover all the categories of your life:

Bar/Bat Mitzvah
Bible Study / Midrash
Children's Books
Congregation Resources
Current Events / History
Ecology / Environment
Fiction: Mystery, Science Fiction
Grief / Healing
Holidays / Holy Days
Inspiration
Kabbalah / Mysticism / Enneagram

Life Cycle
Meditation
Men's Interest
Parenting
Prayer / Ritual / Sacred Practice
Social Justice
Spirituality
Theology / Philosophy
Travel
Twelve Steps
Women's Interest

Stuart M. Matlins, Publisher

Or phone, fax, mail or e-mail to: **JEWISH LIGHTS Publishing**
Sunset Farm Offices, Route 4 • P.O. Box 237 • Woodstock, Vermont 05091
Tel: (802) 457-4000 • Fax: (802) 457-4004 • www.jewishlights.com
Credit card orders: (800) 962-4544 (8:30AM–5:30PM ET Monday–Friday)
Generous discounts on quantity orders. SATISFACTION GUARANTEED. Prices subject to change.

For more information about each book, visit our website at www.jewishlights.com